Mother Was a Gunner's Mate

Mother Was a Gunner's Mate

World War II in the Waves

Josette Dermody Wingo

BLUEJACKET BOOKS

Naval Institute Press

Annapolis, Maryland

To the reader: This story is about real events that happened, although many names have been changed to protect privacy, some biographical details have been altered, and some of the characters in the story are composites. All good sea stories are conflated, inflated, exaggerated, and embellished. This one is no exception.

Naval Institute Press
291 Wood Road
Annapolis, MD 21402

First Bluejacket Books printing, 2000
ISBN 1-55750-960-3

The Library of Congress has cataloged the hardcover edition as follows:
Wingo, Josette Dermody, 1924–
    Mother was a gunner's mate : World War II in the Waves / Josette Dermody Wingo.
        p.   cm.
    ISBN 1-55750-924-7
    1. Wingo, Josette Dermody, 1924–   . 2. United States. Naval reserve. Women's Reserve—History. 3. World War, 1939–1945—Naval operations, American. 4. World War, 1939–1945—Personal narratives, American. 5. Women sailors—Biography. 6. United States. Navy—Biography. I. Title.
D769.597.W568 1994
940.54'5973'092—dc20   94-10440

Printed in the United States of America on acid-free paper ∞
07 06 05 04 03 02 01 00   8 7 6 5 4 3 2 1

Frontispiece: Josette Dermody, gunnery instructor, celebrates her twenty-first birthday in San Francisco.

Contents

To Lowdon

ACKNOWLEDGMENTS

So many people have helped me over the years in getting this story right; among those I want to thank are:

Dr. Dorothy Brennan Kaufman, who was Women's Representative on Treasure Island in 1944-45. Her help and encouragement (and her scrapbooks) have been invaluable.

Portia Joan Dennis, another TI Wave, worked with me for a whole year when I began this book. Marie Bennett Alsmeyer wouldn't let our Wave stories fade away. My roommates/shipmates, Marian Hansen Jahn, Billie Rankin Brooks, and Mary Barber, really did keep me from messing up, but they were much nicer than the composite characters in this story. My friends in Waves National cheered me on, and our buddies in the Armed Guard Veterans provided yarns and details in their newsletter *The Pointer.*

The librarians at the Naval Historical Center and the Naval Library in Washington, D.C., especially Barbara Lynch, were unfailingly helpful. Lisa Brandes at the Navy/Marine Corps/Coast Guard Museum on Treasure Island helped me access the gold mine of memories there, especially the files of *The Masthead.*

Peter Chelemedos, survivor of numerous torpedoings, friend of many Waves, generously sent me the clippings from the *Berkeley Daily Gazette,* January 20, 1945, and shared the details of the sinking of the *John A. Johnson* with me.

Eleanor Harder and Sister Felice Kolda kept me writing and rewriting, as did Sue Fischer, Laura Olsher, Marjorie Fairman, and Jean Aaberg. Christine Mather researched details of Chicago's Navy Day parade.

My friends in the Navy now, especially ATC Mary M. Vernoy, Lt. Cmdr. Cynthia Wilson, and Lt. Cmdr. Donna Fournier, read my chapters and kept me nautical.

Dr. Linda Grant DePauw of George Washington University printed an early version of chapter 23 in *MINERVA: The Quarterly Report on Women and the Military* (Spring 1985).

Norman Corwin gave permission to use excerpts from his broadcast on V-E Day. His is a voice that epitomized World War II on the radio for all of us.

My husband and resident laureate, Lowdon Wingo, contributed the poem in chapter 15 and supported me all the way in spite of having served in the Army Air Transport Command in World War II.

My sons, Tony and Laird, wearied of my sea stories early on and said, "Gee, Mom, you ought to write a book. Nobody believes our mother was a gunner's mate."

And finally, none of this would have come to fruition without my agent, Michaela Cappello, and my editors, Mary Lou Kenney and Therese Boyd. Well done, mates.

Mother Was a Gunner's Mate

PROLOGUE

Birthday

Instant traditions spring up so easily in wartime. The Navy is big on tradition, always has been. Our own instant tradition is going to San Francisco (which we defiantly call 'Frisco, like the sailors) for each one's birthday dinner, just gals, no guys, no sweat. Tonight is my turn. Twenty-one at last, no more M-I-N-O-R stamped in screaming red letters on the face of my ID card. Four of us—Waves, roommates, shipmates, best friends, and enemies since boot camp, antiaircraft gunnery instructors, called Navy fashion by our last names—Corman, Tolliver, Atkinson, and yours truly took the train from Treasure Island and got off at the East Bay Station like we always do when we have liberty. The Navy is unhappy about women standing watch in the gunsheds in the men's area after dark so we theoretically have liberty every night, which makes some people in our barracks unhappy, but what do we care?

San Francisco glitters and pulses with excitement and light. The nights of the blackouts long behind us, this is June 1945. V-E Day, Victory in Europe, has come and gone; the United Nations Organization has been in the city planning the peaceful postwar world to come. Meanwhile the war is tilting toward a feared long and bloody campaign against the Japanese. Tonight the Japanese enemy is far away except for maybe a few submarines lurking outside the Golden Gate. Our great gray ships, secure behind the antisubmarine nets, bob and tug at their moorings in the greasy, crowded bay. Sometimes there are hundreds of ships in the bay before a big push: at irregular intervals we wake up to the melancholy sounds of the foghorns to discover that almost all the ships have upped anchor with the tide and sailed out through the Gate with the dawn. The black and white gulls keen lonesomely, wheeling in the damp empty air; little choppy whitecaps glisten iridescently from the leftover oil slicks. The cushiony fog rolls in and out through the Golden Gate, following some

1

schedule of its own. Eventually the bay fills with ships again, empties again. The war in the Pacific Theater breathes in and out, in and out. That's what they call it. The Pacific Theater, like it's some big show.

Tonight we are just having a good time, nobody unhappy with anybody at the moment, as we elbow our way down Columbus Street. Everything about us says N-A-V-Y, top to toe. *Life* magazine could use us for a cover. The dark blue ribbons around our identical white-topped hats have US NAVY woven in gold thread. Our snappy blue suits have the fouled anchor—an anchor with a rope twined around it—on each round lapel. We wear identical starched white shirts, although mine is ironed only in front, who would know? We have even-ended black ties tied in proper square knots (right over left, left over right, Girl Scouts came in handy after all), we have even seams in our stockings. More or less. Our boxy black leather purses are strung regulation style on a black strap from the right shoulder to the left hip, as spit-polished as our black Cuban-heeled pumps.

We look pretty spiffy and we know it. We are wearing the exact same clothes, for all the world like parochial school girls on an outing, but you can't really say we look alike. I'm short and brunette, Corman medium-tall and "stacked," as the guys say. She has honey-blonde hair and astonishing blue eyes she can turn on and off like a signal lamp. Tolliver is pudgy with wispy blonde strands constantly escaping from her hat. A hillbilly from West Virginia. She hates Catholics. I never cared for hillbillies so we are even most of the time. Atkinson is a raw-boned farm kid from Nebraska, always asking dumb questions, so blunt we almost kill her sometimes. Still, she's in our guncrew and we are used to her. She's the one who bought me the gardenia pinned to my left lapel. Birthday girls always get gardenias. Tradition. As I said, the Navy is big on tradition.

We are so busy talking that we don't see the shore patrol guy unwind himself from the wall he was holding up by the prophylactic station. (We Waves are not supposed to know about prophylactic stations so we play dumb with our eyes in the middle distance as we walk by them.) This guy is so big he fills the whole sidewalk. I feel his truculence before I see him. He plants himself in front of us, his legs enclosed in white gaiters, his white hat drawn down over his eyebrows. He's blocking our way, so we stop, bewildered. He slaps his truncheon, splat, into his gloved palm, hard. "Where ya goin', mates?" he snarls, looking dangerous. Nobody answers, it's none of his business. He pushes his gob hat to the back of his head, allowing his springy ginger hair to fall over his forehead. He leans toward me. I quail a little, not understanding. You can never let them know you are afraid, only way, so I suck in my breath and stand my ground, looking him straight in the eye, my face blank and innocent. "I ast youse a question, din't I? You're out of uniform, Sister." Splat! the truncheon hits his palm again in punctuation.

Holy Mother of God, I think, he's got me dead to rights.

"You ain't supposed to wear no flowers with no uni-form, unna-stand?" His pale green eyes sweep over our little group standing flat-footed here on the sidewalk. I can feel Tolliver swelling up beside me. Corman can feel it, too, and moves quickly to shove Tolliver behind her. Marines and shore patrol make Tolliver nervous and belligerent since her Captain's Mast. Corman has noticed that Tolliver isn't wearing her white gloves, technically out of uniform too. I am frozen, desperately trying to think what to do. All I can think of is the headline back home—LOCAL WAVE ARRESTED IN S.F. REPORTS BREAD AND WATER NOT SO BAD.

Our Duty-Honor-Country shore patrolman sees Tolliver guiltily shove her gloveless hands behind her ample back. "I gotta notion to run the whole lotta youse in." He doesn't notice Corman push her jangly charm bracelet down into her glove as she steps out and smiles her homecoming queen smile at him. We all step back and let Corman bring up the heavy artillery, listening as the Kentucky honey comes out in her voice.

"Really, Coxswain, surely you wouldn't be putting a girl on report on her birthday, would you?" She smiles at him and lets the "birthday" hang there a minute. "It's Dermody here's birthday and we are just going out for a little celebration." Outgunned for the moment, he scratches his head, knocking his gob hat off. He swoops to retrieve it, Corman motions me closer and unpins the offending gardenia. Now I am technically no longer out of uniform. "Tolliver, put your gloves on." With that she hands the perfumed flower to the nonplused boy and chirps, "Perhaps Dermody's flower will brighten your evening, sailor. It must be so tiring to have the duty while everybody else is having fun." She shoos us past the shore patrolman who is dashing the poor flower into the gutter. She herds us ahead of her, giving little "ta-ta" waves behind her—moving out "toot sweet" before the guy recovers himself.

"That was a close one. Thanks, Corman, I thought I was a goner," I say. All of us are giggling. After it's over, it's funny.

"I thought you were going to die right there on the sidewalk, pal. You are *so* chicken-hearted, Dermody. Forgive me, sailor, for I have sinned. I am out of uniform . . ."

"Knock it off, Tolliver." Corman isn't giggling anymore. "Can't you even be nice to Dermody on her birthday? That guy was just throwing his weight around, just sore because he can't get sea duty. You know how some guys are . . ."

Tolliver's round face is pink with excitement. "Didja see his face when you gave him Dermody's flower? He was shi——"

"Oh, stow it, Tolliver. It's over. We gotta get ol' Josie here another flower, then we cel-ee-brate." Corman is still in charge. She hails a little wispy old lady in a babushka who has a flat basket full of gardenias, waxy white blooms surrounded by heart-shaped leaves with droplets of moisture shaking off when you pick one up, wetting the red, white, and blue ribbon bow. I don't even particularly like gardenias, the overpowering cloying smell makes me woozy, but tradition is tradition. Each girl gives her a quarter, she smiles a toothless smile and says, "God bless you all, ladies."

It's incredible that it was only a year ago I was home in Detroit working for Meekin Brothers Plumbing and Heating Supplies, worrying about withering on the vine. Sometimes I wonder myself what possessed me to run away to sea, why I joined the Navy—patriotism, of course, and adventure . . . and sometimes, I think, a great big hole in my head.

CHAPTER 1

Goodbye

My going-away party is just like everybody else's, but this time it's for me. I can't believe that it's happening, that I am actually sworn into the U.S. Navy Women's Reserve, that Daddy signed his permission for me. He didn't have to sign for my brother Michael when he enlisted in the Army two months after Pearl Harbor, but for some reason it's different for girls until you're 21. Anyway, Daddy did sign; I passed all the tests, written and physical; a rotund officer with a very short haircut swore me to defend the country against all enemies, foreign and domestic, I have my service number—766 73 28—and my bag is all packed.

First thing this morning my brother Buddy and I thumbtacked streamers of red, white, and blue crepe paper around the porch pillars. In the living room and dining room we twisted the strands and looped them from the chandeliers to the corners before we walked with Mother and Daddy to ten o'clock mass.

Monsignor O'Callaghan came down to the front of the altar rail beforehand, like he always does, to ask the congregation to pray for our fighting forces. Looks like they will need all the prayers they can get—this morning the *Detroit News* reported that U.S. forces are blocked northeast and west of St. Lo. That's somewhere in France. The Germans are using a new kind of buzz bomb against England. Michael, where are you? Are you okay? It seems like this war will never, ever be over. I'm going to jump out of my skin waiting to get into it, my insides seem bigger than my outside, as though I'm going to explode. Holy Mother, help me.

"This morning we want to ask God's special blessing on Keith Applegate and Josette Dermody who have answered their country's call to arms and will be leaving us soon," Monsignor intoned, but then he had to add, "To be sure, I don't know what our beloved country is coming to when we send our young ladies off to war. Let us pray." My face flamed. Doesn't he know that this is 1944? And hasn't he ever heard of Joan of Arc?

People, all our relatives and friends, keep coming to the party. The living room is so crowded some people sit on the porch, the front steps, or in the backyard. Aunt Cecelia has brought a copy of the item in the *Free Press* last week, "Local Girl Joins Naval Reserve," with my graduation picture. Someday I'd like to see my picture in the paper without "daughter of Mr. and Mrs. Joseph P. Dermody" under it. Mother props it up on the piano where everyone can see it.

Buddy, in his Boy Scout uniform, is running around with all the kid cousins playing soldier, bang-banging with their fingers at each other, making machine-gun noises. Daddy yells, "You, Brian, go outside and take all those rapscallions with you, for Chrissakes." Mother's eyes glisten a little whenever she looks at me, but she won't cry, you can see she's making an effort; she and Aunt Cecelia are seeing among the ladies who wants a nice cuppa and who prefers lemonade. It's that hot. The gents have their beer and whiskey in the kitchen, I can see Uncle Packy in his shirtsleeves popping the tops off quickly.

Everybody gossips and visits, as if most of them don't see each other all the time anyway. "Mrs. Schmidt, across the street," Aunt Teddy says with a stricken face, "has had word that her oldest, Tom, is missing in action. She's taking it hard, refusing to come out of her darkened room or to eat a bite." Tom was just home on leave last winter; I can't think of him as presumed dead. He was one class ahead of me in school, a stocky, rowdy boy who said he wanted to be a priest, but couldn't wait to join the Coast Guard. Aunt Wilma says, "Sometimes there's better news. You remember the youngest Szatiwcz boy—his folks have the butcher shop on Six Mile Road? He was missing for a while, but they got word last month from the Red Cross that he is in a prison camp in Germany somewhere. They mail him soap and socks, cigarettes and salamis every week and hope he gets at least some of them." Nobody asks where the salamis come from, butchers have ways. Buzz, buzz, buzz.

"Attention, everybody," Sheila Rafferty is clapping her hands, "time for presents." Sheila and I have been best friends since third grade, each trying to best the other, to do something first. Sheel's freckled snub nose is out of joint now, she'd never be able to persuade her Da, Rafferty the cop, to sign anything. He has a vile temper and a heavy hand and all of his kids keep as far away as they can,

but she's smart. She's taking over my job at Meekin Brothers Plumbing and Heating Supplies now that I've left. Let them as likes filing
and typing invoices do it. I'm off to my Big Adventure, like the
recruiting posters say. Beat you this time, Sheila.

I open the card on the box she hands me when she finally shuts
her gob for a minute. The card has a picture of a puppy wearing a
sailor hat and the words "We'll All Miss You." Inside it's signed by all
the girls who were in our high school secret club, even poor Edith
Shaughnessy, who nobody is talking about since she got "in trouble"
and had to leave town to "visit her aunt in St. Louis" for the summer.
"We clubbed together for it," Sheila says; "we don't want you to forget
us."

"You're all so nice to think of me this way," I say, interrupting
Sheila who's off on another speech, hey, whose party is it anyway? Inside the tissue-wrapped box with the red, white, and blue ribbon is a
traveling case of blue imitation leather with a zipper around three
sides. It has little containers to hold toothbrush, comb, lotion, soap,
bobbypins. Guys almost always get a shaving kit when they leave for
the service, this must be the feminine equivalent. "Thanks, everyone,
I love it. I'll think of you every time I use it while I am off seeing the
world."

For a while it's like Christmas in August: Aunt Teddy gives me a
sewing kit, Aunt Cecelia a pair of nylons from her prewar hoard, Aunt
Wilma and Uncle Bud a leatherette portfolio with stationery, Buddy a
bottle of Evening in Paris perfume from Woolworths, Aunt Geraldine
a cut-glass container of aqua bath salts. Bath salts in the Navy? Aunt
Geraldine always has her own ideas.

Mrs. Lundgren isn't here, but she sent a card, one of those all-
purpose ones that say in red, white, and blue ribbon letters, "Goodbye" and "Good Luck." Inside it says,

> Good luck and all best wishes
> from those you left behind you.
> You'll never be too far away
> for friendly thoughts to find you.

Arvid Lundgren was pretty upset when I didn't marry him before he
went overseas, but his mother still likes me. It's his father who gets so
red in the face when he thinks how much he hates Catholics and De-
mocrats. Forget about Arvid, megirl, this is a party.

Daddy hands me a slim package, with the gold sticker from

Zauber's Jewelry Store, my going-away present from him and Mother. I squeal when I open it, it's a delicate gold identification bracelet with an anchor on it and "Josette" engraved in script on the front. On the back Mr. Zauber had engraved my service number, free of charge, Daddy says. Daddy looks proud and baffled at the same time, maybe he's sorry he gave me permission to go. Too late.

By the time all the presents are unwrapped, the tissue paper neatly folded for another use, the red, white, and blue ribbons coiled neatly by Aunt Cecelia like the bandages she rolls at the Red Cross every Wednesday, it's cooled off some and time for supper. The sideboard is loaded with the covered dishes people brought: the macaroni and cheese, the tuna noodle casserole, the sweet and sour cabbage from Buddy's Victory garden, the patriotic applesauce with no sugar, the scalloped potatoes. The kids take their plates out into the backyard by the picnic table, then rush back for dessert. Mother and the aunts have outdone themselves; Geraldine's wartime cake, her special egg-less, milkless, butterless wonder, Mother's eggless chocolate cake, frosted only on top with cocoa frosting (delicious) and, oh no, Aunt Teddy's Yankee Doodle prune pie with Victory pie crust. Nobody likes it, it sits like a depth bomb in the stomach for days, but nobody wants to hurt her feelings either. Somehow it disappears. The grownups have more beer or tea, the stuffed children move to the vacant lot to play Red Rover in the Sunday-quiet twilight.

The aunts and girl cousins help Mother clear away, Uncle Bud stands up to tap his glass with a spoon. He's feeling no pain, fat and jolly as always, his watch chain stretched across his "corporation" where his chest had slipped, his hair combed funny so it won't show bald. He rocks back and forth a little as he declaims his famous "There's no muster in Munster like the slap of the sleet on the sails." He really thinks everybody is dying to hear him do it at every gather-ing. Now I suppose he'll do that poem, *Shan Van Vocht*, just what I need, in the Gaelic.

"Bring me another beer, Josie me darlin'." He looks hot and cross, waiting for Aunt Teddy to shush the baby.

"He's cutting teeth," Aunt Teddy apologizes, cringing a little. Uncle Bud glares at poor little Victor, daring him to whimper. Victor sucks his tiny fist and Uncle Bud continues, "Now in honor of our own mavourneen, who is leaving hearth and home and loving hearts" —he takes a swig of beer, keeping his eyes on the baby, daring him to make a whimper—"I'm going to sing a song." He croons, "I'll take you home again, Kathleen." Everybody claps. I do wish they wouldn't encourage him. He really can't sing very well. He puts his arm around me and says, "I've only one thing to ask of you, Josette. Stay as sweet as you are." I almost die, he's embarrassing me. He's squeezing me so hard it hurts. I smile. He gives me a silver dollar for luck. He's not my real uncle, he's Daddy's best friend from the Big War and my godfather. I kiss him on the cheek. He beams.

Thank God, it's Daddy's turn. Daddy always gets real Irish when he's got a snootful. First he puts his arm around Uncle Bud and they do "The Risin' o' the Moon" and "It's a Long Way to Tipperary." Uncle Bud goes to wet his whistle. Aunt Geraldine is waiting expectantly on the piano bench, her floppy lace sleeves pushed back and her wrists poised. As long as I've been alive I've wondered how two people who hate each other as much as Daddy and Mother's oldest sister could make such beautiful music together. Daddy has a tenor that can make a stone cry. His voice soars as he gets into "Danny Boy." The audience is rapt, but I am unmoved. It's so sad, that song. Why are the Irish so melancholy? Who needs sad songs about parting, loss, and death? I'm 20. This is 1944. I'm alive, I'm not biding anywhere, my life is about to begin. Enjoy the party.

The evening star is bright in the west as people pick up their sleeping toddlers and trickle home.

"Goodbye, God bless you, Josette" (hug and kiss).

"Take care of yourself, don't forget to write" (wave).

"Don't take any wooden nickels" (har har).

"The WACS and Waves will win the war" (salute).

"Your Da is proud of you, child" (pat on shoulder).

"Leave some of the handsome guys for us girls at home" (wink).

"Be careful, Josette" (anxious peck on cheek).

"Goodbye. Good luck." Goodbye. Goodbye. Goodbye.

After Mother and I finish the washing up I take all my stuff upstairs and fit what I can into my maroon-striped graduation-present suitcase, which seems to be waiting expectantly by the dresser ready to go in the morning.

I say my prayers; the usual one for Michael, recovering as far as we know from the broken ankles he got on D day when his chute only opened part way; I ask God to take care of Mother and Daddy while I am away and bless Buddy. Please God, don't let me mess up. I can feel the cool links of my ID bracelet on my wrist, I can hear Daddy snoring in the room across the hall. Somewhere a dog is barking. My pillow is damp. Why would I be crying? Just tired, I guess. All that excitement from the party.

"Give 'em hell, Kitten." Poor Daddy has never sent a daughter off to war before. Sweat trickles down the side of his face under his straw boater, he doesn't look as jaunty as usual, must be the heat in this stifling station. Two years ago, when Michael left for the paratroops it was winter and the two of them, Michael and Daddy, stood in the same railroad station mock-boxing and banging each other on the muscle in that manly/palsy way. The day Arvid left, I wanted so much to be there to say goodbye, but he had turned on his heel and walked away without a word when I wouldn't quick-marry him before he left. It would never work, Arvid, I had told him. Our families are too opposed, why don't we just wait? You don't love me, that's it, he said, his long, fair face impassive. Forget Arvid, megirl. He's found an English girl to marry, didn't take him long.

Daddy is saying, "Write if you need anything." He hands me a folded-up five-dollar bill. "Five dollars?" He winks, "Don't spend it all in one place." Once when I was six he gave me a nickel and told me not to spend it all in one place. I dutifully trudged to Old Gus's to buy two Mary-Janes, penny each, then trudged four blocks in the other direction to find Mrs. Malud's Candy Shoppe to spend the rest. I got lost, it was after dark when they found me. What a hue and cry that was, they were sure I had been kidnapped.

"Will do, Daddy. Won't do." I stick my white purse under my arm, put my fingers up in the V for Victory sign, and rattle off the Morse code for V, "dit, dit, dit, DAH. Don't worry so much about me, Daddy." Ever since I was born you have thought I couldn't live unless you were right there. I'm not made of sugar, I don't melt in the rain. It's a good thing for me that Aunt Geraldine convinced Mother that it would be nice for "our Josette" to get out and see the world before she settles down to marry and have babies.

Geraldine and all the aunts made a bunch of novenas for their "intention" but I think it was Mother and Aunt Geraldine wearing Daddy down. He always says he feels outnumbered by Mother's five sisters, especially when they gang up on him. They should name battleships after my Aunt Geraldine. Poor Daddy.

Where is that darned train? I'm suffocating in this crowd. Mother isn't saying anything. "Look, Mother, there's that poster we like." On the poster a pretty, starry-eyed girl in a natty Waves uniform stares off into the middle distance. An older woman with her hair in a bun, wearing a flowered Hoover apron, has her arm around the girl's shoulder; in the window behind them hanging from a blue cord is a red-bordered square banner with a white field containing two blue stars. "He'll be home sooner now that I've joined the Waves," the poster proclaims in large letters. Mother smiles a tiny smile, I squeeze her arm. She never says how worried she is about Michael, but she got one of her three-day sick headaches when she got word that he had been wounded. "Now you be sure to get a new service flag with two stars, one for me and one for Michael, promise?" Mother bites her lip.

All around us in the cavernous station people are saying goodbye, little clots of family groups everywhere, lovers clinging like limpets, fathers looking stoic, mothers blinking back tears. The big iron filigree hands of the station clock don't seem to be moving at all. An angel must have just passed through the station because for an eerie, silent moment all the people seem to run out of conversation at once. Unspoken thoughts and unasked questions hover overhead in the sudden movement of air in the station. Will I ever see you again? Will you come home blind, in a wheelchair? Changed? Will you forget me and love another? Will you ever see the child I am carrying for you? Will you be faithful to me? Will you wait for me to come back? Holy Mother of God, those same questions must be hovering, trapped by the coffered ceiling by the enormous flag, trapped since the Big War and the war before that. The moment passes and the ordinary wartime hubbub resumes.

My feet hurt. My head hurts. My black patent-leather belt is cinched too tight, but I dare not put my orders down to do anything about it. Daddy looks like he is impatient for the train to come, too. "I'll mail my civvies home as soon as I get my uniform. I'll send you a picture of me in Navy blue soon's I can." I look at my mother and think, don't cry. Puh-leeze. Least not until I go. You said I should go, you know you did.

Out loud, I joke, "Join the Navy and see the world, eh, Mother?"

She doesn't even smile, just pushes back the tiny veil on her little white hat so she can see to rummage in her knobby white purse. She fishes out a cellophane packet and hands it to me. "This is a Miraculous Medal, Angel. Monsignor O'Callaghan blessed it especially for you. Keep it with you always." It's a miracle I'm getting out of here, I think, but I reach out and take it, ignoring Daddy's snort. I figure you never can tell about medals and a person like me can handle all the miracles she can get. I look at my mother resolutely not crying beside my father. Has she shrunk? She wasn't always that small, was she? I scrub my finger under my nose like I always do when I am puzzled and I catch Mother's automatic headshake. She's been like that all my life. She doesn't want me to get any bad habits. She wants me to be her angel. She makes me feel like I'm six years old again.

"Hey, wake up, daydreamer." Daddy touches me on my arm. Buddy reappears from where he was talking to some Army Air Corps guys by the four-for-a-quarter photo booth. "I think they are calling your train. A whole platoon of Germans could sneak up on you while you are daydreaming. I hope you don't daydream on duty, young lady."

"Oh, Daddy, you know I won't." I pick up my suitcase and brush Daddy's rough cheek with my lips. "Goodbye, Mother, I'll write every week and tell you everything. Don't worry about me." Mother reaches out for a hug, great whispery clouds of carnationy cologne enveloping me. I'm already holding my suitcase and an awkward hug it is.

"'Bye Mother, 'bye Daddy, 'bye Buddy. Take care of things."

I turn and run across the dirty marble floor to where a group of civilian girls forms a raggedy line under the officious whistle of a brisk young woman in a Navy uniform. How long before we exchange our silly flowery dresses for the neat and natty uniforms? I turn for a final wave at my parents, standing exactly where I left them. As I catch their eyes they wave vigorously, like windshield wipers moving back and forth. Neither is crying. The Lord at least has spared me that.

"All aboo-oo-ard." The trainman leans way out of the door.

"Ten-shun. Forward, harch." Our colorful group straggles up the platform, following the sign held by the Navy lady who is our shepherd, and mashes its way into the crowded cars. With a sudden jerk and a great whoosh the train roars out of the station.

CHAPTER 2

Boot

The barracks, called Building E, when we get to it toward the end of the first day of boot camp is a surprise. In all the war movies barracks are ugly wooden buildings surrounded by a sea of mud. This one is a regular apartment building on the corner of 197th Street and University Avenue in the Bronx. Inside is a regular apartment lobby with a black and white checkerboard floor. A Wave wearing an armband with the letters MAA on it (for Master-at-Arms) sits at a desk. She is abrupt and bossy, like almost everybody else we have heard all day. "The elevator is only for officers and people on important Navy business. Enlisted walk up or down. Move it."

Thank the good Lord for small favors—it's only a five-story building. Dermody, Josette P. is billeted on the top floor, I find out, not exactly to my surprise. Top deck, *deck*, not floor. You're in the Navy now, megirl. I hoist my gear and trudge up the stairs. The Navy insists it's a ladder. Everything has a different name, but this looks like a plain old stairway to me with a banister stuck into the bumpy tan stucco walls. Longest ladder I ever climbed, which goes with the longest day in my whole entire life.

When I woke up on the train I wondered where I was. I pushed up the shade to look out just as the sun was coming up. A broad river—must be the Hudson if we are this close to New York—was sparkling far below in the fine morning. Anchored in the middle was a fat, white oceanliner. First one I ever saw in real life. The back of the ship said *Gripsholm*. I drew in my breath; she was the ship we saw in the newsreels bringing refugees away from Hitler, as many as she could. I'm glad they got this far. That is pretty much what this everlasting war is all about, getting everybody away from Hitler. He looks so funny, talks so funny, and does so much damage. It's hard to figure out, but we will beat him, *and* Tojo. Then everybody can go home.

We got off the train at Grand Central Station, bigger and more echoey than the station back home, but it had the same four-sided clock with the filigree hands, the same bustle, the same "Buy War Bonds" posters. Our brisk and efficient temporary mother-hen gathered our rumpled, confused group together and checked off our names from a list on her clipboard, like she wanted to make sure she hadn't mislaid any government property during the trip. Once she was certain we were all present and accounted for, she about-faced quickly and descended into a dark stairway with us behind her, trying to keep up, chirping and cheeping as dumb as any new chicks. The tracks ran every which way like a nest of snakes, but our fearless leader knew exactly which one to take to get us to the Bronx and Hunter College. The subway was scary, dark, and noisy, I was glad I wasn't alone as we hurtled along. When we emerged into daylight again I put down my too-heavy suitcase for a minute to catch my breath and have a look-see. The Bronx looked peaceful and quiet after the subway, the morning sun slanting all green and goldy through the trees in that almost-end-of-summer way. Not quite what I expected of New York. Our Wave leader shouted, "Compa-nee, fall in!" but all we did was troop along the sidewalk behind her in a raggedy line that would have set Sister Monica up for a sick headache. (Poor Sister Monica, still scaring the bejabbers out of six-year-olds, most likely, like she did me long ago. She told us over and over that our Lord did love an orderly line. We never asked how she knew.)

We reached a gate. On the brick gatepost was a brass sign,

U.S. NAVAL TRAINING SCHOOL (WR)
NO VISITORS

The curly-haired Wave shore patrol waved us right on through. Should I salute? Nobody else does, forget it. I'm really here, in the Navy. The U.S. Navy. Joan of Arc was Army, of course, khaki underwear and all that. Poor thing. Navy is the way to go. Are there any sailor saints? No one I can think of, but there is always Holy Mary, *Maris Stella,* Star of the Sea. Have to do, I suppose.

The Navy took over Hunter College when the admirals decided to have thousands and thousands of Waves. They like to call it the USS *Hunter,* as though the red brick buildings (some covered with ivy) and the grassy lawns were a gigantic seagoing vessel. Anchors painted everywhere didn't change Hunter all that much; it was still what it had always been, a pretty campus. "You will be trained at the finest women's colleges," the glossy recruiting brochures had promised. So far so good. We walked along the sand-colored flagstone walks that lace the green lawns. There were stone benches here and there, but nobody was sitting on them. Planted along the walks at regular intervals little triangular trees stood at attention, not like any tree I ever recognized in Michigan. Where's the ocean? All the water I could see was across the street marked Goulden Avenue. Behind a cyclone fence twinkled a wedge of water with tiny waves lapping sedately at the rock walls forming its borders. Must be some kind of reservoir. I felt cheated. Anyone would think if she went to all the trouble to join the Navy she'd see an ocean. Atlantic, Pacific, Indian, take your choice. Maybe that comes later.

We marched, sort of, toward a big building that looked like a fort. In front, Old Glory was snapping against the blue of the sky. Patriotism, one of the unequivocal virtues. Thank God, there is at least one. Our guide left us inside the fort, which was really a National Guard armory turned into a receiving station for the Navy. It was dim and cool after the brightness outside. I got in line and waited. And waited. And waited. The dozen girls who came from Detroit, none of whom I knew, were just a small number of the people being "processed." The line didn't seem to move at all. I wondered what Mother and Daddy were doing now. Daddy probably hung up the service flag with two stars as soon as he got home. He would. He never liked hiding Dermody light under a bushel. Did Buddy win the scrap-metal drive his troop was putting on? Did anybody write Arvid Lundgren that I enlisted? I expect his mother would have. Does anybody miss me yet?

On the wall near where I was shifting from one foot to the other was a large poster. Across the top large letters proclaimed, "Through These Doors Pass The Most Essential Women In The World." I felt at least two inches taller. They must know what they are doing, all those admirals. And Mrs. Roosevelt, too, of course, she's the one who kept after them to allow women in the U.S. Navy like the British had their Wrens. In the middle of the poster was a picture of a pretty, perky girl with her shoulders back and her hands on her hips, wearing a Waves uniform. Somebody named Mainbocher had heeded the request to make the Navy girls some "glad rags" and so had designed the spiffy outfit as his contribution to the war effort. Spiffiest thing I ever saw, so much nicer than the Army or Marines, in my opinion.

"Gangway, gangway. Heads up." A bustle of activity around me, a raspy voice yelling in my poor ear. "Look alive, Seaman Recruit. Didn't you hear the 'Gangway'?" The owner of the voice elbowed me aside, the rest of the girls parting like the Red Sea, as a tall officer with a square jaw strode dryshod up to the processing desk and said something to the Wave sitting there, then whirled and clacked out the same way she came. No time wasted by that one. The sea of people closed together again. The raspy-voiced woman gave me a dirty look as she passed by me. How was I supposed to know "Gangway" means "Get out of the way"? Why didn't they just say so?

Sighing, I returned to examining the poster. Nothing else to do. The pretty, perky girl was still smiling her painted smile. No wonder. She wasn't hot and crowded and pushed around by people yelling "Look alive" in her ear. I rubbed one ankle with the other foot and muttered to no one in particular, "Hurry up and wait."

"Pipe down, Seamen. No talking in the ranks." The voice snaked out like a cat-o'-nine tails as I tried to look invisible. I innocently examined the border of the poster, which had pictures of the insignia patches that told the world what you did, like a red cross meant hospital corpsman. I recognized some of the insignia from the recruiting pamphlets that always told you what glamorous, interesting, war-winning jobs you could have in the Navy. Please, God, don't let them make me a hospital corpsman, I wouldn't be any good around sick and wounded people.

"Shake a leg, Seaman Recruit. Look alive. You're holding up the line." The commanding voice was definitely directed at me. This wasn't beginning well at all. The line had reached the scarred desk where a red-headed Wave held out her hand expectantly. I handed over the getting-grubbier-every-minute envelope containing my precious orders. "Sound off," she said, as she opened it. I just stood there. The girl behind me nudged me and hissed, "Tell her your name, backwards."

"Dermody, Josette Patricia," I squeaked.

"Your service number. Your rank."

"766 73 28. Apprentice Seaman."

"Seaman Recruit," the redhead corrected. She looked down a checklist, ticked off my name, handed me a sheaf of papers and cards. She looked directly at me and said, "Welcome aboard, Sea-man." Does that mean they are glad I am here?

The rest of the day was a blur as we whirled from station to station, handing in a card here, signing another form there. They gave me a Waves hat, a spanking white upside-down pudding bowl with a brim, which looked ridiculous with my civilian clothes. At another stop they fitted us with clunky black shoes, shoes not for show but for marching. They might as well have had wings on their heels for me. I felt happy with them until the girl who had nudged me from behind in line sat down next to me for her fitting. She stretched out her foot, flexed her pretty ankle, and grimaced, "Ugly, ain't they? My sister says they are the very devil to polish. You have to use spit."

"I can't imagine spitting on my shoes. That's disgusting." Maybe this wasn't going to be as easy as I thought.

She laughed and tucked a long strand of black hair behind her ear. "Darlene, that's my sis, says you do a lot of things you never thought you could do. You get used to it. There's a war on, you know."

"Look alive, Seamen. Look alive, look alive." Someone was hurrying us off to somewhere else. JesusMaryandJoseph, I've only been here part of one day and already I am tired of it. Bossy people are yelling at me from all sides to look alive, on the double, make way, gangway, now hear this, move it. Most of it seems to mean "hurry up." Navy sure makes a girl step lively.

Just before I expired from starvation they marched us into the mess hall, really just a cafeteria that smelled of steam and long-ago meat. Somebody barked over the clank of silverware and trays, "You've got exactly 23 minutes to get in and get out. We've got 5,000 hands to feed here." I plunked my tray, loaded with Swiss steak and gravy, carrots, baked brown potatoes, and apple turnovers, down next to the dark-haired girl who was blowing on the coffee in her handleless mug. She was the only person I knew to talk to in the whole place.

"Hi again. Need a throat made of asbestos. My name's Helene Baskerville."

"Josette Dermody. Your sister in the Navy, too?"

"Yep, she joined up last year. Aviation machinist's mate at Pensacola."

My mouth was full of steak and gravy. It tasted okay but needed quite a bit of chewing. I looked at my new friend. She's nice. When my mouth was empty again, I asked, "She like it? The Navy?"

"You bet. Good duty in Florida, all those gorgeous flyboys. She talked so much about it I signed up soon's I was 20. She says you get the hang of it sooner or later and then it ain't so bad." I winced at the "ain't." The last time I said "ain't" was ten years ago and Sister Veronica Louise whacked me one with the edge of a metal ruler that I can still feel.

"She give you any advice?"

"Lots. Watch out for sailors named W. T. Door." She laughed at my puzzled look. "You'll find out." I followed her as she got up to dispose of her tray under the sign that said, "Take What You Can Eat. Eat What You Take." "Okay, okay," I said to the sign. "Aye, aye, sir." Now I'm talking back to Navy signs. A bad sign, megirl.

Helene, alas, wasn't assigned to Building E. Nobody I had ever seen before was. I stop to get my breath at the door of apartment 5-D. A heavy-set girl with straw-like blonde hair pushes right by me and says, "Dibs on the bottom bunk." Doggone. Drat. Dibs is dibs. The other two bunks already have somebody's gear on them. "Linen room, c'mon." The blonde girl disappears and reappears with an armload of sheets and a blanket. She makes up her bunk and flops in one of the chairs, watching me as I flounder with the sheets on the top bunk. "Catholic, eh?" She says it as though "Cath" is three syllables. *Ca-aa-th-o-lick.* I feel for my specially blessed Miraculous Medal on the silver chain around my neck. "Back where I come from, we don't give Catholicks the time of day," she continues. I can feel my face flaming. I can't breathe. What should I say? What should I do? I can't get into a fight before my first day is over, can I? Before I can think of anything my new bunkmate continues, "You don't look too bad, though. Least you ain't a nigger. Them's the worst. Name's Tolliver. Coralee Tolliver. I'm from Johnstown, West Virginia. Where you from?"

I barely fight back an impulse to tell the fat fool my name is Joan of Arc. Claudette Colbert. My head is swimming. I can't remember when I have been so mad. Holy Mother, give me strength. If this Hillbilly-Sassenach person has no manners, I have. "I'm Dermody, Josette P. That's the way the Navy says it. I'm from Detroit. How do you do?"

"Glad t'meetcha," she says, as though she hadn't just been insulting. "You meet Corman and Jones yet? They're the other two." Before I can reply, one of the rhinestone buttons on her purple rayon dress pops off. "Drat. You got a safety pin? Thanks. Us Tollivers always serve. My great-granddaddy on my daddy's side, he was with Stonewall Jackson." She pauses for breath, I am just about to tell her I'm for Abe Lincoln all the way when there is a hiss and a staticky blurp before the squawk box spits a barely intelligible "Now hear this." Somebody wants us to do something on the double. Tolliver and I look at each other and shrug; nothing to do but follow all the girls pell-melling down the ladders to line up in the middle of the street wearing our new Navy white-topped hats with our motley civilian outfits. Somebody yells something that sounds like "Par-aye-rest!" I look around to see if anybody knows what we are supposed to be doing, because I sure don't. Tolliver is standing in the row in front of me off to one side. A movement ripples through the ranks, and I see Tolliver stand with her feet apart, solid, and fold her hands in the small of her back, her elbows sticking out. All the others are doing it, too—so now I know about parade rest. So much to learn. A very tall Waves officer with a high squeaky voice makes a welcoming speech about the privilege of serving in the oldest service. I'm so tired and so mad at Whatzername that I don't pay much attention to the speech.

Somebody yells "DIS-missed!" and we drag our weary selves back upstairs. A different somebody hollers, "Lights out!" before I have time to say anything more than "Where you from?" to my other two roommates who introduce themselves as Barbara Lee Corman from Louisville, Kentucky, and Mildred Jones from College Station, Kansas. They seem pretty nice. Plenty of time to get acquainted tomorrow. If there are any more like Tolliver I swear I'll go over the hill. Don't be silly, megirl. You'd end up in jail. You're in for the duration and six months. Every time anybody turns over or even moves, the bunks creak and the springs squeak. I can hear the different rhythms of other people's breathing all around me in the strange, dark apartment turned into a barracks. I almost forget my prayers, everything is so strange. Did Michael feel this way when he arrived at basic training? He'd never admit it, big brothers never do. You've made a lot of dumb moves, a lot of mistakes in your life, Josette, megirl, but this one gets the blue ribbon. Even if you could go home, everybody would laugh and say, "I told you so." Remember, sailors don't get homesick. Sailors don't cry. You're in the Navy now.

Barely have I gotten to sleep when a horrible, insistent buzzer jolts me out of a sweet dream about a picnic at Walled Lake with Errol Flynn. I bury my head in the pillow but the reverberations won't let up. This must be reveille, but how can that be? It should be a melodious bugle—you gotta get up, you gotta get up, you gotta get up this morning. So far life in the Navy isn't at all like those movies we watched at the Coolidge or the Fox back home. Maybe it gets better as it goes along. More like the movies.

All around me the humps in the other bunks stir and groan. I look at my watch. 5:30. Too early. I groan, start to roll out of bed, just in time remembering that I am in the upper bunk. I jump gingerly to the deck, the wooden floor slippery and cold under my bare feet.

In the head I discover that "my aunt from Red Bank" has arrived early. All I need is the Curse. Nothing for it but to borrow a Kotex from Tolliver who has fortuitously provided herself. "Remember, mate. You can't have cramps in the Navy."

"Whatever are you talking about?" I am still half asleep.

"There's a war on. Sailors don't get five days off a month." She looks like a fat yellow cat that has just swallowed the whole book of Navy regulations.

"Oh, knock it off, Seaman. You make me sick."

"How 'bout that?" the pretty tousled girl in the other lower bunk whose name I remember is Corman, gets up and laughs at us standing clench-jawed opposite each other. "You two better stop squabbling and get ready for chow. Shake a leg. We've only been here one day and already we're talking Navy."

CHAPTER 3

Ripples

We march raggedly across the pretty campus in the pearly morning light. The sun, barely up, tints the apartments across the reservoir a faint pink. Platoons of "old" Waves in their summer grays swing their black-gloved hands in unison as they march briskly toward the mess hall. As each group swings into range and they see us in our goofy mixture of Navy hats and shoes with our flowery summer cottons, they chorus in cadence, "Here come the Ripples. You'll be *sor-ree.*" Each platoon has an officer who feels compelled to squelch them with "Eyes in the boat, seamen. Pipe down." That bunch immediately pipes down, having made the point, but the platoons follow each other like carriers in a task force and each yells derisively, "You'll be *sor-ree, sor-ree, sor-ree.*"

"I can do anything you can do, honeychiles. Just you wait and see," the girl called Corman mutters under her breath as she marches next to me on the right.

"That goes double," I say, skipping a skip-hop to get back in step. Who do they think they are, anyhow?

Two helpings of French toast with bacon and several cups of steaming coffee revive my flagging spirits somewhat. "Why do they call us Ripples?"

"Little Waves, silly girl," Corman smiles. She's tall and very, very pretty. She could do for one of those wide-eyed, perky girls on the recruiting posters with her heart-shaped face, dimple in her chin, and wide blue eyes exactly the color of cornflowers. She acts like she's known she's pretty all of her life. She wipes her mouth daintily on her paper napkin and asks, "Why do they call a ship a she?"

"Give up," I say, playing the game.

"'Cause it costs so much to keep her in powder and paint."

"Doggone," Tolliver pulls a mouth like she's really upset. "Here I always thought it was 'cause she loves to ride on the bosom of a

21

swell." Everybody groans. It's just about the last laugh we have for a
while. Boot camp is turning out to be an obstacle course to weed out
the faint-hearted, the cry-babies, the pusillanimous. One thing Dermodys never were, quitters. Everybody knows the story about the girl
who packed her suitcase, lugged it down to the quarterdeck (what we
used to call the lobby), and asked the petty officer on duty to call a
taxi because she had had it and was leaving for home. Now. This
minute. The MAA didn't turn a hair, just kept on sorting out the
mail, and said, "I'll pretend I never heard that. I'll pretend I never
saw you tonight. You just turn right around and put yourself where
you are supposed to be. Move it." She moved it.

The scheduling office has our days laid out for us minute by
minute. Never a chance to think. Just follow along. Keep going by
pure stubbornness. I hate swimming—going around the rest of the
day with damp, stringy hair. But swimming isn't as bad as physical
training, all those jumping jacks are hell on shot-swollen arms. The
physical exams are horrible; the chest X-rays with the guy corpsmen
pointedly ignoring the lines of bare-breasted women; the pelvic exam
is worse, but soon over, unlike the shots, which are a foretaste of Purgatory. Honest to God, they make us cranky and sore, and just about
the time the effects wear off they give us another set. We line up in
the so-called daisy chain, roll up our sleeves, and grit our teeth. We
Waves never faint at shots, point of honor, because we know the guys
often keel right over when they get theirs. T.S., Sailor, we might have
said, but of course we never did.

Always slightly feverish and more than a little disgruntled, we
move, always in a crowd, from one place to another. Training films,
uniform fittings, selection interviews and tests. Along the corridors
are signal flags and ship silhouettes so we won't even waste a minute
standing in line. At one office I stand in line to sign up for war bonds
to be taken out of my $55 a month. If the war lasts long enough I'll
be a rich lady civilian someday. At another, I designate my mother
beneficiary of $10,000 dollars of GI insurance. "Makes me feel I'm
worth more dead than alive," I say to Jones, our fourth roommate.

"Don't worry about it," she comforts. More than she usually says.

The days turn into weeks, racing by on the double. First-aid
demonstrations. Fingerprints. Real dogtags with name, serial number, and blood type. Religion, too, in case anybody ever needs to

know. ID photos, scheduled, of course, immediately after swimming. I look like a pop-eyed rat fished out of the East River on mine. When I meet Helene one day at the Betty Boot Beauty Shop, she laughs at my complaint; her platoon had their ID pictures taken right after a gas-mask demonstration. Figures, a girl really looks her best with her eyes red-rimmed from tear gas and her hair all mashed from the gas-mask straps. Dontcha know there's a war on?

We know there's a war on, all right. We have movies, the training-movie kind with the triumphant patriotic music, a series called "Why We Fight" or "The Battle of Britain." We get briefings and war reports from a Wave officer with a pointer, large maps and charts, little ship figures denoting tonnage. "We" have more. Tonnage. To get stuff from one part of the world to another, in case anybody asks. "They" used to have more U-boats. Now we think our destroyers and our planes got most of the wolfpacks that were sinking our convoys. One day the news reports that some unhappy German officers tried to blow up Hitler, but the bomb didn't kill him. Too bad. Paris is liberated, but there is still fierce fighting everywhere in Europe. Our Marines invaded Tinian, a tiny speck on the map. I hear from Michael, too, still in that hospital in England. He brags about landing in the water and still keeping his rifle dry. That would be Michael all over, he doesn't mention his broken ankles. At least he's still alive.

I send letters home a couple of times a week, making it all sound so funny. Look Ma, no hands. Yep, Daddy, the old moxie is still there, you know I would write more if they didn't keep us so busy all the time. I have to be careful what I write. It doesn't seem kind to tell them I would rather be here than there, we like to agree I'm just doing my patriotic duty. On the other hand I can't write them when it's awful, when I'm so tired I don't care if I die right there on the drill field and the whole platoon marches over my inert body, when I get so fed up and frustrated with stupid rules and insane regulations that spending the rest of my natural life in solitary in the brig seems like a vision of a peaceful vacation. Fortunately, these black moods don't last long and don't often get into the letters home. I don't need to be reminded, as the women in our family have been all the way back to Eve, that I had made my bed and now I must lie on it. Or what if Aunt Geraldine, who has had her run-ins with the bishop and probably would take on the pope, decides to take on the U.S. Navy? All I need is for her to write a letter to Eleanor Roosevelt and demand that conditions surrounding her goddaughter, Seaman Recruit Dermody, Josette P., be investigated right away. What if Mrs. Roosevelt does show up? She just might, you know. I would die of mortification. Better to keep it funny, so I write about the marching songs we have:

Oh the coffee that they give us
they say is mighty fine,
good for cuts and bruises
and tastes like iodine.
Oh, I still love the Navy
and I don't wanna go
I don't wanna go home.

I know Michael would understand, but we aren't supposed to write "down" letters to people at the front—we are supposed to keep up their morale.

In some ways boot camp is like a harder Girl Scout camp; much harder, of course, with the purpose more deadly and serious than the carefree days of youth and summer. Here they fill us up to the Plimsoll line with lore and lingo: the rooms where we learn naval traditions are full of glass cases with exquisite models of historical ships, the *Bonhomme Richard,* the *Constellation,* the *Monitor,* and the *Merrimac.* Buddy would be fascinated, he loves models, fills his room at home with balsa-wood planes hanging from strings. Something is magical about these ship models with their teeny tiny brass cannons and all that complicated rigging. President Roosevelt loves ship models, that's easy to understand. If I ever got to be president I'd have lots, too.

Modern ship recognition is harder. How will I ever learn to tell them apart? The models are all made to scale—twelve inches for our big new battle wagons and the carriers; the older battleships and the others, cruisers, destroyers, get littler and littler, down to the bitsiest ones. The whole set looks like a baby's bathtub fleet painted gray. I write in the little looseleaf notebook I carry everywhere with me: "Iowa cls btlshps, nwst, bggst, recog lng rsng prw, sistrs, Misuri, N.Jer. Wisc."

Tolliver is wonderful at aircraft recognition. Flash one at her and she can name it just like that. I hate her. It's pretty much the same as ship recognition except that all the little models are painted black. Teachers keep flashing them at us, we are supposed to learn them like we learn a friend's face, by conformation. There are so many: bombers, fighters, dive bombers, torpedo planes, dihedral wings, gull wings. We don't have to remember the Japanese names for their planes, thank the good Lord. They mostly have nicknames like Emily and Betty and Zeke. Sometimes Zeke is Zero. Write it down. German planes, British planes, Russian planes, Heaven help us. From the top, from the side, from the bottom. American planes have names and numbers: F4Fs are Hellcats, B-17s are Flying Fortresses, the newer B-24s are Liberators. That's the official name. The guys call them Flying Prostitutes because of the narrow wings. No visible means of support. Get it, get it? My mind goes wandering off . . .

Arvid is a bombardier on a B-17. I hope his war bride English-Eileen-person can cook. Arvid's mother is a baking machine. She makes her own bread, Swedish rye, and braided prune-filled coffee cakes with almonds and white frosting. Before sugar rationing she baked mountains of cookies that looked like pale pretzels with sugar instead of salt, cookies with anise, cookies that looked like rosettes rolled in powdered sugar.

The last time I saw Arvid he was home on leave before he left for England. We had gone to see *Mrs. Miniver* and crunched home through the snow. Arvid always looked handsomer in the winter; the cold flamed his pale cheeks and made his blue eyes bright. He has a big friendly smile, but he got serious. "I'm asking you for the last time. Marry me, Josie. Marry me now before I leave." Arvid was determined to have everything signed, sealed, and delivered before he went overseas. Most of the guys said they wanted somebody to come home to and lots of people rushed their weddings. He had been asking me for a year, but I wouldn't say yes. I really liked him, but this wasn't love, was it? He put his arm around me and kissed me on the mouth. His skin was cold from snow and wind, his breath tasted like coffee and almond cookies. He was so tall he had to bend over to kiss me. I stood on tip-toe, sheltered from the icy wind by his greatcoat. I just wanted to stand there forever, safe and passive, warm and sweet, but after a minute I pushed him away.

"It would never work, Arvid." My breath made a cloud between us. "Your father hates me. My family would never let me marry a Protestant . . ." I almost wished he could convince me it would work. I took my rose mittens off and blew on my fingers.

"Don't be such a scaredy-cat, Josie. Pa really likes you. He just has those old country ideas about religion and politics. That wouldn't have anything to do with us." He leaned down to kiss me again, more insistent this time. He was so big I felt overwhelmed. I took a deep breath and drew back.

"I just can't, Arvid. I just don't want to be married yet." A little voice deep down inside of me whined, 'I don't fancy being a nineteen-year-old widow, probably with a baby. I'd have to live with my parents forever.' I couldn't tell Arvid that I was more scared of that than of his crusty old father with his pipe and gruff ways. There was a moment there when time seemed to stand still and neither of us breathed, a crystalline globe like haloes around our heads, where if he had said something romantic like "Love conquers all," I would have given in. I hadn't turned down all that many proposals, but I'd seen lots of movies and read tons of books. Maybe he didn't really love me. Maybe it was just the war. My head whirled, my heart raced, and I couldn't find anything to hang on to.

"If that's the way you want it," he said. The shining globe shattered into a million shards as he turned to go—it was just ice crystals from our breath after all. I looked at him. He looked back at me, but didn't say anything. His boots squeaked on the snow as he strode down the porch stairs and down the walk. I went into our warm, dark house, where everybody was, Thank you God, asleep, and curled up in a ball in my bed. Why does it hurt so much? He left the next day without a phone call or anything. Just left. Like that. In one way I felt a big sense of relief, but another part of me was sad and mad and empty at the same time. I told everybody I was sick, shut the door to my room, and wouldn't tell anybody what was the matter. They were already unhappy enough with me for going out with somebody who wasn't Catholic. Mother had an idea of what had happened but I didn't want to talk about it. I was glad I hadn't when I heard he'd married somebody in England.

I'll probably never be in love again. It's not fair. That was last year. I mostly don't think about him, but I can't help myself when I see the newsreels showing the waves of bombers on a raid over Germany. Flocks of planes in the sky, like mechanical geese in a wedge. Sometimes a puff of flak collides with one of the planes and it spirals slowly to the ground like a maple seed twirling toward the sidewalk in summer. Time stops. It takes an awful long time. Sometimes you see the chutes pop out and open with a white jerk—the plane on the grainy, gray film keeps twirling slowly, trailing smoke and debris, until it hits the ground and digs halfway in. I do wish Michael hadn't explained, one time when he was home on leave, that when a plane like that goes down the centrifugal force will sometimes pin guys against the bulkheads of the spinning plane and they can't get out. When I see those newsreels my heart pounds and my palms get sweaty. What if one of those chutes is Arvid, down behind enemy lines? What if he was still on the plane when it hit? Holy Mother, nobody would notify me. I'm not his wife.

Corman notices that I am daydreaming and jostles me with her elbow, pointing with her head at the instructor who was saying something about the maneuverability of the Japanese Zero. Pay attention, she mouths. Nuts, I hiss back. I can recognize a Zero. Actually, it's a real pretty little plane, trim and graceful like flight itself. Don't suppose it would be particularly patriotic to say so, and I don't suppose I would have time to think how pretty they are if there were several on my tail. I make a notation in my little notebook. "Zke, manuvable, no armr." The voice in the front of the room drones on. All I want to do is sleep. Sleeping on duty is a capital offense, punishable by death. In boot camp? Sometimes I think they are just trying to scare us. You never can tell though, there is, after all, a war on.

Saturday at last. Corman, Tolliver, and Petrelli, the Italian girl from the other bedroom, have been harmonizing like the Andrews Sisters, or trying to, all afternoon. We have a little bit of free time on station liberty, a nice change from having every minute "look alived" for us. Their voices rise, pure and sweet, even though some of the songs are silly.

"Don't make my girl a sailor,"
  the weeping mother said.
"Make her a Wac or send her back
  to Lockheed school instead.
She's always been a homegirl,
  she's never been to sea.
A man in every port is not
  is—zz-z not
  the life she learned from me."
They collapse in a heap of giggles.

"Haven't seen a man in any port yet," Petrelli says.

"Haven't seen a port, either."

"This place is like a convent. Sorry, Dermody," Corman laughs.

"Don't sorry me. In a convent they don't talk about sailors and boyfriends and husbands all the time. Even you ought to know that . . ." I am not going to let them get on my nerves.

"Let's do 'Bell Bottomed Trousers' next. If we get real good maybe we can go on the Navy Bulletin Board program on Station WOR." Petrelli has big dreams about being a radio star when the war is over. She has a sweet alto, has already tried out for the Singing Platoon.

"That would put recruiting off. Probably set the war effort back six months." Being with people all the time is certainly not helping my disposition any, but I can't help myself.

"What are you trying to prove, Dermody, eh? Always acting so superior, so ugly?" Corman stands there, pigeon-toed, arms akimbo, her head cocked to one side, like she always does when she is exasperated. "Tolliver here reads comic books all the time and she'll likely make ensign before you do."

"You ain't just whistling Dixie." Tolliver flops heavily on her bunk; with a grunt of satisfaction she pulls out a raggedy comic from under her mattress.

"All of you make me sick." I can feel my Irish rising, my face getting red. "Why are you always picking on me?"

"Well, podden me." Petrelli flounces back to her own room.

"You shouldn't be so touchy, honeychile." Before Corman can continue inventorying my sins and shortcomings a horrible klaxon splits the air. "Drat, why do they have to do this every night?"

"Doggone it all to hell." Tolliver rolls off her bunk and begins closing the windows, first shoving her comic book under the mattress.

"Dermody, Jonesy's in the shower. Take her her raincoat and shoes. Coralee, ladies don't swear. Turn on all the lights." Corman has her take-charge voice going as she stows stuff in the lockers and slams the doors shut.

"This is so goddamn stupid," Tolliver complains even as she obeys. "Why do we have to turn on the lights for a stupid fire drill?"

"Ours not to question why . . . ours but to do or die. So the firemen can see, I reckon. Shake a leg you all, they're timing us."

We clatter down the ladder, all of us, ladies or not, ready to swear at anyone who bumps our sore shot-swollen arms—double tetanus and typhoid shots this time. We form up on University Avenue, looking as dignified as we can with our rosebud or striped pajamas sticking out under our raincoats, our bare ankles showing about our black shoes, our hair wet or in curl rags under our white-crowned hats. Our civilian neighbors, those who hadn't been emptied out of their nice apartments when the Navy took over Hunter and environs for our boot camp, are taking the air and watch us idly. The little kids fall in behind our platoons and ape everything we do. When we sound off they yell, too, their little faces aching with solemnity as they clench their grubby little fists in the small of their backs. When we "To the left, harch," they do, too. When we march back into the building a very pregnant civilian lady rushes into the street and grabs a little guy by the back of the belt just as he's about to follow us inside. "You, Arnie. Stay outta the street. I toldja a million times." Poor Arnie. Lucky Arnie. Stay out of the street? Stay out of the war, kid.

CHAPTER 4

Waves

Fire drills or air-raid drills every night are only the half of it. The Navy is conditioning us not to waste time asking questions, we should just respond to the drill. A misbegotten granny knot could screw up the whole war, whether it is in the tie of a yeoman striker in Cedar Rapids or in the cable of a ship of the line in a North Atlantic gale. An un-proffered salute could dissolve centuries of discipline, possibly leading to mutiny and death and all of our grandchildren speaking German or Japanese. Nobody puts it quite that way, but they make every little thing so important. Growl you may, but go you must. That's what the Navy says. By this time we have all learned to growl under our breaths. Aye, aye, sir.

My little dog-eared notebook grows fatter and fatter. "Salut cmding ofcr whenevr meet him," I write and draw a little picture of a shoulder board and a sleeve with four stripes. "Aye, aye, sir" means "I understand and will comply. *Does not mean yes.*" I underline that last part twice, they make such a big deal out of it. "To pass ofcr, cm up on ofcrs lft, trn bdy sltly to rt, salute, —say, 'By yr leave'—hold salute." When they say officers they always mean men, otherwise they say "Women Officers," who have "cmd only ovr wm—wear blu braid insted gold."

I have by this time a permanent case of writer's cramp, my middle knuckle has a permanent ink stain because my fountain pen leaks a little, and I am developing a permanent head cramp from trying to remember all this stuff getting crammed in so fast. Tolliver and Corman, not so much Jonesy, laugh at me with my conscientious little notebook permanently stuck in my palm, but they borrow it to study at night in the barracks when I am writing letters. Everything is so different here, even the alphabet. Able, Baker, Charlie, Dog, Fox, Easy, no, dummy, Easy, Fox. That's not so hard, but there is a flag that goes with each letter with a special meaning like "We have smallpox on board" or "We need a pilot" or "Leaving port."

***

"Lord have mercy, what are they teaching us all this old, old stuff for?" Tolliver hates anything historical unless it has something to do with what she calls the War Between the States. She's crabbing her way through the lecture today. She looks a little feverish, I guess we all do from the latest battery of shots. I think history is exciting; in all the historical novels I borrowed from the library back home everybody always has such interesting lives, meeting pirates, dashing guardsmen, superheroic saints, and having romances and adventures at every turn.

Up in front of the lecture hall the instructor is going on. "*Naval History* and *Traditions* are *So Important* to the *Esprit* of the *Oldest Service.*" We can hear the capital letters as she emphasizes points with the little ship models she holds up.

"I love the ones with sails. Wouldn't you love to sail on one?" I ask, sotto voce.

"Sure you would," whispers Petrelli. "I saw this movie once where they flogged the sailors. Just beat them all to hell till their backs was bloody meat."

"I saw that one, too." Tolliver brushes a tendril off her damp cheek. "*Mutiny on the Bounty*. That Clark Gable now, he can put his shoes under my bed anytime." She brightens up perceptibly at the very thought.

"Knock it off, Seamen." The square-faced officer, ignoring the lateen-rigged model she has in her hand, is searching, radar-like, for the source of the inattention.

"Too bad she hasn't got a cat-o'-nine tails handy," Petrelli can't resist saying, her angelic face immobile. We have to hide a small fit of mutinous giggling by coughing.

"Knock it off." We knock it off.

There must be a whole department in Washington, in the Navy Department somewhere, that does nothing but dream up tests for us poor overworked boots to take. Today we have to go to one where we listen to *tones* through earphones. I can't distinguish one from another and they make my head ache so much my teeth hurt. Oh well, who wants to be a radioman anyway?

The next one is really easy, but I blow it. Not so much blow it as torpedo it. I didn't tell anyone about my devious little plan to avoid yeoman school in the middle of Oklahoma. I figured the Navy might not have learned how to read minds like the Sisters can. It isn't easy to mess up on the clerical aptitude part because I have to suppress visions of Sister Victoria Albertine looking surprised, amazed, and downright indignant as I put "eldest" after "Eldorado," "Oregon" before "ordnance." They can't make me a yeoman if I can't spell, can't file, and can't capitalize, can they? If I wanted to file papers I could have stayed home and not left poor Mr. Meekin shorthanded like I did. Besides, there are plenty of girls dying to learn how to roll seven different colors of onionskin paper, in the proper order, of course, into the typewriter and how to make the Remingtons clackety-clack at breakneck speed. Not me. I cross my fingers and hope nobody finds out I cheated backwards.

By this time we are accustomed to doing everything the way the Navy wants us to. We march from training classes in Davis Hall to the mess hall to the gym to the drill field singing, "Give me a kiss by the numbers, I want to do things the Regulation way." I'm beginning to get the picture—if I survive the Navy I will be a different woman, strong and sturdy, able to march perfectly (well, almost), but only activated by a voice barking orders to "Move it, forward harch, shake a leg." I probably will have forgotten how to kiss anybody, by the numbers or not. Nobody to check it out on around here. No wonder all the gals went crazy when Frankie-boy Sinatra sang at one of the morale-building entertainments they put on for us—even that skinny little twerp looked good.

My biggest problem right now is Tolliver and her ignorant braying laugh. She figures it is her duty or something to get my goat. I never met a more annoying person in my whole entire life. I miss Consuelo and Sheila and Edith, poor Edith, but when I write to them I realize that they won't have a clue about what I'm telling them. Old stick-in-the-muds.

Corman is much nicer than Tolliver. She has a molasses accent, too, but hers is soft and pretty, except when she gets bossy, then it is no-nonsense time. She gets more mail than anybody, mostly flimsy V-mails from her beaux. That's what she calls them, her "bows."

We hardly ever hear much from our fourth roommate, a tall, dark girl with a space between her two front teeth. Her black hair is straight as an Indian's and chopped off right below her ears. When she talks she talks like regular people, but she hardly ever opens her mouth. She spends her time studying in the pool of lamplight on the wooden table in our cubicle with all the hub-bub around her. All she wants to do is finish boot camp and join her Dwayne at Storekeeper's School in Milledgeville, Georgia. Dwayne's picture is tacked up inside her locker door; he has an enormous Adam's apple, his ears stick out under his rakish gob hat, he's as blond as Jonesy is dark. When Jonesy isn't studying she's writing mushy letters on pink stationery, the kind that's punched out around the edges to look like lace. She joined up when he enlisted, they haven't been married very long. She isn't really unfriendly. She's just here. She's already married.

Eight of us live for now in apartment 5-D. We share a kitchenette as a place to store luggage. The Navy insists on making us swab the decks in the whole apartment; none of dares to ask what all that watery, soapy mopping is going to do to the varnished parquet floors. I know Mother would just die, but we are here to follow orders. We also share the single head, a small bathroom still retaining its prewar pink tiling and pink toilet, little black and white hexagonal tiles, some of them cracked, on the floor. The head is the only part of the stripped-down apartment that isn't as bleak as a CPO's heart, but none of us ever gets to really enjoy it for long, what with someone always banging on the door hollering "hurry up" or threatening to bang the door down, cut your only nylons up, or do something really desperate unless you get out of there toot sweet.

Is it because the Allies are in France that nobody ever says "right away"? Certainly since John Paul Jones, of sainted Navy memory, our sailors haven't had that much contact with the French unless you want to count "Mademoiselle from Armentiéres" way back in our dads' generation. Howsomever, it's "toot sweet" we all use. It's part of our new vocabulary along with "port" and "starboard." When I was 5 Mother put a red mercurochrome mark on the back of my right hand and on the tongue of my right shoe so I could learn the difference between right and left. Now I am 20 and grappling with the difference between port and starboard. We all are. Tolliver bursts into our cubicle, looking pink and cheery after a phone call home to those hills.

"Hey, Dermody, didja hear about the ninety-day wonder who kept running below to look at a paper in his safe? Wouldn't tell anybody

what his secret was. When his number came up Kwajalein they
opened the safe and . . ."

"Yeah, yeah, it said 'Port = Left. Starboard = Right.' I heard it a
thousand times."

"The trouble with you Catholicks is you ain't got no sense of
humor."

On Sundays we sort ourselves out, the Catholics going to mass in
the chapel and the Protestants to an all-purpose, all-denomination
service with their chaplains. Petrelli's bunkmate, a gangly, freckly gal
from California called Millie Davis, gets to spend a couple of luxuri-
ous hours each Sunday morning in the empty barracks/apartment,
with the head all to herself, because she had said she had no religious persuasion. It's too late for the rest of us to put that on our
records even if we had the nerve, so off we go. Mass is mass everywhere in the Church Universal, but it seems so different here with so
many flags in the church, no babies crying, no families a-tall. I'm so
tired by Sunday that the minute I hear that *Introibo ad altare Dei* I fall
almost asleep, just wake enough to stand up and sit down with the
rest of the uniformed congregation and walk up to take Commu-
nion. Our Heavenly Father will just have to hear my prayer and over-
look my sleeping at mass just like he overlooks eating meat on Fridays by our brave boys and girls giving their all for God and country.
Best I can do. Hail Mary, you understand, don't you? Explain it,
please.

Mother writes her weekly chatty letter that jumps from subject to
subject so she can get all the news of the week on a couple of pages:
the ration board has cut the fat and sugar rations again, fortunately
there are enough coupons traded around in the family to get Buddy
new shoes for school . . . He's growing like a weed, Josette, you won't
recognize him when you come home . . . Consuelo's almost ready for
her interim vows . . . Aunt Teddy is in the family way again and isn't
totally happy about it with Victor only nine months old . . . We don't
hear much from Michael, we don't even know if the packages of
cookies and shaving soap are getting through. I saw Mrs. Lundgren
at the market—the papers are full of the Eighth Air Force on bombing runs every day and she can't help but worry about Arvid . . . The
Germans are so stubborn . . . Daddy is working two shifts at the plant,

some secret hush-hush project he won't talk about . . . His bronchitis seems better . . . He sends his love . . . Take care of yourself, Angel. Get enough rest.

Yes, Mother.

"Hey, Dermody. You look just like Dopey in that raincoat." Nobody had ever told Tolliver if you don't have anything nice to say about somebody, don't say anything at all. Still, she does have a point. Even without a long mirror, I can see the Navy blue material covers my knuckles. Too big. Too bad.

Uniforms come in two sizes. Too Big and Too Small. Take the Too Big, common wisdom whispers, with all that good Navy chow you will soon grow into them. Actually, the New York department stores like Macy's and Gimbels had sent out fitters, New York ladies with accents I found hard to understand even when they didn't have a mouth full of pins. They measured, chalked, and pinned as I stood tall and still, trying not to fidget. "Not to vorry, Sweetie," the tiny, gray-marcelled lady on her knees pinning up the hem of my skirts had promised, "we make effryting perfect, just you see." Now two weeks later, the fitted uniforms have arrived and somehow a gremlin got into the works so Too Big is Too Ridiculous. Where is the pretty, perky, spiffy Wave of the recruiting posters? Not here, surely. This raincoat would be perfect for Boadicea, the Warrior Queen, whom all the books show with her stylish stout bosom encased in outsize armor. Wearing this coat she could shelter several of her ravaged daughters at the same time. 'Sfunny, I never thought of it before, but Boadicea looks just like my Aunt Geraldine—or is it the other way around? Sigh, I'll never, ever be a Warrior Queen.

"Hey, snap out of it. What are you standing there daydreaming for, Dermody?" Corman rushes in, balancing a toppling pile of gray, white, and Navy blue government issue. "Shove it over, honeychile," she snaps at Tolliver. She tumbles her gear on her bunk, she has her stencil cards with her name cut out on them in her hand. We have to put our names on *everything*. "I asked the storekeeper where my bell-bottomed trousers are. That's the trouble with this man's Navy. No sense of humor. None a-tall. Dermody, skedaddle down right quick and turn in that raincoat for a smaller one: somebody made a mistake. Move it."

"Fair enough?" I swear I'm getting stupider and stupider. Corman always knows what to do. I dash down the five flights to the main deck to explain my problem to the crabby MAA. (They are always crabby, so I don't pay any mind.) I rush over to Davis and attach myself to the end of a long disbursing line, get myself a raincoat that fits. Holy Toledo, life is so simple when you get the hang of it.

"Hate-the-Navy Hate-the-Navy Hate-the-Navy." Rain drums a tune on the window when we awake this morning. The green, gauzy days of August have dissolved into rainy fall, turning the world dark gray and wet. Not so gray and nasty, perhaps, as the gray, gray newsreels where our Good Guys, looking grimy and hollow-eyed from exhaustion, are chasing the recalcitrant Germans mile by bloody mile out of France. Still, it's gray enough. The usually placid waters of our little reservoir across Goulden Avenue whip and froth like a miniature sea in a typhoon. The little trees, so precisely planted along the flagstone walks in our pretty campus, bend and bow away from the wind like so many Rockettes, but when the wind changes direction and gusts, sending rainwater scudding in gray sheets into our formations, the frantic trees toss their branches wildly and try to shed their still-green leaves. I feel as frustrated as the trees, dancing to the buffetings of wind and weather, rooted in the Bronx with nowhere else to go.

Every morning when I wake to hear the tattoo of rain on the window I burrow back into my government-issue pillow. Between the buzzer and the time to actually hit the deck there is time to castigate myself. Dummy. Stupid. Retarded. Misguided. Simpleton. Foolish girl. You could have gone to work in a war plant, with your hair in a snood and a big paycheck, I tell myself. There, if the person you work for is an idiot, you don't have to salute. (Fingers together, thumb tucked inside, looking at the backside of those fingers.) You could have married Arvid and be at home with his mother, living on your allotment and learning how to cook lutfisk and bake fancy coffeecakes. Nobody to shout at you all the time, "Seaman this and Seaman that," never even a "Seaman, if you please." I'm never going to get out of bed again, no matter what.

"Last call, Dermody. One more minute—we dump you on the deck. You're making the rest of us look bad."

"You don't need to yell in my ear." Only a couple more weeks and I'll never have to see Coralee Tolliver's whey face again. I roll over and ease myself out of the covers carefully. No sense in messing them up this close to inspection. While I was lollygagging in bed they changed the Uniform of the Day three times so all I have to put on is the last one, which includes raincoats and havelocks. Havelocks are named after some loser general in the Crimean War, but funny name or not they cover our hats and shoulders with rubberized material and keep us dry. Dryish. We would look mighty peculiar all "hup-two-three-four"-ing with umbrellas, so we march in the rain looking for all the world like black mushrooms trying to be nuns. I slide into my place in formation seconds before Ramsey, our platoon leader, calls my name. Why are we standing here in the downpour taking roll? Do they really think we are likely to go over the hill—AWOL—to hide ourselves in some attic somewhere, growing gaunt and crazy till the war is over? However tempting the idea might be at times, it would never work. Daddy, probably wearing his too-tight American Legion uniform, would think it his patriotic duty to turn me in. I swore an oath, didn't I?

CHAPTER 5

Impressions

The rain stops this afternoon as the hurricane, for that is what all the rain was about, has moved out to sea. We don't have hurricanes back home in Michigan, so I guess it counts as an adventure hanging on to each other on the way to chow so we won't get blown away. We heard on Tolliver's little radio that authorities were worried that the roofs of the barracks might give way so they posted security people on the top decks all night—that was night before last, but nothing happened except it was harder to get to sleep worrying about the wind, which sounded like it was trying to blow the windows in. Now the drill field is squishy but usable, and marching is easier when it isn't too hot. I love marching, it's so neat, so precise and exact. I love the feeling of all of us acting in unison, like we are some bigger thing; I feel platoon-sized instead of just me.

The skinny Wave officer who is our drill instructor strains her vocal cords, making her soft voice assume the Habit of Command mode. "MARK TIME MARK. FORWARD HARCH." We move forward, counting the cadence, singing, "*Left, Left,* I hadda good job and I *left.*" Oops, I missed it. I slide a foot to get back into step and hope nobody notices. "First they hired me, then they fired me, then, by golly, I *left.*" We march up and down that muddy field until we are all ready to drop, but there's no rest for the wicked or anybody else in this Navy. It could be worse. At first they had Marines for DIs. Helene's sister told her how the tough guy in her platoon had yelled and cussed and got all red in the face when people didn't do it right. Sometimes he made people cry and then he would look all nonplused and helpless. Maybe he put in for sea duty. That's what we are here for, so all the guys can go off and fight.

Time for eliminations. Go ahead, try us, DI. Our company got the E for Excellence flag last week. We're good. She starts us off easy. TO THE LEFT, HARCH. TO THE OBLIKE, HARCH. TO THE REAR. Gotcha. Didn't say HARCH. About ten girls drop out and move over to the edge, laughing and giggling. The commands come faster and faster. It's dizzying. I see Tolliver look disappointed after she turns right instead of left and has to join the others against the cyclone fence. A few fat raindrops spatter down, the TO THE REAR HARCH follows the ABO-O-U-T FACE so fast we lose another five. Soon there are only five of us left, Corman, Petrelli, and two girls I never knew to talk to. We turn and move with magic feet for about ten minutes: like my Grandma Scanlon used to say, there are some days you just can't put a foot wrong. Petrelli tangles her feet on an ABOUT FACE, Corman moves without a HARCH. The other two girls are rosy-faced and damp with exertion, and then both goof at the same time. I'm the winner, standing there like the Cheese in "Farmer in the Dell." The others crowd around and thump me with congratulations. We form up again and swing off, singing, "Be kind to your fine-feathered friends, for a duck may be somebody's moth-er."

I still can't believe that I actually won. The feeling is the same as the time Michael persuaded the other guys to let me have a turn at bat and I heard the baseball connect with exactly the right spot on his Louisville Slugger and we knew I had hit a home run. Ka-thunk. I'll write Michael and tell him. He'll say, "'Ray, Josie," and make one of his jokes. Could it be that I am cut out for this Navy life after all? Last night I dreamt of three shining golden ships with sails of apricot or crimson silk, carrying sailors dancing hornpipes because the war was over. When reveille came too early at 0530, the war wasn't over, the weather was fouler than ever, but the vision of the beautiful ships with shimmering sails stayed with me all day, filling me with ginger ale bubbles of elation till lunch, and now this. I can drill better than anybody in the whole company. How 'bout that?

If Jonesy has a fault, it is quoting her Darling Dwayne so much. She's more talkative now than when she first met us and was so shy and silent. She tells us that her husband is an expert on the Japanese. He always calls them "those yellow-bellied, bandy-legged bastards" like most of the sailors do. He has been learning how to distinguish a Japanese from a Chinese. He shares this new knowledge by letter and phone with his wife, who has never seen a real live Japanese person either; she shares his insights with us, reading aloud from Dwayne's latest letter at night while Corman puts my aggravatingly straight hair up in curl rags. The Japanese are the enemy—Remember Pearl Harbor and all that—the Chinese are our allies. Dwayne worries about a potential disastrous misunderstanding should he ever get out of Milledgeville, where he's teaching basic accounting to storekeeper strikers. In his spare time Dwayne studies "Terry and the Pirates" comic-book training leaflets, chock full of information. "The Japanese have a separation between their big toe and their next toe from wearing sandals with a thong from a very young age," she reads aloud in her earnest, flat Kansas voice.

"Too bad the Imperial Marines wear Army boots," I say. Corman yanks the hair she is rolling for me as a "stow it" signal. Jonesy doesn't pay any attention, just keeps right on reading.

"The Japs mix up the sounds of 'R' and 'L'. If you capture one and you aren't sure which is which just ask him to say 'Lallapalooza.' If he says 'Raraparooza' you can be pretty sure you haven't nabbed Chiang Kai-shek by mistake." Noted. Lallapalooza. Just in case. Every week new lessons, Dwayne is a font of information.

"Wouldn't it be funny if the Japs thought all Yanks look alike, like they do?" I wonder.

"You got locks in you head, Amelican sailo," Tolliver says. She throws her pillow at me, but misses. Terrible aim.

A cold and rainy Sunday afternoon. We decide to forgo the official recreation offered and gather in our apartment lounge to watch Jonesy do impressions, like we used to do during skits at Girl Scout camp. We were all surprised at Jonesy, who's so quiet, but she's good. She can change her long, lanky body and undistinguished features into anybody she wants. We drape ourselves over the overstuffed chairs and watch her as she pushes her neck into the back of her collar, squeezes her elbows into her ribcage, and says through clenched teeth, "Seaman, sound off-f-ff. You're on REE-port."

"Ramsey, Ramsey," we all yell at once. Nobody has ever seen Ramsey smile. People speculate about what kind of boyfriends she has, if any. She's our platoon leader and natural enemy. "Do another, Jonesy."

Jonesy puffs out her cheeks and sticks out her lower lip. She seems to become short, square, and solid. She frowns and walks around the lounge rocking back and forth on her heels threateningly. She runs her finger in her imaginary white glove along the top of the window molding, shakes the finger in dismay and disgust, looks around truculently for a culprit. Most of us are doubled over laughing, but someone chokes out, "Lieutenant Adams."

I think momentarily of doing Chaplain Huntdziger buzzing through mass so fast his Sign of the Cross looks like he's brushing away gnats. Better not, megirl, it's probably sacrilegious. Besides, Jonesy is so much better. She can do Hitler and Mrs. Roosevelt, Betty Hutton, Martha Raye, anybody. She gets everything just right, like the way some of our officers, bright and nervous as thoroughbred horses, talk with their lower lips and jaws immobile. I tried it a couple of times, "Eyes in the boat, Seamen," I would spit out, but I found it impossible to keep my lower jaw from wagging up and down like ordinary people. Jones can do it easy. She says it is the way ladies learn to talk at Smith. How'd she know that?

"Izzat so?" says Tolliver, who's only half listening. "Who's Smith?"

"Smith College, dummy, where Officer Training is," Petrelli answers, hands on hips, waiting.

"You're So smart, Miss, Miss . . ."

Oh God, if Tolliver calls her Miss Dumb Dago again there's going to be blood on the moon. That dumb hillbilly doesn't realize that people don't like it if you call them names. Corman jumps between the two of them, smiling like she's pouring honey on pancakes, and says, "Maybe we should do something else for a change. Let's sing." We join her in "If you're nervous in the service, and you don't know what to do, have a BA-bee, have a BA-bee." Mother would just die over that one, I don't want to think what Daddy's reaction would be. What's happening to Mother's Angel and Daddy's Kitten? Not much, actually. I smile to myself because I have an image of dear, simple Sister Alphonse Terese, who must have gone to the convent straight out of kindergarten, saying how nice that Uncle Sam's sweet sailor girls are planning to adopt a dear little war orphan to give her a good Catholic home. Yeah, Sister. I reach over and take a cig from Petrelli's rumpled red pack of Pall Malls. You've made it so hard for me to embrace a life of wickedness and vice, Sister, but I'm doing my best. The harsh tobacco makes me cough and I crush the cigarette out in the overloaded ashtray. I'm feeling bloody minded. "Hey, Jonesy, maybe you better write Dwayne to knock it off about all that stuff about the Japs. That's likely classified information, you know. Even the walls have ears."

Jonesy looks affronted. For once, Tolliver takes my side. "Dermody

here's right, you know. My Pappy won't sing 'It's a Long Way to Tipperary' anymore. He don't want the Germans to know." Trouble with
Tolliver is you never can tell if she's putting on, but "Tipperary" is a
great song.

When Michael and I were little, before Buddy was born, we used
to sing it with Daddy in the car, along with "Pack up your troubles in
your old kit bag and smile, smile, smile." Who feels like smiling? I
had a letter from Aunt Cecelia yesterday with a P.S. that said Joe,
that's Daddy, hasn't been well since I left. My family is enough to
drive a person crazy, always telling me things but never saying
enough. Poor Daddy. What can I do? I suppose I can try to get a
long-distance phone call through soon's I get paid. Sometimes all I
want to do is *go home*. Time for camp to be over. Tolliver senses my
mood and gives my shoulder a hard squeeze. "Only three more days
until liberty in New York Cit-ee, pal."

Affirmative. Only three more days. Liberty. New York City. Now
that's more like it, the kind of thing I joined the Navy for. Before
Michael shipped out for England two years ago he sent us a long
strip of postcards, the kind that fold up into a fat packet closed with a
tab. It had pictures of everything: the Manhattan skyline, Rockefeller
Center, Central Park, the Chrysler Building, St. Patrick's Cathedral.
He had drawn an X over the Rose Window and scribbled, "X marks
my room, Ha Ha."

My Grandma Scanlon always said that Michael was a boyo born to
be hanged. He was her favorite, she thought he was D'Arcy, the only
Scanlon son, who was killed at the Marne. Me, she always called Bernadette, my mother's name. There are so many girls in the family
she didn't bother to tell one from another. When Michael was 10
he crashed his sled into a wall and lay in the downstairs bedroom
for days, unconscious, with his head wrapped in white bandages.
Grandma sat beside him, crooning and keening like she did when
somebody was dead, moving her rosary over and over through her
arthritic fingers. I was frightened.

"Grandma," I ventured, halfway in and halfway out of the door of
the darkened sick-smelling room. "Grandma, is Michael going to
hell?" The old lady sort of growled and turned her near-sighted eyes
toward me. I scrunched a little farther out of the door.

"Whatever makes you say that, *machushla*, have you taken leave of
your senses?"

"You always said he was born for to be hanged. Bad people get hanged. Bad people go to hell."

She clasped her rosary convulsively and glared at me, mostly all behind the door by now. "And sure, wasn't Robert Emmet himself hanged by the Sassenach, and him the most blessed thing that ever walked this earth?" She rocked back and forth. I guessed that the Sassenach were the English. Everybody knows they do bad things. Michael stirred and murmured a little, but didn't wake up. I held my breath, waiting for Grandma to continue. "He'll be up there at the right hand of God along with all the other heroes, Cuchulain, Cormac, Owen, Red Hugh." She nodded off in her chair. I wanted to ask her if there were any girl heroes but Grandma never liked questions much. She scared me. They said she had the Sight, the Second Sight, and could tell when people were going to die. She died when I was nine. When I was older I prowled the library at St. Aloysius' and found some old books with each page bordered with a design of twining leaves and flowers that told me about Maeve and Deirdre, Grania and Boadicea. Girl heroes, heroines, each one more beautiful and brave than the last: sweet, sad, and doomed, most of them, but worthy.

The whole week before our long anticipated liberty, the Navy overloads us with lectures, warnings, and instructions. We sit, as always, in a crowd outfitted identically in the Uniform of the Day in the same stuffy lecture hall. I find myself nodding off as the intense, anonymous officer up front ticks off her points: We must, it goes without saying, comport ourselves to the credit of the service; we must do nothing, re-peat nothing, to disgrace the uniform (the UNIFORM); everyone will be looking at us; we are no longer civilians, we are *Navy;* most important, we must get back On Time. Dire things happen to Navy people who don't get back On Time. Must be because ships might have to leave without you.

Petrelli pokes me. I snap awake when I hear the voice in front say, "W. T. Door." Hot diggety dog. At last. After all the pokes, giggles, and warnings, it's not so much after all. Sailors, it seems, are not above a little hanky-panky on liberty. The hall ripples with nervous excitement, none of us having had any chance to find out for the last six weeks. Said sailors, continues the officer in that maddening maternal way older ladies have of warning you about things without actually mentioning whatever it is that they are warning you against, said sailors prefer avoiding the consequences of such mischief by giving the unlucky or unwise young lady in question a false name. A favorite false name, for reasons lost in the midst of naval antiquity, is W(ater) T(ight) Door. Surely no modern Navy woman, wary, aware, and forewarned, would fall for an old barnacle like that. C'mon, I wish she would come right out and say straight out—"Don't get pregnant. Don't get VD. You'll foul up the entire war effort if you do." No way, I guess she figures we have all seen enough of all of those gruesome VD movies to last a lifetime. All she said was "DIS-missed."

CHAPTER 6

New York, here I am at last, worldly and sophisticated as I've always known my true self to be—just like the recruiting poster with two leggy Waves (they look like they had been painted by that artist Petty) in summer dress whites who stride in step in front of the Manhattan skyline. Underneath it asks, "Are you going to miss the great adventure?" Not me. Nobody looking at us could know that I was plain old Josie Dermody from St. Aloysius', former file clerk at Meekin Brothers Plumbing and Heating Supplies.

Petrelli gave us the drill for the subway; it seems years instead of weeks since the noise, blackness, and flashing lights had frightened me so. "Push, shove, use your elbows, hang on. Look at nobody. Nothin' to it," she said. She'd been doing it all her life. Petrelli has the face of an angel and, except when she sings, the voice of a parrot. No kidding. When she talks she squawks just like the baseball announcers on the radio. Her first name is Theresa, she's Catholic like me, but she sure acts different. Maybe it's because she grew up in New Yawk, maybe because she's Italian, maybe because she's got so many brothers and sisters; whatever the reason, she sure doesn't take nothin' from nobody. She told us so several times and suggested we do the same. Maybe so. I mean, if you aren't from New York, would it work? I imagine how the flowers on my aunts' hats would tremble with indignation if I arrived home and announced, "I don't take nothin' from nobody." Heart attack junction. Mother would look teary, after all that working so hard to keep me from developing any bad habits. Aunt Geraldine, at least, would recognize Petrelli's spunk, even if her words were, shall we say, a little strong. Unladylike?

We pile off the subway at Grand Central, champing with excitement and armed with enough warnings, battle plans, strategies, maps, cameras, and injunctions for a major task force to invade an archipelago. New York, it's the biggest city in the whole wide world.

Naturally America would have the biggest city with the tallest buildings, no wonder those Germans and Japs want to take it away from
us. I feel like I'm in one of those dreams where everything grows
more than life size and you have shrunk down to the size of an ant. I
fill my lungs with air and expel it with a whoosh and hope nobody
notices. Once more, and I'm my own size again. I look at my shipmates. Their faces shine with excitement and anticipation.

All of our careful battle plans go wrong immediately, because it
turns out everybody has a different priority target. Right in the middle of Fifth Avenue Corman and Jonesy start arguing with Tolliver
and Petrelli about whether to go to the Empire State Building or
Staten Island first. Petrelli waves her hands around so much she
smacks Corman in the shoulder. Corman swerves around and her
black leather purse swings on its strap and hits Tolliver in the middle
of her back. Just as it looks like it's turning into a donnybrook I see a
shore patrol guy striding toward us purposefully, watching for us to
do something to disgrace the uniform so he can run us all in, looks
like. "Let's go, shake a leg," I say in a swivet. The others see him at
the same time, about face, and execute that classic military maneu-
ver—getting the heck out of there. Even Julius Caesar did it sometimes, but I've forgotten what "strategic retreat" is in Latin. No matter. Seems like I'm forgetting everything I learned before I enlisted.
We amble through Central Park for a while, just like being in the
country on such a pretty fall day.

We window-shop, looking in the windows of Tiffany, Cartier, Saks
Fifth Avenue, Macy's. We look for but miss Gimbels somehow, but all
our heads jerk backwards to look up when Tolliver whistles at the
Empire State Building. "How's that for high? Where's King Kong?"

"Reckon he's gone to war with Lucky Strike Green. Don't you ever
think of anything but movies, Tolliver?" Corman says.

"Not me. Let's go." Tolliver elbows her way through the crowds
until we reach the line for the Free for Service People elevators. We
change elevators three times before we get to the top. Actually, it's
not the very top, where they have that point to hook zeppelins onto,
but it's pretty high. I hold onto my hat and peek over the side. The
people look like ants and the cars and streetcars tiny toys. Wonder if
that's what it looks like from heaven? Naah. Heaven's higher up. Just
then Griffin's hat blows off to tumble and roll along the parapet.
Griffin's from near Corman's hometown in Kentucky—they ran into

each other in Central Park. She makes a dive for her hat and misses it. A big guy in a Marine uniform grabs it just before it flies away like a Navy blue and white pudding-bowl kite. He holds it up high and laughs as Griffin reaches for it. "Say pretty please."

"Pretty please." The wind whips her dark hair into tendrils around her heart-shaped face as she mock-battles him.

"Put some sugar on it." He raises it a little bit higher, she jumps, grabs her hat, jams it tight on her head, and laughs. Corman takes a picture of them together; they are both smiling, he so blocky and farm-fresh, she so tall and thin and almost delicate, her gloved hand clutching the strap of her purse. One of those fabled wartime romances begun in unusual circumstances that sentimental people love? How would we know? After that day we would never see either of them again, but the picture was sweet and young. When we all have had our fill of the magical view we make our way down the three elevators to the street. Griffin and her Marine go north and the rest of us go south.

"Lordy, I always thought that old gal was so shy," Corman remarks. "Must be a good omen for the rest of us."

"Let's eat." Tolliver is always hungry. "My granddaddy always said an army travels on its stomach." We troop into Jack Dempsey's Restaurant. Jack isn't there, but on the walls are lots and lots of framed autographed pictures of him with just about everybody who was famous in the whole world. Too bad. Daddy did love to go on and on about how he won all the bets on the Dempsey-Firpo fight. That must have been a big deal a long time ago. Sheila's dad calls her "Firp" because he was at the fight the night she was born. The waiter gives me a menu for a souvenir for Daddy. It's certainly a nice change to eat at a proper table with regular dishes and cups and napkins.

When we come out I pose in front of the restaurant sign so Corman can take my picture, looking as patriotic and military as I can, for the folks back home to put in the album, to show the grandchildren some day. We whirl along, marking off places on our maps. We pose in front of Prometheus, all golden frozen-motion statue in Rockefeller Center, then by the stone lions in front of the big public library. Corman teases me as I line up my fingers on the seams of my skirt, heels together. "Just the spot for a bookworm like you, honeychile. You can send a copy to those nuns with men's names, Sister Alphonse or Raymond—let 'em know you aren't getting into trouble."

"That's what you think; there are ideas in libraries, don't you know, books on the Index. A person could lose her faith in a library, ideas are dangerous. That's trouble. Hurry up."

"Honestly, Dermody, sometimes I don't understand a word you say." She lets her camera fall on its strap so she can salute a handsome young man with a dimple in his chin and a silver bar on each shoulder. He returns her salute but keeps walking. "Let's go, mates," she burbles. "The world is full of handsome officers and men today." She's right: French sailors with red pompoms on their hats, Canadian soldiers in their heavy, scratchy-looking khaki wool, wiry paratroopers swaggering by in their boots and their cords of colorful braid looped under one arm, Marines so braced that the material in their dark green and red uniforms strains the material by their buttons. The prettiest uniforms, except for the good old U.S. Navy, of course, are the ones the British airman, RAF, wear, blue wool grayed to the color of a winter sky after a snowfall. Demurely, we look them all over. It's been a long six weeks on the USS *Hunter* where the only guys were in Ship's Company and never close enough.

"Why are you saluting that one for, dummy?" Petrelli swats me one with her folded map. "That's a doorman."

"How'm I supposed to know—all those brass buttons and gold braid?" I pout, drop back to the rear. A portly gentleman with ruddy jowls rolls down the sidewalk toward us. His uniform is spanking white, he has one of those gold loops over his shoulder, his sleeves are loaded with gold stripes, the bill of his cap a scramble of gold braid. He frowns and harrumphs until Petrelli recovers herself and salutes.

"Good afternoon, sir," she says, her madonna face innocent. He returns our salutes and sails majestically on by. We stand snickering at her, can't help ourselves. "Looked like a doorman to me," she says. Somehow our walking and gawking have brought us back to Rockefeller Center. My feet are beginning to hurt, my camera's heavy, I'm tired of carrying my carefully folded raincoat over my arm. I am looking for a place to sit down, humming, "My father's name is Rockefeller, he shovels diamonds in his cellar," not paying any attention when Corman hisses, "I need you-alls picture here on this bench." She pushes and shoves us hastily into line. Some people are swifter than others. Tolliver and Jonesy grin and put their arms around each other, posing prettily. Petrelli hisses at me to wake up. Corman fusses with the camera, looking helpless, which she is anything but. A good-looking ensign with dark curly hair who looks a little like Glenn Ford comes up to her. "May I help you, Miss?"

Corman dimples prettily and salutes when she sees the stripe on his arm. Some salute—she still has the camera in her right hand. "Would you, sir? I just can't seem to get the hang of this old thing." She hands him the Kodak and scrunches herself at the left of the group on the bench. He clicks the shutter. Nobody's surprised when he doesn't hand her the camera back—instead he asks her to go with him to the Plaza for a drink. How's that for glamorous? He starts to take her arm, but she shakes his hand off, remembering just in time the Uniform. She gives us a see-you-all-later smile and leaves.

"Hot damn," Tolliver mutters. She smiles a come-hither smile at the next officer she sees, a stuffy Army bird colonel who looks all beetlebrowed and pained until she salutes him. "Good afternoon, sir," she says aloud. Under her breath she mutters, "Up yours."

"Tolliver!"

"Forget it, you make me sick." Tolliver has such a sulk on that her creamy pale skin has turned all mottled red. "I'm going to the Women's Service Center, they're having a tea dance. You coming?"

"No, thanks. I've got something I've got to do." She wheels and stamps down the street, her head turned to look in all the windows so she won't see the people she's supposed to salute. She's a case, that girl. The rest of our bunch race after her, except Jonesy, who is looking for a USO to get a free long-distance phone call in to Darling Dwayne, pining away in the pine forests of Georgia. I guess they all figured what I have to do won't be all that interesting.

First I stop at a kiosk and buy postcards for everybody back home, to make sure nobody forgets that Josette Patricia Dermody is off seeing the world. I keep walking till in front of me, right there on Fifth Avenue, is St. Patrick's, buttery yellow in the sunlight and gray in the shadows, against the sky the towers silhouetting convoluted stone squiggles, the big round stained-glass rose window in the front, exactly like the picture on Michael's postcard. The doorway carvings in stone point upwards so that if you weren't paying attention your spirit would sort of whoosh out of you and fly heavenward. That's Gothic for you.

Inside it's cool and dim, except for the jewel-colored patterns of light on the stone floor from the windows. I cross myself at the font

and stand in the nave, waiting. I'm so aggravated at the others for
their ease at going off with other people and leaving me behind, I
need to cool off. I sit down in a pew where I can see the statue of
Saint Patrick, not my favorite saint by any means; he seems so crabby
in his single-minded way, no fun a-tall. There were lots of nice saints,
of course. God knows we spent enough time reading about their lives
in school; we even wrote little plays about them. Once we borrowed
Auntie Cecelia's black and yellow canary for a play about Saint Francis. First, he wouldn't sing, then he got away and flew frantically
around the ceiling of the auditorium. There was the devil to pay, but
finally one of the eighth grade boys captured the poor, trembling
thing. Saint Bridget freed all the slaves in Ireland, now that's something to be remembered for. Saint Elizabeth with her basket of roses
was pretty and she helped the poor. The best was Joan of Arc, a girl
after my own heart, not one of those simpering ones who just kneel
around with eyes rolled up toward heaven. Poor Joan came to a bad
end, but it's hard to tell whether it's really bad, if she went to heaven
and became a saint. I can do without the burning-at-the-stake, dear
God. All this is making my head muddled. I sit, watching the dust
motes dancing in the almost deserted cathedral in the lonesome,
echoing silence, not feeling very holy at all.

I get up and go into the Lady Chapel, light a taper for my parents
and another for Michael. I figure it is probably a couple of dimes
well spent, even though I'm no longer sure of what it all means. I
wish I didn't have all these presentiments about my brother. I hope I
haven't inherited the Second Sight; that would be horrible. I pray
that Michael will come home from the war, whole and sound, to join
the American Legion like Daddy. I turn to leave, reflexively dusting
off my knees, but turn back toward the bank of little smoky lamps,
flickering crimson in the gloom, to light another, right at the top,
for Arvid. I don't care whether the blessed candles work for Luther-
ans or not. I don't want him to die. Why does anybody have to die?
Why does anybody have to die so young? Why do people start wars,
anyhow?

Well, megirl, you've worked yourself into a fine state, haven't you?

The sky is coloring a little when I come out of the cathedral. Almost time to head back. One day in New York is not enough. When
the war is over I'm going to come back for a whole week, go to all the
museums, shop in all the stores, eat in a different restaurant every

day, even take a boat ride around Manhattan, climb to the lamp of the Statue of Liberty, and go over the Brooklyn Bridge. I walk along, just enjoying being there, saluting everything in uniform, just in case, till I realize I'm all turned around and lost. Which way is Grand Central? I flatten my map against a newsstand to look. A cop with a ruddy Irish face a little like my Uncle Tim's, the same red jowls and twinkly, squinty blue eyes, leans down from his horse, "Could you be needin' some assistance, now, Miss Sailor?" He points me in the direction of Grand Central Station. I don't want to be late. AOL—Absent Over Liberty. I hurry, zigzagging through the crowded sidewalks, my purse flapping out behind me on its strap.

Griffin and her gyrene materialize out of the crowd by chance. They greet me like long-lost friends. Farmboy (I never did learn his name) introduces me to the guy they had with them, one of his Marine buddies from Camp Lejeune. "Durmoney, wantcha meet Duffy here."

I look at Duffy, skinny, pinched little face, rabbity teeth, watery blue eyes, a jagged adam's apple that bobbles up and down in his skinny throat, little flecks of saliva at the corners of his mouth. "Duffy? Polish, eh?" I say in the automatic tribal greeting we use back home.

"Nope, Irish." This one's dumb, too. "Where you been all my life, gorgeous?" He must think he's leering invitingly. Errol Flynn he's not.

"I've been where I've been, but I know where I'm going," I say crossly.

"Wait a min—where ya' goin' in such a rush?"

"I'm heading for the subway to meet my mates and go back to the base."

I quicken my pace. His skinny freckled face puts on a cajoling look, like Michael when he wanted to bring Mother around. "Aw, don't be that way, sweetheart. Me and my buddies here are shipping out tonight. We need a little lovin'. C'mon, what's the harm?"

"I'm not interested, Buster."

"Dontcha wanna serve your country?" He puts his arm roughly around my waist as I twist out of his way. I smell the sickening whiskey smell on his breath—he's full of Dutch courage. Tanked full. His problem. What does he mean, don't I want to serve my country? What does he think I am doing in this spiffy, spanking new uniform? Thank God, Grand Central looms ahead. I push his arm away, which makes him more belligerent than ever. He's not very big, but he's probably stronger than I am. He grabs my purse strap and I jerk away. I'm getting really mad. Where have Griffin and Whatzisname got to, anyway? "Go away," I say. Doggone, all you Sisters who were supposed to prepare me for Life, which one of you is going to tell me how to get rid of this guy? He's too drunk to take a snappy brushoff. I give him a good push and almost run into the station where I see some of my friends waiting under the big clock.

"What's with you, Dermody? You're all out of breath and red in the face. Your hat's on crooked."

"Some gyrene just got fresh, that's all. Oh, oh, there he still is." Duffy has followed me and lurches up to where I'm surrounded by my safety-in-numbers shipmates.

"Hey sweetheart, I'll give you another chance."

"Sorry, not interested." I turn my back, I don't want to hear what he mutters as he goes away. I don't owe him anything.

"Holey smoley, Dermody. You better watch those fatal charms. Where'd you pick him up? It's a wonder your mother lets you out alone."

"Oh, stow it, Tolliver. We were formally introduced, I didn't pick him up. Griffin and her friend were doing me a real big favor." I giggle. "Should have told him my name was W. T. Door (USNR) WR."

When we get back to our cubicle in Building E, I take off my shoes, climb up on my bunk, and rub my poor tired feet. Corman is putting her hair up, humming happy tunes with the bobbypins in her mouth. The others have gone off to the lounge for a last smoke before the smoking lamp goes out. Tolliver's probably telling sea stories about French sailors falling in love with her or something. I get out the postcards and lay them out on the bedspread to look at the colored pictures of everywhere I went today, along with some places we didn't get to this time. I joined the Navy to see the world, didn't I? New York is a good beginning. When I write to Mother—I'm too tired tonight—I won't mention whatzisname, Duffy. Nothing happened and what Mother doesn't know won't worry her.

The next day they post the duty stations. Jonesy has to go to cooks' and bakers' school. Griffin got storekeepers' school, her second choice. Petrelli will go straight to Oklahoma to yeomen's school. She'll like that. I finally find my name along with Corman's and Tol-

liver's: Great Lakes Naval Training Station, Specialist (G). I'm so re-
lieved that it's not typing school, let them as likes it do it, but what's
Specialist (G)? Tolliver lets out a whoop as she reads the list over my
shoulder. "Wow-ee. Antiaircraft gunnery instructor." She pounds my
shoulder hard. "Wait till I write my daddy. Us Tollivers always been
crack shots."

"Wow-ee." I echo her. "Poor Jonesy. She won't be with her Darling
Dwayne. Fortunes of war, I guess. Let's go tell Corman, Gunner." An
hour later it hits me. The good Lord had answered only half my
prayer. Doggone, I won't be rid of Tolliver after all.

CHAPTER 7

Gunners

I wiggle my jaw to relieve the tightness of the chin strap of my helmet, but it doesn't help much. My jaw aches from keeping it stretched open to equalize the pressure on my eardrums, while I concentrate on leading the little drone target plane as it comes into my gunsight. I have to stand tip-toed. The glare off Lake Michigan is making me squint. Gunny is yelling at me, his weatherbeaten face all open mouth and tonsils. He makes chopping motions with his big, square hands. All the guns on the line are going off at once—20-millimeter Oerlikons and big Swedish Bofors 40s. How does he expect me to hear anything? I have to read his lips and guess, even though he is shouting so loud the cords in his throat stand out like ropes.

"Short bursts! Short bursts! Dammit!" He turns and yells at the other end of the line. "Lead him! Lead him! Jeezus." I feel my forehead wrinkling into a frown as I strain to translate the demonstration lessons into reality with a real gun. Holy Mary, what do I know about vectors and angles? What do I care? It's really hard not to just lay into the trigger and keep firing crazily until the magazine runs out—the tracer shells flaming red against the Madonna-robe-blue Indian summer sky. Gunny would kill me if I did that. Waste all the ammunition at once. The noise is so loud I can feel it through my feet as the concrete emplacements resonate under the pounding guns.

There is a hole in the noise around me. My gun isn't firing. My bottom hits the ground with a heavy thunk before my head realizes what has happened. Gunny had appeared by my side, unhooked my shoulder harness, knocked me away, and jerked the magazine off the Oerlikon in one smooth motion. My bottom hurts and I have the wind knocked out of me. Gunny puts the big metal cylinder down on the ground, away from the gun emplacements, and wipes his sunburned brow with the back of his hairy hand. He grins sheepishly at us stupefied girls standing around the silent gun. "Cook off," he says.

"Cook off? What'd I do?" I'm sputtering, trying to get my breath back, and mad as a wet hen. "Why'd you knock me down?" He has a nerve.

"Magazine jammed. Guns get hot. She'll explode in seven seconds. Sorry, mate. Hadda do it." He reaches out a huge hand to pull me to my feet.

I still don't get it. Seven seconds. I suppose I should say a thank you to my guardian angel, but it was Gunny who knocked me out of the way. He sure doesn't look like any guardian angel I ever saw. Not that I ever saw one, but we had plenty of pictures in grade school, sissy-looking young guys with big white wings and a hand on some child's shoulder. "Thanks, Gunny." My voice comes out in a croak. I'm not sure he heard me.

"Whaddya mean, magazine jammed?" Tolliver demands, with an undertone of hysteria in her voice. Gunny, who doesn't seem to have any other name, just the nickname for gunner's mate, stands there surrounded by our guncrew, a circle of smudged female faces, all one big anxious question.

"Somebody wasn't paying attention. Loaded a shell in crooked. It jammed." He gesticulates with his big hands, demonstrating. "Gotta pay attention. We ain't playing beanbag here, nohow."

"You mean Dermody here could have been killed?" Corman asked, for once forgetting to be charming.

"Who knows? Maybe the whole frigging shebang. Them shells will stop a Zero. Easy blow up a gun and crew. Happens." He shrugs and starts to turn away. He's regular Navy and all business, kind of good-looking in a rugged sort of way, if you like that type. Big and solid and reliable, not dashing. Like a battleship.

Tolliver pushes her helmet back and shoves her face into his, or tries to. She only comes up to the triangle of white skivvy that shows at the vee of his dungaree shirt. "Wait a minute. Wait just a doggone minute here." She leans her head back to yell up at him. We freeze, watching her. How does she dare? "From now on, let us Waves load our own magazines, hear? I din't join no Navy to have no dumb sailor get me killed on no gunnery range." Gunny looks her in the eye. I see her breath coming fast and shallow, but she holds his look.

"Suit yourselves, ladies." He turns to the guncrews on either side who had stopped to watch the show. "Resume firing."

Most of us had heard about the ammunition ships in California blowing up while being loaded before going to the Pacific just this summer—flattened a whole town, but no one wants to talk about *that.* Corman puts herself into the shoulder harness even though it is still technically my turn. I take over as loader, striving for coolness, as I swing the heavy cylinder and listen for the click that locks it into place. Nobody looking at me can tell, I don't think, that I am a person who was seven seconds away from looking St. Peter in the face, but trickles of sweat run down the hollows on either side of my spine, shivery even in the midday heat. LOCAL GIRL REPORTS NEAR MISS ON GUNNERY RANGE. No way, thanks.

The target plane putt-putts into view off to starboard. It looks like a real plane that's far away, but it's really a little model controlled by a radio. As it comes within range, all the ack-acks open up at once. We open our mouths as far as we can, tasting the incredible noise; each of us would rather die than stick our fingers in our ears, going deaf is nothing, nothing, to the disgrace of that. From where I stand, waiting to reload, I can watch Corman, beads of sweat on her delicate upper lip and a smudge of gungrease under her eye, get the simulated enemy plane in the third ring of her gunsight, swing the gun around just a little. She holds for a second, squeezes the trigger toward her once, twice, three times. With a pou-f-f the tiny plane explodes and dives into the lake. The Waves who have been watching the trajectories cheer. "You got him. You got him."

"We splashed one." Tolliver always knows exactly what to say because of the movies. "Hurray for us. Hurray for our side." She tries to hug Corman, who is still buckled into her shoulder harness attached to the gun, looking both bewildered and pleased. Tolliver can't stop jumping up and down, "They should let us Waves have a real shot at those Nips. Look out Tojo . . ."

"Make way, make way." Gunny muscles his way through the gathered Waves. All the guns have stopped firing because there is nothing to shoot at except maybe a few mare's tails way up high. Corman looks expectant, but then surprised, as Gunny takes a spanner and adjusts the gunsight, turns it out of alignment five degrees. He glares at her, turns, and glares at all of us. "You dumb broads costing Uncle Sam too damn much money. Dontcha know how much them drones cost?"

"We're supposed to hit the target, aren't we?" I yell at Gunny's departing back. "You make me sick." I don't care if he hears me or not.

Atkinson puts her hand over my mouth. She's a big, gawky girl with a muddy complexion, another member of our guncrew. "Cool down, Dermody. You know there's a right way and the Navy way." Atkinson may not be all that swift, but she hardly ever gets flustered and I've never seen her mad. She straps herself into the harness for her turn. Nothing to shoot at, no chance of hitting anything anyway, with the gunsight skewed, but what else can we do? Somebody is forever telling me to cool off, cool down, knock it off, stow it. Don't they feel how stupid it is much as I do? Why shoot at something you can't hit, for instance? If that's the Navy way, that's real dumb. How are we going to win this war, anyway? Nobody asks my opinion around here.

On this go-round I am just the observer, so I don't have to do much. October is such a pretty month with the sky such an incredibly clear blue and the air paradoxically hazy. The Indians around these lakes used to call it the Season of Smoke. After the hurricane and all that rain at boot camp, it was a relief when we got here and could dry out before we all grew barnacles.

Great Lakes Naval Station must be near, I think, where Hiawatha paddled his birchbark canoe on the glittering surface of Gitchee-Gumee. That was a long time ago. Now it's just Lake Michigan, no more birchbark canoes, just the long, silent freighters passing along the horizon out beyond the range of our guns.

The old part of Great Lakes is as different from Hunter as can be. It wasn't converted from anything else, it was built as a naval station before the Great War, of bricks that have turned rosy and look older than they are. The buildings have big wide windows with half-moon tops of wavy glass. Somebody told me they still have hooks embedded in the walls—the bulkheads—where old-time sailors used to sling their hammocks and dream fitfully of the dusky girls in Pago Pago who wear flowers behind their ears and no blouses a-tall. Nowadays the pretty buildings are chockablock with triple-decker bunks. We can see them as we march by on our way to the gunnery range by the shore, singing, "Shipmates, stand together, don't give up the ship. Fair or stormy weather, we won't give up, we won't give up the ship."

"Take five!" Gunny yells at last. I tug off my helmet and sink down to the sun-warmed cement in the meager shade of the gun. Tolliver pulls out a rumpled pack of Lucky Strikes and offers it around. I wave it away, then change my mind. What's one more bad habit?

"Wonder how much one of those cute little drone planes costs, anyway?" I wonder out loud to no one in particular.

"About a zillion dollars, I reckon," Tolliver laughs her braying laugh through the curls of cigarette smoke.

"Honestly, sugahs, sometimes I wonder about you all." Corman rubs her sore shoulders as she talks. "Gunny doesn't care a fig how much that li'l old drone costs."

"Why'd he turn the gunsight, then? How we supposed to hit anything when he does that?" Atkinson's broad face is flat with puzzlement. I wonder also, but I count on Atkinson to ask the dumb questions.

"Because," Corman stretches her arm out and wiggles her fingers for a cig and continues, "because one of us Waves hit it. You know how the guys get when they can see gals doin' things better'n them. The other crews weren't coming within a mile . . ."

"That's dumb. That's really dumb." I'm tired, I'm filthy, I'm fed up, and I'm mad. "We're all in this together to beat the Germans and the Japs, aren't we?"

"Gonna have a hard time beatin' anybody if our brave boys can't hit the broadside of a barn." Tolliver giggles and gets another cig out of her almost empty pack. She's out of matches, but she borrows Corman's precious Zippo lighter, which just happens to have belonged to the handsome officer who asked her to the Plaza when we were in New York. He's been writing her mushy letters every day and Corman implies they are sort of engaged.

"Calm down, honeychile," Corman says, ignoring Tolliver after she retrieves her lighter and stows it in her pocket. Zippos never fail, and if you have one you are careful to hang on to it. She never pays much mind to Tolliver, but she's after me again. "You can't change the world by getting so mad all the time, Dermody. My grandmother used to say 'Honey catches more flies than vinegar.'" With that she gets up and dusts off the seat of her greasy dungarees, as though it would do any good. But who wants to catch any flies? I don't say.

Atkinson says, "Here comes Gunny. It's my turn to load." We take up our stations around the gun, waiting for the signal to resume. Tolliver starts singing, in that hillbilly voice of hers, "But it's diff'rent, oh so diff'rent, since the Navy put a uniform on me." The girls in the adjacent guncrews join in; we start over at the beginning of the song, "Give me a kiss by the numbers, I want to do things the Regulation way." It's different, all right. Sometimes the only thing to do is laugh, even if I am probably going to be deaf for the rest of my natural life.

Shooting the big guns is actually kind of fun, but breakdown is awful. When the sun sets, we have to take our guns apart and stow them securely before the guys can finish theirs and stand around teasing. Worst part of the day on the gunnery range. Worst part of my life. Taking the guns apart isn't all that hard, Lord knows we practiced it enough with the wooden mockups that are easy because they have the firing systems painted red. We can all, by this time, break down a machine gun blindfolded and race some instructor's stopwatch to put it back together. Nothing to it. Easy as pie. Just remember that the sear pin is in the correct position if it looks like a highchair, and don't mention it out loud when the guys are around. It drives them nuts when we use a feminine image like a highchair for remembering. Too bad.

The problem is, the real guns, the Oerlikons, are heavy machined blue steel. It takes me and Corman, one at each end, to carry the long barrel. Atkinson struggles awkwardly with the shoulder harness, leather half-moons that catch her legs as she walks toward the gunshed. Tolliver carries the empty magazines, big as bowling balls and twice as heavy. Dombrowski is the fifth member of our guncrew, she's clumsy and always in a hurry, so she treads on Tolliver's heels as she lugs our five helmets. "Shake a leg," she grumbles to Tolliver.

"Kee-rist. I'm hurryin' as fast as I can." Too late. The sailors have secured their guns and are waiting for us. They chant, "Release a man for active duty. Har har. It takes five of you broads to do what two guys can do." We have to walk right by them, looking as confident and unwinded as we can. Let me tell you, it's not so easy to look dignified and ladylike under these circumstances. Only thing to do is ignore them, but I'd sure like to have a word with the genius who dreamed up that slogan, "Release a Man for Active Duty," for the Waves. The guys won't stop. "The WACS and Waves will win the war. What the hell am I here for?" Holy Mary, I could be home, doing my part by serving cookies and jitterbugging in my aqua prom dress at the USO with our brave boys who have to behave nicely there. Too late, megirl. You'll never get the gungrease out from under your fingernails.

Wearily waiting for the cattlecar bus that will take us back to our

barracks, showers, and the sack, I don't notice the strange yeomen
with their clipboards at first. What are two yeomen doing on the gunnery range so far from their typewriters, anyway? Looking over the
Waves in an official seeming way, that's what. Not much to look at
this time of day: dirty, baggy dungarees, blue chambray workshirts
so encrusted with grease and dirt that our stencilled names are almost obliterated, broken fingernails, sunburned faces, hair all wind-
blown and mashed from sweating under the heavy helmets all day. So
what's to stare at, fellas? I am standing here trying to decide if I want
a shower or chow first or if I'm too tired for either.

"Seaman. You. Look alive." One of the yeomen, the taller one with
the pimples, looks straight at me.

"You talking to me?"

"Affirmative. Sound off."

"Dermody, Josette P., Seaman, Second Class." I will never, ever,
never get used to having a backwards name.

He looks down his list on his clipboard. Nods. "766 73 28?"

I nod. I hope he's going to skip the old chestnut about "able-
bodied" seaman. I'm in no mood for jokes. I'm starving. My bottom
hurts where I landed on it. My jaw hurts from straining all day to
spare my poor eardrums. I want a shower. I smell like a goat. I'm sick
of sailors giving me a hard time. It's been a long day, fellas. Where is
that bus?

The other yeoman, who is shorter, with curly blond hair that
pushes his white gob hat back rakishly, nods to his companion. This
one is kinda cute, but I'm too tired to care. I paste a patient look on
my face and wait, since they won't let me pass. "What's up?" I ask.

"Skipper told us to pick a Wave for the Navy Day parade in Chicago
next week," he says, swelling up with his Important Mission. He looks
dubiously at me and then at the short, cute guy, who nods again.
"You look like the best bet."

"Thanks a heap. I really appreciate the honor. What do I have to
do?"

"Report at 0600 Friday week, full dress uniform, at the Ad building. They'll take it from there."

"Is everybody crazy? I'll have to get up before reveille."

He tucks his clipboard under his arm and they turn on their heels
and walk away. "You'll have to take it up with the skipper, sweetheart.
Dontcha know there's a war on?"

***

Today is the day that almost wasn't, I mean yesterday my naval career almost ended in total disgrace and defeat. The gunnery range I can handle, the teasing guys are no worse than my brothers, but Motivatin' Joe is something else. The first time I saw him, I knew he was trouble. He's the most frustrated person I ever met in my whole life. He's got that kind of wiry, exploding body that comes from growing up poor, I would have known him for Shanty anywhere, except he's not Irish. Bohunk or something. His lank, dirty-blond hair always looks greasy. He swaggers when he walks, he has a chip on his shoulder the size of a baseball bat. Wonder how he ever got to be an instructor, anyhow? We have to take a class from him to learn how to motivate people to learn antiaircraft gunnery. Now isn't that dumb? We couldn't tell that to Joe. We couldn't tell him anything.

What happened yesterday is all my fault. Lately I've been crawling into the sack at night and falling right asleep without saying my evening prayers; transgressions like that always catch up with you sooner or later. Sooner, in my case, why else did he pick my workbook to check, first thing as we slouched into the classroom, still half asleep?

"Kee-rist, Jee-zus H. Kee-rist on a raft." He flung the workbook, with the last two mimeographed pages not filled in, at my head. I ducked. Good reflexes are important in a career in the Navy. Remind me to put that in a recruiting brochure. "Dermody, you dum-dum. You've been gold-bricking long enough. Do this over. Do it right. Ya hear me? Otherwise you'll find yourself a civilian with an Unsuitable Discharge. Out on yer ear. O-U-T spells Out-Goes-You. Crazy broads anyway. No job for a man, teaching dumb stupid broads. Nothing but bitches and lezzies."

A proper fit he'd worked up to. Do the medics know he's over the edge? They probably don't care. I turned back to my desk, not saying anything.

"Can we help it if you can't get sea duty?" Tolliver muttered in a semiaudible way.

"You, Dermody. Repeat what you just said." Spit sprayed out in a fan in front of his little pointed teeth.

"I didn't say anything." I looked him straight in the eye, keeping my face expressionless. I braced my shoulders and tried to look as much like the embodiment of Duty, Honor, Country in too-big dungarees as I could manage. Joe glanced wildly around the room. All of the other Waves sat still, faces blanked of expression, at the same time subtly shaking their heads no. He'd lost again. Too bad.

"You dames is all hopeless. All of youse bring in your completed workbooks tomorrow. Completed. Shipshape. Unnastand? DIS-missed."

We filed out, edging past his baleful glare. Tolliver, you can always count on that girl, said out of the side of her mouth, "T.S. Sailor. Better get your ticket punched." Joe exploded again, I could see him as I looked back, pounding the desk with his fists. Section Eight coming up.

"I don't see for the life of me why the two of you, Dermody and Tolliver, waste your time tormenting that poor man." Corman was mother-henning us again.

"He asks for it." Tolliver pirouetted ungracefully, kicking gold leaves like gold coins that had fallen on the walkway. "My daddy always raised us Tollivers to give as good as they got. He hates us."

"What makes you say he hates us? He's just trying to do his job, like everybody else." Corman's forever taking up for people. Must be the influence of that grandmother of hers who always had something nice to say about everything and everybody. Some kind of grandmother saint. Personally, I like my saints dead and carved out of marble. My own grandmother was crabby and fierce, called me Bernadette, and had Second Sight. I don't know if I want to be like her.

Even stolid Atkinson was incensed. "Always calling us dumb broads, telling us we're stupid, Dermody's right. He hates us."

"Calling us bitches and lezzies." Tolliver was getting madder, I could see her face getting redder, as she thought about it. She saw my mouth open. "Don't ask, Dermody. If you have to ask, you ain't old enough to know. Why didn't your mother tell you what you need to know before you left the house?"

I hate it when people keep telling me I don't know anything, especially when they seem to be right. "Makes me wish I'd gone to Stillwater with Petrelli," I said, feeling more and more sorry for myself. "Wouldn't have to learn all of crazy Joe's psychological mumbo-jumbo, stimulus/response, all that junk. I wouldn't have to take any more of his guff. I won't take any more of his guff. I don't care. I'm never going to his stupid class again, ever." I heaved a great breath and tossed my workbook into the trash barrel. I felt a great, crazy sense of freedom, watching my future life arc into the innocent wire barrel. I strode ahead, ignoring the others and their gasps.

Corman grabbed my shoulder, turned me around to face her. "You get that workbook back. Hear? Right this instance, Josette Dermody. Move it."

"Won't."

She shoved her exasperated face into mine. I looked away.

"What do I care?" The others gathered around as we stood arguing where the walkway branches off toward the mess hall. Corman handed her books to Dombrowski.

"You all go ahead. Me and Miss Priss here have got something to talk over." When they were out of earshot she says, "Okay, Dermody. Time to grow up. You're in the Navy. Fish that out."

My head felt like a thundercloud, all gray and shot with lightning looking for a place to discharge. "I thought you were my friend."

"Knock it off, Dermody. You give all of us Waves a bad name if you act this way and get into trouble. Don't you ever think of anybody but yourself? Honestly. Look alive now." She had her arms on her waist, elbows out. If I ever remember Corman when I am an old lady, I'll think of her, standing pigeon-toed, arms akimbo, pretty face flushed with exasperation, chivvying me, willing me, saving me, actually, from totally messing up.

"I still hate him."

"Hate away, kiddo. Only two more weeks and we never see that handsome face again. If you don't foul up, Dumbo, we'll all be off to our new duty stations in another month. C'mon, pal, there's a war on."

I walked back the way we had come, retrieved the duotang-covered notebook, and brushed it off. "The next time I get a notion to enlist I hope my mother ties me to the bedpost."

"Me, too." She tagged my arm. "Race you to the mess hall."

So I copied Corman's notes and handed the workbook in today. Joe was sullen and hung over. He didn't say anything, just kept his back to us, as he drew diagrams and arrows on the blackboard till the hour was up.

I promised Mother I would write about everything, but she'd have another sick headache if I told her about cook-offs that aren't about coffeecake. She wouldn't be proud of me if I told her about Joe, even if I try to make it ha-ha funny, like I'm having a lark at gunnery school. I'll ask her to send me the old iron, forgot to bring one. She'll be happy to learn that I'm to be in the Navy Day Parade. She's always been so proud of having once been chosen Queen of the May.

CHAPTER 8

Parade

The gray Navy bus lets us off at the staging area on Columbus Street. What a mess, all confusion and crowding. The early morning chill hasn't dissipated yet. I see our float, could hardly miss it. It looks just like a tugboat pulled by a Navy gray jeep. Along the gunnels on either side a long sign in red, white, and blue letters says "Great Lakes Naval Training Station Service School." The pimply yeoman who had chosen me is there with his clipboard. Too bad it isn't the cute one. This one peers at me through his specs. "You Dermody?" He sounds puzzled. I almost ask him if he's expecting Rita Hayworth, but shrug an affirmation. "You sure look diff'runt." You bet, I think. It's diff'rent, oh so diff'rent, since the Navy put a uniform on me. He continues in his nasal voice. "You're supposed to sit on this here torpedo, see, and try to look glamorous. Cross your legs." He sounds more than dubious, but he gives me a boost up onto the deck of the little fake boat. I hoist myself up onto the shiny steel surface of the huge torpedo that sits cattycorner on the deck. It's cold, metallic, and shiny-smooth, so much so that I slide right off and land with a jar.

"Hey, mate," I yell down through the hub-bub to the cute yeoman who has shown up after all. He is busy checking off the other personnel who are going to ride as crew on the float. "How's anybody supposed to ride on this thing?"

"Ain't my problem, sister. You figure it out. I gotta war to run." He doesn't even look up from his clipboard. Forget about him. The wind off Lake Michigan is whipping up, freezing cold. I stand on the deck, feeling like bursting into tears of frustration right in front of God and everybody. Sailors don't cry, megirl, not even a single trickle. I can see the headline in the paper back home. LOCAL GIRL SLIDES OFF TORPEDO. MARINE BAND MARCHES OVER INERT FORM. RIP.

I give just a tiny little sniffle at the thought and then I hear a hearty Southern voice above me. It comes from a rangy, rawboned signalman holding his rolled semaphore flags under one arm and offering me a steaming mug of java with the other. "Hey, mate. Don't give up the ship." I drink the coffee gratefully, then he says, "Ups-a-daisy," and boosts me back up onto the shining deadly beauty of the torpedo. He shows me a handhold. He has tattoos on his hairy fingers. If I had only known what I was getting into, I could have stopped at a tattoo parlor on my way to boot camp and had my stubby fingers artistically embellished with H-O-L-D on the fingers of my left hand and F-A-S-T on the right, just like Flags here. In years to come my grandchildren could twiddle with my arthritic fingers and prattle sweetly, "Tell us, dear Grandmother, about when you were young and fair and saved the world for democracy."

Parades take forever to get going. It is, as Aunt Geraldine would be wont to point out, the nature of the beast. I wonder where Tolliver and Corman are—they are supposed to meet me after the parade with the rest of the gang. Tolliver is still a little miffed with me—EXTRA, EXTRA, READ ALL ABOUT IT—since yesterday, when I bumped into her on my way to the head. She was skating around the hallway, singing "Chattanooga Choo-Choo," with two big wads of steel wool under her feet. "Heads up, Miss Priss."

"We-ull. Excuse me. Why don't you look out yourself?"

"Gotta do the 'Great Lakes Shuffle.' Woo-ah, woo-ah. Shine that deck. Tote that bale." She reached the end of the hallway, turned, skidded back so that she was peering right into my face. "What in tarnation you so crabby about, anyway? Motivatin' Joe passed you, din't he?" She paused to put more wax on the left wad of steel wool and mopped her dripping brow. "Give us a hand, will ya? A foot rather. If the war lasts much longer, these goldurned decks will be worn right through." She's probably right, I thought. The cheap pine floorboards were shiny with wax all right, but so worn that the knots stuck up like little islands. Tolliver took off in a long glide.

"Sor-ree. No can do," I said. "Already finished my section. Corman's going to cut my hair, make me look glamorous. Says we got to uphold the honor of the Oldest Service, the good old U.S. Nav—watch it, mate, you'll be putting in for a Purple Heart next." She had collided with a bucket of floor wax and landed on her ample bottom with a teeth-aching thump. "They can put it in the paper back home, LOCAL GIRL DECORATED FOR WAR INJURY—REFUSES TO DIVULGE LOCATION. If anybody back in them thar hills can read."

"'Tain't funny, McGee." She lumbered to her feet, rubbed her injured denim-covered derrière, and resumed her skating on the splintery overwaxed decks.

I skipped out of her way. She'll get even sooner or later, like she always does, but I can't worry about it.

The shower room was empty for once. I hate, hate, hate taking a shower with a lot of other girls all the time. I stripped off my filthy, sweaty work clothes and left them in an unshipshape heap on the deck. I turned on the lovely hot water, enjoyed it for five minutes, only to jump out quickly and grab my towel as a sudden freezing stream threatened to make me an icicle. I danced my way into my flannel pajamas, wrapped my towel around my wet head, and skedaddled back to our cubicle. Corman was waiting for me. "Guess who sent me his picture?"

Jolt. A bugle call in the distance must mean "Move on out." Sure enough, the Marine band behind me strikes up "Anchors Aweigh," and the little fake boat starts up with a jerk. It takes all of my strength and concentration just to hold on. Who has time to think about looking glamorous at a time like this? As I shift to maintain my balance, I feel my left stocking pop at the garter. Just what I need, a runner. I spit on my free fingers to try to stop it. No way. It goes *zing*, right down the front of my leg. Now all of Chicago will be treated to cheesecake with a runner. Too bad. Fortunes of war. We only move half a block and then stop again. It's boring waiting—I go back in my mind to last night in our dorm. Corman did her best to make me glamorous.

"Don't you think he looks a bit like Glenn Ford?" she showed me the picture of the dark-haired ensign with a twinkle in the corner of his mouth who had taken our pictures in New York.

"All your beaux look like Glenn Ford. This one is a dead ringer. Another fiancé?"

"Well, he did write that he has his ship and would I wait for him till the war's over? I'm not goin' anywhere. Might as well." She thumbtacked the picture to the inside of her locker door right next to the glossy of the Army guy she knew from back home—he's a tank commander in Europe somewhere. "Sweet dreams," she said, with a kissy noise to the pictures. "Ready?" she pointed with her scissors to the chair next to the mirror propped up on the table. I sat down, she began. "Hold still, Dermody, 'fore I cut your ear off."

"Sorry. Don't know why they chose me for their parade anyway. You're much prettier."

"Who knows why the Navy does what it does, honeychile? You have nice eyes and a pretty smile. Wait till you fall in love again, it does wonders for the complexion."

As she talked she snipped and then deftly turned my brown non-descript hair for a pageboy, tying it up on the inside layers of Kotex, which work better than rags every time.

"I'm never, ever going to fall in love again." I stifled a feeling-sorry-for-myself sniffle and reached for a tissue.

"You still moping about that Norwegian boy from back home who married the English girl? He's just part of your interesting past now, sweetie. Trust ol' Auntie Barbara Lee. You ain't seen nothin' yet, as they say. There, you're finished."

"He's Swedish. Not Norwegian," I said automatically. "It will never happen to me. Not to me. Thanks for the hairdo."

The parade finally starts, lumbering down Michigan Avenue in the watery Chicago October sunlight. I decide to enjoy the ride and wonder about whether true love will ever come my way another time. The tall signalman who helped me stands by the fake gunnels. Nobody ever calls them "gun-whales," which is what you would think. He snaps his red and white signal flags smartly, like a big overgrown Boy Scout. I can see the servicemen and ex–Boy Scouts lined three deep along the curbsides mouthing the letters as he sends them. I can't read semaphore very well, especially backwards. "Hey, Flags, why are all those guys laughing? What are you sending?"

"The Wacs and Waves will win the war. What the hell am I here for?" he chants without breaking his rhythm.

"Don't you guys ever get tired?" He acts like he doesn't hear me. I already know they don't. That's okay, fellas. We're here. We'll win the war, and if anybody asks we are having a great time.

More and more people join the crowd watching the parade. Navy Day is a big deal, posters had advertised the event for weeks. Yesterday Winston Churchill made an announcement that we are on the last lap of the war, we and the Russians. Everybody is feeling perky because we had given the Japs another shellacking somewhere on the long road to Tokyo. The littlest kids sit on the curbside between the legs of the grown-ups waving their little American flags. People crammed in the windows of the stores and offices wave and cheer. I wave back with the hand that isn't hanging on for dear life, thinking, "Look glamorous" and "Buy war bonds, all you patriotic people." The music is bright and brassy. I love parade music, the way the brass notes loop around and around, the drumbeats boom, boom, boom. I move my free hand in a windshield-wiper wave, caught up in the euphoria and the excitement. This sure beats being the May Queen back home, which I never was. I'll have to write Sheila about it, and poor Consuelo, shut up in that dark convent with no fun a-tall. Don't think about home, Dummy. You'll come over all homesick while you are having fun. Most of the folks watching us are cheering, but some are crying and wiping their eyes when the colors go by.

As we stop and start again by Marshall Field's I notice a Marine officer, standing next to a pretty civilian lady in a forest green coat, who is wigwagging his arms. Flags, most imperturbable of signalmen, falters and stops sending. "Hey Flags, what did you signal to him? What'd he send back?" I tug on his sleeve to get his attention.

"You're on report. She's my wife." Flags is turning red under his sunburn.

"Don't worry about it. He won't know who you are. There's thousands of guys in this parade."

"Hope you're right, mate."

I'm not your mate, doggone, but let it go.

"Hey, girlie." The extra deep voice young guys use sometimes is definitely addressed to me. I turn away from my adoring crowds and look down. A young Marine bandsman has marched ahead of his formation to draw abreast of our tugboat. "You got a run in your stocking."

"How 'bout that?" I can't do much about it, but I do cross my legs the other way, almost losing my precarious seat on the torpedo.

"Whatcha doin' after the parade, babe?"

"Nothin' much. Goin' shootin' with Admiral Halsey, then a spot of tea at the Edgewater Beach . . ." He looks affronted. I never met a Marine who can take a joke. He's practically a baby, really. He drops back into formation. I keep waving to the crowds, automatically making the V for Victory sign. This must be what movie stars feel like. Flags keeps semaphoring innocent messages like "Loose lips sink ships" or "Buy war bonds." The band behind is rousing us all with the "Stars and Stripes Forever." I can feel the shiny metal of the torpedo warming in the sun. Holy Toledo. What if this thing is armed? They wouldn't put an armed torpedo in a parade, would they? Would they? What am I doing sitting on top of all this explosive? Daddy? It won't detonate, will it, unless the driver of the jeep goes berserk and plunges us all into Lake Michigan. Steady, girl. Nothing I can do about it, but I make an Act of Contrition just in case. Over the loud-speakers set up along the line of march a voice booms—"Ours is the best—and the best trained—Navy in the world." That's for damsure, I think. I shock myself. Ladies don't swear, megirl, but sailors do.

Well done. The Navy always says "Well done," even if all you did was not slide off a torpedo for the length of Michigan Avenue. I like hearing it, anyway. I meet the others waiting by the Water Tower, looking as spiffed up as I am in their dress uniforms and gleaming white gloves.

"Musta made you feel proud, eh?" Tolliver's enthusiasm is making her voice squeak. "Didja see Admiral Carpender? Mayor Kelley was here and the governor. You got a run in your stocking."

"Yeah, I saw 'em when we passed the reviewing stand. I know I've got a run." She's the strangest girl, always acting like she doesn't know I hate her, ever since that first remark about Catholics. All my signals just roll right off her thick skin. "You're right. It does make me feel proud. I had a good ride, too."

"You missed the midshipmen rowing their boat all the way. They were behind you. Bet they had sore shoulders even if they were only pushing air." Corman's excited, too.

"Yeah, you missed the BAM with the ugly dog mascot, too. She was way in front of our float."

"Tolliver, don't say 'BAM.' That's nasty. She's a lady Marine." Corman had her schoolteacher's voice out again. The guys try to kid us that BAM means Beautiful American Marine but we know better.

"Well, that's one ug-lee bowlegged dog. Let's go to Ireland's and get some decent chow." Food is always number one with Tolliver.

"Is Ireland a fish place? I hate fish."

"Here we go again," Atkinson says. "You got a terrible attitude, Dermody." Who asked her? "Why aren't you more like Petrelli? She's Catholic and she's not crabby all the time like you are."

"She is now. Had a letter from her last week. She hates yeoman school. She wants out of the Navy."

"Well, she's in for the duration and six like the rest of us," Dombrowski pipes up.

"Unless she gets preggers." I can't believe I am saying this.

"You getting nervous in the service, Dermody? Who's the lucky fella you got picked out?" Atkinson is being obnoxious today, not like her. A commander with his uniform sleeves weighed down with gold braid comes toward us, we each snap a salute. Because we are strung out along the narrow sidewalk he has to return six salutes to our one. That's a game we play sometimes, let the brass get saluter's elbow. Don't they know there's a war on? It gets tiresome quickly so we just window-shop as we walk along, looking at all the civilian things in the store windows, things we gave up when we enlisted. Actually, not all of us wore spike heels and filmy negligees much ever. Not me, anyway.

I choose shrimp at the restaurant, which tastes okay with lots of sauce on it. No beans. I just love eating in restaurants now, one of the reasons is they never serve us beans. I ask the manager for a souvenir menu for my scrapbook. When we come out we are full and happy. Corman stops to talk to a paratrooper from the 101st by the USO. He's a big guy for a paratrooper and Viking-blond. When she learns he is from Murfreesboro, Tennessee, she accepts his invitation for a drink at the Palmer House. "Ta-ta," she waves at us. Just like New York.

"Nothing will come of it." Tolliver says.

"How do you know so much?"

"He doesn't look a thing like that movie star, Glenn Ford. You'll see. I know lotsa things . . . Miss Prissy."

There's something in her voice. "Tell me, Tolliver."

"Fair enough. You talked me into it. I know where you are going. Right after you left the duty station list went up."

"Did you see my name? Why didn't you tell me earlier?" I am about to shake her, but the rain that had been threatening most of the day begins to spatter fat raindrops. We crowd into the white-tiled alcove doorway of a cigar store.

"You're not gonna like it."

"Go ahead, shoot. I regret that I only have one life to give for my country." You have to kid around with her, it's either that or kill her.

"You're going to Treasure Island, California. That's the good news. The bad news is that me and Corman are going with you. Atkinson, too. Dombrowski and the others are posted to New Orleans."

"California? I can't believe it. I actually got what I wanted." I hugged her.

"Take it easy, pal. It's just a good thing for all of us that you didn't queer the dew with Motivatin' Joe."

I back off, which isn't easy in the crowded doorway. "Coralee Tolliver, how can you say that? You gave him a hard time, too, worse'n me, always telling him to get his ticket punched and all those nasty things . . ." An elevated train rumbles by and nobody can hear anything.

Tolliver has to yell. Her face is red. "I don't know what I done that I gotta spend the whole damn war with you. Maybe you should ship out or something."

Likewise, I'm sure.

California. Land of dreams. Far away, mountains, the terrific Pacific, sunshine, oranges. Wow-ee. Now I'll have a lot to write to Mother about.

CHAPTER 9

Home Leave

Buddy is outside kicking a football around when I walk up the steps from the sidewalk where the dried leaves are swirling around in little whirlwinds—it feels like winter is on its way. For a minute I think Buddy is Michael, all arms and legs and elbows; he's grown since I've been away and looks like Michael used to look. His jaw drops when he sees me. "Hiyo, Sis. We weren't expecting you till this afternoon. You look great. Wouldna known you in that uniform."

"I caught an earlier train to surprise everybody. Hey, watch out, you'll knock me down, Buddy." I put my suitcase down to return his hug. "You've grown."

"You sound just like all the other grownups, Sis." He pulls a face and hunches his thin shoulders in exasperation.

"Sorry, fella. Don't be mad. I brought you a real sailor hat from Great Lakes."

"I'll go tell Mother you're here." He races up the steps by where the jack o'lantern left from Halloween is just beginning to go soft. He lets the screen door slam and screeches for all the world to hear, "Mother-r-r. Hey, Josie's home." His voice is changing, too, no more baby brother for me.

Our house looks the same. Daddy hasn't taken the awnings down yet or put up the storm windows—it's way past time. Sure enough, the red-bordered flag in the front window has two blue stars, one for Michael and one for me. I wince when I look across the street to the Schmidts', where the star on the flag is gold for poor Tom. The maple trees along our street are almost leafless, just a few survivors tugging in the wind. Doggone, I missed the flaming arch the maples make across the street in the fall. My favorite time of the year. Some-one is burning leaves in the neighborhood, I can smell the smoke.

"Josette angel. We didn't expect you so soon." Mother comes out on the porch wiping her floury hands on her apron. She looks flustered, like she always does when something catches her off guard, her hair all in wisps like she hasn't done it yet.

"Caught an earlier train. Wanted to surprise you."

"Well, you certainly did. Let me take a look at you." She puts her hand on my shoulder and draws back, eyeing me like when I was little and she was trying to determine if I was coming down with a fever. "I must say, the Navy seems to agree with you." I smile. You should only know, Mother.

"Didja shoot any Japs, Sis?" Buddy is varooming around the porch like a fighter plane, making rat-a-tat noises in our ears. That kid was born loud. I had forgotten.

"I'm a gunnery instructor, not a real gunner, Buddy. I'll tell you all about it later."

"Let's not keep Josette standing here on the porch, Brian. Take your sister's suitcase upstairs. Come into the kitchen with me, Angel. I'm making a peach cobbler. We've saved all of Michael's letters for you."

The kitchen is just as warm and cluttered as I remember it, the floor as shiny clean, the refrigerator humming. The calendar from O'Donnell and Malone—Funerals with the blood-red picture of the Sacred Heart has today's date circled in red with "JPD coming home!!" in Mother's tiny handwriting.

Mother puts the biscuit topping on the canned peaches and cinnamon already in the pan as she talks. I have the queerest sinking feeling that there isn't anything to say. Mother doesn't notice, just rattles on, her long graceful fingers working nervously over the dough. "I thought we would just have the immediate family tonight. Geraldine wanted to have a big gathering but I told her to wait till Sunday after mass. You will be here through Sunday, won't you? Monsignor O'Callaghan asks after you all the time."

I bet. I watch Mother check the oven temperature and put the cobbler in. I just sit there on the same stool where I always sat waiting for the spoon to lick. Mother doesn't pause for breath.

"Mrs. Lundgren asks for you whenever I see her. I saw her in line at the butcher's yesterday and told her we were expecting you. She said you should come see her if you have time. Mrs. Rafferty tells me that Sheila is engaged to that second Murphy boy, Owen, I think. I never thought those Murphy boys amounted to much, but Sheila says she knows her own mind and this is love. Consuelo is going to take her next vows as I wrote you. Geraldine is taking on airs about it, you'd think Consuelo was being elevated to the College of Cardinals or something. Theodosia's Cornelius thinks he has a vocation. If you ask me, I think 16 is too young to decide something like that." She pauses at last, pushes a stray tendril behind her ear, and says, "But you're not saying anything, Josette. You must be tired from your trip. Perhaps you want to lie down before dinner. You know the way. We can talk later."

I know the way. How can anybody get a word in edgewise in this house? I take the pile of V-mails from Michael off the top of the radio to read upstairs. There isn't any news in them, even less than the letters he writes to me. He must figure he has to keep it light, too, not to worry Mother and Daddy. Is it very bad where you are, Michael? I bet you wish you were home, too—Daddy would make you take the awnings down and put up the storm windows and Mother might talk your ear off.

Daddy gets home late. They are putting in a lot of overtime at the plant, making all sorts of gizmos for the Army that are supposed to be secret, things for bombsights and gunsights. He looks tired, his face looks gray, he looks older. "Look what the cat dragged in," he says when he sees me, still wearing my whole entire uniform for the effect. He acts like he doesn't even notice. "Good to have you home, kiddo. How long you staying?"

"Ten days."

He grunts and sinks down into his old armchair and flaps the paper open. "Says here," he reads aloud, "your Admiral Chester Nimitz announces that the U.S. Naval forces have destroyed 73 Japanese ships and 670 planes in the last week. That seems like a lot. Looks like you're on the winning side, kiddo." He picks up his beer and disappears behind the *Free Press*.

Kiddo? I bite my lip, take off my hat, gloves, and jacket, and go out to set the table for Mother.

Buddy insists on wearing the white sailor hat I brought him all through dinner. Daddy asks me, "They treating you right, Kitten?"

"Sure, Daddy." Would I tell him if they weren't? Dunno.

He doesn't say a word after that. Mother is so fluttery and nervous she passes the mashed potatoes twice in two minutes. Buddy's hat is too big for him and keeps sliding down his forehead as he bounces around in his chair asking one question after another. I

keep feeding him sea stories about marching till we dropped and firing our big Bofors 40s till our trigger hands were numb; can I help it
if he believes his big sister was the one who splashed the little drone
plane and made Gunny furious? Lies. Sea stories. Did you do the
same thing, Odysseus, patron saint of all us voyagers, getting carried
away by the wide eyes and will to believe of your homefolks and making up those stories? Scylla and Charybdis? Mermaids that sit singing
on rocks combing their long seaweed hair? Magical dolphins that
save children from the sea?

"I sure hope the war lasts until I'm big enough to get into it,"
Buddy says.

"Dear God in heaven," Mother gasps, "that would be six more
years." She crosses herself and disappears behind the swinging door
to the kitchen.

Daddy grunts, "We've got the Jerries on the run. It won't take that
long, Bud. Now that Josette is after them."

"Say something Navy, Sis, like they do in the war movies. Two
points off the starboard bow. Fire one!" He curls his fists in front of
his eyes like binoculars. "Fire two. Ka-pow. Scratch one flat-top."

"Knock it off, little brother, or I'll put you on report. How's that?
You can have the last pork chop."

Daddy gets up from the table and goes into the living room and
turns on the radio to listen to Gabriel Heatter. He didn't even wait
to have any peach cobbler. "Your father hasn't been feeling well,"
Mother sighs when she brings it to the table.

I feel the sun hit my closed eyelids and my heart begins to race. I
must have missed reveille somehow. Now I'm in for it. I groan, open
my eyes. Yellow gingham curtains, Jesusgod, I'm home. I turn over to
go back to sleep but decide it's a shame to waste a day lollygagging in
bed. It's already ten o'clock, according to the Snow White clock on
my bureau. I had painted all of my bedroom furniture white when I
was fifteen—pink is so babyish. I call to Mother who's vacuuming
downstairs that I'm going to take a long bath. Biggest treat in the
world, a long private, soaky bath with Aunt Geraldine's left-behind
bath salts.

Soon's I'm wrinkled as a prune I'll get dressed and let the whole
world see me in my uniform. No more just the little Dermody girl,
but Seaman Dermody, United States Navy Women's Reserve. Hot
diggety dog.

Mousy Mr. Meekin is out when I pop by the plumbing shop, but Sheila is there. She smiles when she sees me and thrusts out her left hand; sure enough, on the third finger is a ring with a little chip of a diamond in it. I admire it. Sheila looks almost pretty, she's shining so. Owen Murphy was a snitch at school and kind of dopey at that, but maybe he has improved in the two years he's been in the Army. Sheila's real smart, she was almost valedictorian instead of me, except that I'm better in Latin. What can she see in a dimbulb like Owen? No accounting for tastes, Grandma used to say.

"How do you like the Navy?" Sheila asks, but never gives me a chance to answer, just gushes right on. "I'm so grateful to Daddy now—he wouldn't let me go into the service with you when I wanted to. If I had I wouldn't have been here when Owen came home on leave." She smiles a self-congratulatory smile. I have to admit she looks good, her long civilian hair in a stylish upsweep, she looks businesslike as she answers the phone and writes down the message. It's a funny-peculiar feeling to see her in my old job. No sweat. She can have it. I turn to go.

"Mother and I are going to Zauber's this afternoon to pick out the pattern for my silver club. You want to come along?"

"No thanks. I've got lots else to do. Lots of luck and happiness, Sheel. Send me a wedding announcement. Tell Owen I said he's a lucky guy."

"Too bad you won't be here so you could be one of my bridesmaids. I think I'm only going to have six, that's enough, don't you think? You couldn't get off for the wedding, could you?" she asks, kind of halfheartedly.

"I doubt it, Sheel. There's a war on, you know."

"Too bad—you'd look good in sea-green taffeta. I'm thinking of waltz length dresses with pink rose bouquets. We can't be sure when it will be because we don't know when his next leave will be. I hope it's soon."

There's something in her voice. Could it be? We'd been best friends since third grade, but she won't tell me anything now, somehow we're practically strangers. "Sorry, Sheila." I straighten my shoulders and feel my starched white uniform shirt crackle. I almost throw up but think better of it.

"Too bad you can't be here." She admires her teeny tiny ring which is making a miniature rainbow on the wall, enlivening the dusty girlie calendars with sparkles of colored light.

Like bloody heck, too bad, Sheila Rafferty. Come back soon,
Owen Murphy. Sheila needs the wedding sooner rather than later.

The relatives all want a piece of me, come to dinner, come to
mass, come to a novena, come to see us, see us, visit us, validate us.
The aunts surreptitiously check me out for signs of lost innocence,
the uncles tease because they don't know what to say. Somehow I am
a credit to the family, or they feel obligated to make sure that everybody in the parish sees it that way. They drag me to call on Monsignor O'Callaghan, who seems to have shrunk somehow, he's turned
into a little sawed-off guy with a terrible temper, beautiful silver hair,
a terrifying loud voice, and ears that stick out. He and I manage to
dance around the ceremonial visit Cecelia takes me to; he doesn't
bring up Saint Paul and I don't bring up Joan of Arc. I can't believe
he's so little. When Geraldine finally has her big family come-all-ye at
her house, he sends the Saint Sebastian–like beautiful curate with
the asthma, Father Malloy, instead of coming himself—we can't take
it personally, though, because the Doyle family had just got word on
the same day that their Barry, their firstborn, was missing over Yugo-
slavia somewhere and that Hugh, their baby, their fair-haired semi-
nary student, was dead, his ship torpedoed, no survivors. Monsignor
has his hands full comforting the Doyles, not so much comforting
them as showing them how to keep their faith. When something like
that happens to a family, somebody has to explain it. Even so, it
doesn't make any sense. Nobody mentions Michael, but he is there,
the oldest of the cousins, everybody's favorite. He has never even
seen Aunt Teddy's Victor, our war baby, our hope for the future, our
howler with two teeth and more to come.

Edith Shaughnessy meets me at Sanders on Woodward, not ten
blocks from our old high school. We sit at the green marble counter
on the high swivel stools and order hot fudge cream puffs. "Next I'm
going to have a Tin Roof. They never heard of them at boot camp.
I've really been wanting one." I tongue the ice cream off the upside-
down spoon. Bliss.
    "Maybe they are a Detroit special, like Vernor's ginger ale. They
didn't have them at my grandmother's this summer either."
    She knows and I know that she wasn't at her grandmother's this
summer, but naturally she doesn't want to talk about her slave-days at

the Good Shepherd Home or the little ghost-baby that was there and
then wasn't there. Put up for adoption, most likely.

I look at her in the mirror behind the fountain. Her rose-colored
twin set is a little tight for her and she has delicate violet shadows
under her eyes. Her fingernails are bitten to the quick. She chatters
on, a screen of conversation to keep communication at bay. "Next
semester, I'm enrolled in Marygrove. I'll major in art history, I
think." Jeezus, Edith, I don't say. The whole world is exploding. Fas-
cism is taking over, do we need art historians? Edith always liked
Gothic church paintings. She's so quiet now, not jokey like she was
when she and poor Tom Schmidt used to tease and argue. I swivel to
look at her, it comes to me. It was Tom's baby. Bound to be a priest,
even bishop/cardinal Tom. So Tom is killed in the war, his baby alive
and adopted by a good Catholic family in Kansas, Edith sits here
putting her life back together and talking nonsense about admission
policies of Marygrove College. I can't think of what kind of medal
there is for her kind of courage, she never told. I wave for the bill
and pay it. The gray-haired cashier only charges me half because I
am in uniform.

I phone Mrs. Lundgren and tell her I will be in her neighborhood. I have been putting it off, but I'm due back in two days. On
the way, I walk by St. Aloysius' School, the whole place is humming
with enclosed activity, everybody is in class doing their multiplication
tables or whatever, so I don't bother. They've all seen me at mass on
Sunday anyway. I push open the gate to the Lundgrens'. Mr. Lundgren is an engineer at the plant where Daddy is a foreman. He really
is from Sweden, but Arvid is American—it's dumb to keep calling
him Swedish all the time. So what if his family's Christmas tree has
strings of paper blue and yellow Swedish flags instead of tinsel, and
they have a little red leprechaun type called Tomtem instead of Santa
Claus? Mr. Lundgren is an engineer, but mostly what he does is grow
roses. This time of year the bushes are bare and banked into little
hillocks of manure and straw. Inside, the house is always full of flowers, even now in November, smelling deliciously of rose petals,
orange peel, and spices.

Mrs. Lundgren kisses me on the cheek as she draws me inside to
the warmth. She holds me out at arm's length to admire my uniform. "So this is what they have done with our *lilla flicka*," she says.

"We shall have coffee." She brings out a tray with an embroidered tray cloth, a china coffeepot, and two delicate little cups and saucers with forget-me-nots painted on them. She sets the tray down on the coffee table and disappears into the kitchen to return with an almond ring and two delicate plates.

Her tawny dress that almost matches her hair whispers silkily as she bustles back and sits down.

"We bake with honey now," she says, cutting the coffee cake and handing me a laden plate. "So you like the Navy. I got your postcard from the Empire State Building. I think it is so nice that young people get out and see the world." She pours me a cup of coffee in one of the forget-me-not cups. I'm used to GI mugs and the delicacy throws me off balance so I almost spill it, recovering in a swooping motion, the tiny silver spoon chattering in the saucer. Mrs. Lundgren doesn't notice. "I had a letter from Arvid last week. He reports that his wife is learning to cook while she is waiting for him in London. Can't do much with the rationing, but she's working at it. I send them some sugar and some Spam. I have her picture right here." My blood pounds in my ears. Steady, girl, Arvid is part of your interesting past now, remember? Mrs. Lundgren turns to the sideboard where she ruffles through some letters. The cup and saucer rattle so in my hands that I have to put them down, but even so some of the dark, black coffee sloshes messily into the saucer. I fake a coughing fit. "Ah-ha. Here it is, a little blurry but she seems pleasant enough. Nice. Her name, it turns out, is not Eileen, but Gillian. Arvid's handwriting is not what it might be. Are you all right, my dear? Can I get you a drink of water?"

"Please." My coughing fit is no longer a fake. I drink the water, pick at the almond ring, and leave as soon as I decently can.

I have to talk to somebody. I miss my shipmates, who seem much more experienced in affairs of the heart than anybody I know. Mother and Daddy never liked Arvid because he's a Lutheran and I'm afraid they might say something dumb like it's a blessing from God or birds of a feather or something. I suppose I can trust Aunt Geraldine, my godmother and stalwart partisan all my life. Just because I didn't want to get engaged to him doesn't mean Arvid should turn around and marry somebody else just like that. She doesn't fail me. "He's not the only pebble on the beach," she says. "Trust me. You'll get over him. Scanlon women are strong. Do a whole lot better, maybe."

I shake my head. I'm only part Scanlon, not strong a-tall. Before I can start to feel sorry for myself, she continues. "Tell me, Josette, how are you and your father getting on?"

"He doesn't talk to me much," I blurt out, so surprised I forget to guard my tongue. "It's like he's mad at me or something."

"He's pining for you, child. It's like he can't get over your actually up and leaving."

"That's crazy. I can't be seven years old and a Little Sunbeam in the pageant all my livelong life. It's not fair." I'm mad. I feel like crying. Why is he doing this to me?

"No, it isn't fair. As you know, Josette, I was the one who thought you should go. I still think I was right. No one ever dreamed he would take it so hard." She heaves a sigh. "Perhaps when you are a parent, you will understand it better. Meanwhile, don't fret about it. He'll come around."

What about me? Well, in two days I will be on my way to Californ-eye-ay. Everybody will just have to muddle along without me as best they can. I'm off again to see the rest of the world.

CHAPTER 10

Challenger

We are on our way to California at last. Tolliver is sitting next to me on the Challenger—a rackety-packety big old green train with worn, not-so-clean, green baize seats and opaque windows, retreaded from Lord-knows-what boneyard to carry troops from one side of the country to the other. We board at Chicago, the train already so crowded that seabags in the aisles double for seats and bunks. We had started off all together, all the new gunnery instructors destined for the West Coast, but somehow people had drifted from car to car, and only Tolliver and I are sitting on the backwards facing seat by the door in this car. Lounging opposite us are two sailors, who had been teaching us to play acey-deucy until we got tired of it somewhere around Iowa. Culligan, the string-bean tall one, is cute and funny with his pointed eyebrows that make him look devilish. The other guy, whose name seems to be Sparks, obviously a radioman, is one of those guys who comes on like gangbusters. Tolliver strung him along for a while, but she's really not interested. He makes a crack about flat tires, we've heard that one before, and takes Culligan off with him to see if they can hustle up some beer or some live ones.

Outside the cloudy windows there isn't much to look at, except an occasional isolated farmhouse by a slowly revolving windmill. "How come you're so mopey, mopier than usual, I mean?" Tolliver asks in her usual complimentary way.

"What's it to you?"

"Bad time on home leave, eh? Me, too." She heaves a big sigh.

"Mine wasn't bad or anything. It just wasn't what I expected, I guess," I tell her. For the life of me I can't figure out why I'm feeling so forlorn.

"Mine made me feel so bad, like maybe I shouldna joined up. How 'bout that?" Tolliver bites her lower lip, where her lipstick is all chewed off.

"Really, what happened?" Talking helps to pass the time.

"Remember my sister Rosalee? The one that everybody thought we was twins but we aren't because I'm ten months older?"

"She the baby in your family?"

"No, there's Finus, the caboose. He says he wants to be a doctor like his great-great-granddaddy was, so he's always reading, like you. Rosalee's the boy-crazy one. Mama couldn't do a thing with her after Daddy and the big boys took off for Akron and Dee-troit to work in the war plants. Mama thought she'd settled down when she up and married Randall John Byrd." Tolliver fishes out her cigarettes, then puts them back, this is a no-smoking car. She sighs.

"He the one that went down with all hands? I remember you telling us your sister was pregnant. How's she doin'?"

"Don't know. That's the problem. She had her baby, he was early because of the shock, you know. He's getting fat and sassy now, but they didn't know if he'd make it at first, he was that tiny." She holds her pudgy hands about ten inches apart. "I bought him a little bitty sailor suit from Ship's Stores. He looks right cute in it."

"What's his name?"

"Randall John Junior. He's the spit of Randall Senior. I shook his teensy hand and said 'Howdydo, Randall Junior. I'm mighty proud to shake the hand of the son of a gen-u-wine he-roh.'"

My problem with Tolliver is that I can't always tell when she's joshing and when she's not. It's hard to follow the point of her stories sometimes, because they almost always involve several generations of Tollivers to way back before the Civil War. "What did Junior do?"

"He smiled right at me, but Mama said it was probably just gas."

"That must have been nice." It's stuffy in this car, even with the constant opening and closing of the door behind us. I stifle a yawn.

"Not hardly. Rosalee can't stand the sight of Junior. Says every time she sees those little jug ears and that dimple in his chin it reminds her that Randall John is never coming back and she chokes right up."

"Poor Rosalee."

"Poor everybody. Right before I got home she left Junior with Mama and ran off to Norfolk to work in the shipyards. Nobody's heard from her since. Mama's frantic with worry. Besides, Mama's getting kinda old to have a baby on her hands."

"She left her own baby? I can't believe it."

"You don't know Rosalee. She's always been notional. I'm the only one can talk some sense in her head and I wasn't there. I shouldna left Mama."

"Don't blame yourself, Tolliver. This war makes everybody crazy."

"That's for damsure." This time she lights the cigarette and puffs great clouds of smoke into the fetid air.

"Why did you enlist anyway, Tolliver?"

"Lotsa reasons. I love my country. I'm going to beat Hitler and the Japs. Adventure. Then I'm going to catch me a handsome young officer and live in a big house on the hill all the rest of my life." Now the old joshing Tolliver is back.

"Rotsa ruck."

She stands up and stretches. "I'm gonna go see if those old boys rassled us up any beer. Wanna come?"

"No, thanks. I'm off beer." Never been on it, but there's no need to mention that. Daddy drinks enough beer for all of us—now where did that thought come from?

In my melancholy mood I stare out the window. The farms all look the same this time of year, the fields all bare and stubbly, the farmhouses standing two stories high and isolated with nothing but their windbreak trees for shelter in the flatness.

Poor little Randall John Junior. Born a boy. Just so he can grow up to die in a war. Hope he has a good time first. Randall Senior was only 19 when his life ended. The Great War, the one Daddy was in, was supposed to be the war to end wars, and here we all are, all crowded together in uniform creeping across this flat, flat land. I doze off, lulled by the rocking of the train.

I am at Great Lakes by the big swimming pool. I'm on my way somewhere else, but I stop to watch a drill. There are ghostly figures of young sailors up in the shadowed rafters. The gym smells of gasoline. Somebody throws a match. Roaring tongues of flame dance angrily up toward the guys standing on the rafters. "Jump" comes the order. The figures fold their arms and plummet into the water feet first. I feel the heat of the flames on my face. "This must be hell," I hear myself saying.

I am in the water. It isn't the gym at Great Lakes. It is an endless, dark sea. A big, black listing hull looms to starboard. A klaxon is still sounding. Must get away from her, I say to myself. She'll suck me down. I kick off my shoes. The water is covered with flaming oil. I can't remember the drill. I panic. Nobody taught me the drill. Something about push the flames away and come up for air. There is a baby wearing a little blue sailor suit in the water next to me. It is my baby brother, slick with oil. I grab for him, but he slips out of my hands like a soapy child in a bathtub. I bob desperately, trying not to breathe in the scorching air. I can't fight it anymore. I'm going down. I feel a hand grasping mine.

"Wake up, mate." It's Culligan, tugging at my hand. "Rise and shine, mate. We're coming in to North Platte."

"North what??" Still entangled in my dream, I draw shuddering breaths. The air in the overheated car is dry and scorching. "We've stopped at every rinky-dinky town on the prairies already, some places weren't even towns." So I sound cross. I am.

"C'mon, you'll see." Half asleep and groggy, I allow him to lead me by the hand outside onto the wooden platform. The fresh, nippy air feels wonderful and I want to stop and just breathe, but Culligan has my hand firmly in his and he doesn't let me stop until we get to a row of tables set under the wide eaves of the ocher and brown station. Under a sign that says "North Platte Welcomes Our Servicemen and Women," a group of motherly looking ladies are passing out pieces of homemade cake. I never have seen so many kinds of cake outside of a bakery before. What's with the ration coupons, folks? Not for me to know. Culligan, still clutching my hand, smiles boyishly at the nearest nice lady and indicates me, rumpled and still a little groggy, standing next to him. "It's her birthday, Ma'am."

"Is it, dear? How sad to be so far from home on your birthday. What kind of cake do you like?" She waves a plump hand at the table.

"She just loves coconut," Culligan answers for me. I don't have a chance to declare forthrightly that my birthday is in June. He swoops up the snowy white cake nearest him, towing me behind him with one hand, juggling the sticky-frostinged cake with the other. He turns and waves from the step of the train, all earnestness and charm. "Thanks, Ma'am. God bless you."

I turn and look back, ready to die from mortification. It is November-cold on the platform, so the ladies are wearing their winter coats, some of them with voluminous flower-sprigged aprons over them. I catch the eye of the lady Culligan conned the cake from; a tiny smile tickles the corner of her mouth. She's raised rascals of her own, the smile says. Not so dumb. A cake for a God bless you and the war goes on.

"Dammit, Culligan." I'm still sputtering at his using me like that. "Least you can do is give me a piece. Thanks. Why'd you lie like that?" The whistle blows and the laggards on the platform make a dash for it. Some of them are balancing cakes, too.

"Buddies told me," Culligan says through a mouthful of coconut cake. "When troop trains go through Kalamazoo, dames come out with baskets of sandwiches wrapped in paper that says 'I Got a Gal in Kalamazoo.' Like the song, see?" Yes, dummy, I think, we all know the song. He goes on, "Well, in North Platte, Nebraska, they give you a piece of homemade cake," he stuffs another piece into his gob and licks a smidgen of frosting off his thumb, "but if it's your birthday they give you a whole cake. Figured they'd believe you."

"Gee, thanks a lot. Thanks a whole lot." I start to swat him one but he grabs my wrist and grins. "Now I'm famous far and wide as a reliable liar."

"Aw, don't be mad, mate. Nothin's too good for the good old U.S. Navy nohow. Howsabout you and me going to get some chow if the lines ain't too long?"

"Might as well. We've already had our dessert. No funny business, though. I don't trust you."

He pretends to look hurt, pulling a long face that makes me laugh. This must be what Michael is like when he is larking around with girls away from the family. Culligan splays his long fingers over where his heart would be under his heavy woolen jumper. "I swear, I am the soul of honorable intentions. Will you marry me, fair maiden, and save me from myself?"

"That's the best offer I have had all day, but I cannot marry you, alas."

"Why not?" Sincerity radiates from his face under his quizzical eyebrows.

"You don't even know when my birthday is."

"Too bad. You are missing a great catch. The catch of the century, if you want to know. Howsomever, the order of the day is 'Chow down.' Make way, make way." Using his long arm as a divider he leads our way to the dining car. The food isn't half bad, just cold. Culligan persuades me to go to the club car with him after supper. When that gets too roisterous, not to say too smoky, we go outside to that little balcony place they have at the end of the train, holding hands and watching the stars in the midnight sky, large over the prairie. He's nice.

"Gotta fella? You engaged or anything?" I find I can't answer him because he is kissing me. My so-called interesting past is swallowed up in my interesting present.

Third day on the train. It's as claustrophobic and crowded as ever, but no longer hot. Something has happened to the heating system overnight. Gritty cold eddies from the edges of the windows and nips at our ankles. Brr-rr-r. I need coffee. Hot coffee.

"How'd you get along with the guy with the eyebrows?" Tolliver asks companionably as we plow our way toward coffee and breakfast. We are going through the cars that are not part of the troop train, full of young civilian girls in pearls and little hats who are probably going out to the West Coast to get married before Mr. Wonderful ships out; others seem to be going back home, puffy-eyed and disconsolate after a brief weekend honeymoon, to wait out his return. Young service wives are traveling with their sticky-faced babies who are distressed and letting the world know about it. Toddlers in little overalls are playing pattycake with whatever friendly serviceman is in the seat behind them, or playing peekaboo from behind the uniform jackets hung so carefully from the hangers by the windows. It's pandemonium. *Life* magazine and the government keep urging civilians not to travel, but some feel they must. I would, too, in their place, but a trip on this old train isn't any advertisement for the romance of faraway places.

"Well?" Tolliver waits for the answer to her question, when we are in a quieter car.

"I didn't commit a mortal sin, if that's what you want to know," I answer crossly. I follow Tolliver's broad back and frouseled hair through the packed aisles. No point in asking her where she had spent the last chilly night. She'll tell me.

"Maybe I committed a mortal sin, whatever that is, but let me tell you, 'twasn't worth it. That old Sparks had so much beer his powder was damp," she chortles. I giggle just as though I understand it all. I sort of do and sort of don't, but they laugh at me when I ask and my head is getting muddled. I wonder where Culligan has got to? He's not in the dining car.

Outside the train it is beautiful, the day has dawned crystal clear and sparkly. Not exactly frost, the dew lingers and refracts the early sun. You can't tell much from inside the stuffy train, but I am exhilarated and stand on the platform behind the dining car and hang out gingerly, whooping and yelling. Tolliver comes over all worried and hangs onto the back of my uniform jacket. "I can see the mountains up ahead," I shriek. There they are, dead ahead, all jagged edged in the crisp cool air. "First mountains I've ever seen in my whole entire life."

Tolliver laughs at me. "First thing I ever saw when I opened my eyes was the side of a mountain, and mine was blue." She doesn't let go of the back of my jacket until I tire of the cinders in my eyes and duck back inside.

Mysteriously, the mountains seem to stay in the same place all day long. Whenever I lean out to look they never seem any closer. We can feel the train chugging and straining like we must be going up a grade even if it still looks flat and boring outside. It must have taken those old pioneers such a long time to walk all this way. I never imagined it was all this far when I read about it in history class.

Corman, who had seemingly forgotten her mother-henning duties for a two-day-long bridge game with a couple of Glenn Ford near look-alikes in the club car, suddenly comes to and begins to check out her flock. Atkinson is okay, she's found a civilian girl from her hometown who has two babies with her; she's spelling the girl so she can go get some food. Culligan comes by, devilish and mock-gallant as ever; he looks fresh this early in the morning, he smells of Aqua Velva, his blond hair wet from his comb. I introduce him to Corman. He tries to entice us into an acey-deucy game, but Corman grabs me by the arm and herds me into the tiny head at the other end of the car.

"Dermody, whatever have you been up to?" She hisses at me, even though nobody could hear us inside the head, and grabs my upper arm so hard she hurts me.

"Adding to my interesting past, I reckon. Let go of me." I twist and pull to no avail.

"He's married. He's got a baby. He was showing people pictures in the club car. You want to be a homewrecker, Miss Priss?"

"Ow, that hurts." I never question whether she's right. She just has a nose for things like that. I sure don't. I'm not lucky in cards, or lucky in love. Frantically, I pull away and fan through my conscience. Is an almost mortal sin worse with a married man? Do I get a wartime dispensation? I really don't know. He had practically proposed.

Corman is full of concern when she lets go of my arm. "Watch it, sugah, you just might get hurt." She's right, of course, and I put on my best brave face. "Doggone. Now I suppose I'll have to tell him to go back to his wife and kiddies."

I could kick her. I really like Culligan. We were getting a good thing going. Why didn't Corman at least wait till we got to California to tell me? Didn't anyone ever tell her ignorance might be bliss? Some friend.

"New York, here I am at last, worldly and sophisticated as I've always known my true self to be—just like the recruiting poster with two leggy Waves in summer dress whites who stride in step in front of the Manhattan skyline. Underneath it asks, 'Are you going to miss the great adventure?' Not me." (AUTHOR'S COLLECTION)

Don't miss your great opportunity..

THE NAVY NEEDS YOU IN THE **WAVES**

"The first day was a blur as we whirled from station to station, handing in a card here, signing another form there. They gave me a Waves hat, a spanking white upside-down pudding bowl with a brim, which looked ridiculous with my civilian clothes." (U.S. NAVY PHOTO)

"The shots are a foretaste of Purgatory. Honest to God, they make us cranky and sore. We line up in the so-called daisy chain, roll up our sleeves, and grit our teeth. We Waves never faint at shots, point of honor, because we know the guys often keel right over when they get theirs." (U.S. NAVY PHOTO)

"I pose, looking as patriotic and military as I can, so Corman can take my picture for the folks back home to put in the album. Nobody looking at me could know that I was plain old Josie Dermody from Detroit, former file clerk at Meekin Brothers Plumbing and Heating Supplies." (AUTHOR'S COLLECTION)

"The scheduling office has our days laid out for us minute by minute. Never a chance to think. Just follow along. Keep going by pure stubbornness. Always slightly feverish and more than a little disgruntled, we move, always in a crowd, from one place to another. Training films, uniform fittings, selection interviews and tests." (U.S. NAVY PHOTO)

"Eight of us live for now in apartment 5-D. The Navy insists on making us swab the decks in the whole apartment before Captain's inspection; none of dares to ask what all that watery, soapy mopping is going to do to the varnished parquet floors. I know Mother would just die, but we are here to follow orders." (U.S. NAVY PHOTO)

"I returned to examining the poster on which the pretty, perky girl was still smiling her painted smile. The border had pictures of the insignia patches that told the world what you did, like a red cross meant hospital corpsman. I recognized some of the insignia from the recruiting pamphlets that always told you what glamorous, interesting, war-winning jobs you could have in the Navy." (U.S. NAVY PHOTO)

"I love marching, it's so neat, so precise and exact. I love the feeling of all of us acting in unison, like we are some bigger thing; I feel platoon-sized instead of just me." (U.S. NAVY PHOTO)

"Gunny gesticulates with his big hands, demonstrating. 'Gotta pay attention. We ain't playing beanbag here, nohow.'" (U.S. NAVY PHOTO, COURTESY NAVY/MARINE CORPS/COAST GUARD MUSEUM, TREASURE ISLAND)

"More and more people join the crowd watching the parade. Navy Day is a big deal. I love parade music, so bright and brassy, so boom, boom, boom. I move my free hand in a windshield-wiper wave, caught up in the euphoria and the excitement, thinking, 'Look glamorous' and 'Buy war bonds, all you patriotic people.'" (U.S. NAVY PHOTO)

"I caught an earlier train to surprise everybody. Our house looks just the same. Sure enough, the red-bordered flag in the front window has two stars, one for Michael and one for me. Buddy is outside kicking a football around when I walk up the steps from the sidewalk. 'Hiyo, Sis. Wouldna known you in that uniform.'" (AUTHOR'S COLLECTION)

"Treasure Island belies its name. The little pancake of artificial land is jam-packed with barracks, mess halls, a brig, a multifaith chapel with interchangeable altar hangings, ammunition storage areas (way at the farthest end), embarkation areas, athletic fields, and even a prisoner of war camp. Berths for ships and water-taxis and even a couple of sailing ships, looking nautical but odd among all the gray painted steel ships." (U.S. NAVY PHOTO, COURTESY NAVY/MARINE CORPS/COAST GUARD MUSEUM, TREASURE ISLAND)

"Poor Daddy never sent a daughter off to war before and wishes the consarned Navy would let me stay home where I belong. But Mother says, 'Well, I must say, the Navy seems to agree with you.' I smile. You should only know, Mother." (AUTHOR'S COLLECTION)

"It isn't hard. Easier than Great Lakes. Mounted on top of the guns, where the cylindrical magazines of shells would ordinarily be, are suit-case-shaped metal boxes containing the projectors. Our job is to thread the projectors with a large reel of film of incoming Japanese planes, know how to turn the machine on, encourage the reluctant boys in blue to use the ringsight to hit the planes. A GI imitation of an arcade shoot-ing range." (U.S. NAVY PHOTO, COURTESY NAVY/MARINE CORPS/COAST GUARD MU-SEUM, TREASURE ISLAND)

"It started as just an ordinary date, another sailor and another Wave taking the A train to 'Frisco for a Sunday afternoon. A stroll through the park, a restaurant meal, a kiss in the moonlight. I want it to go on forever, but Blackie says, 'Don't get engaged or nothin' while I'm gone, Toots. Ship's leaving.' How can you do this to me, God? First he comes and then he goes. (AUTHOR'S COL-LECTION)

"Lurching around the gunshed all those times with Jackson, Boy-Baptist-Junebug, was preparation for just such a moment. It really is heaven with the band playing swing and jazz, but mostly swing. Blackie is a hundred times better dancer than Jackson will ever be. Sometimes he twirls me so energetically the others back off to the edge of the dance floor to watch us and cheer." (U.S. NAVY PHOTO, COURTESY NAVY/MARINE CORPS/COAST GUARD MUSEUM, TREASURE ISLAND)

CHAPTER 11

Treasure Island

Ice-cold rain runs down the backs of our necks, under our collars, as we tumble at last off the gritty Challenger in Oakland where we are to transfer to fabled Treasure Island. "So this is Sunny California." We all say it.

"I shoulda stood in bed," Atkinson grouses. Who can blame her? She already has a cold. Like a rock hitting a greenhouse window all of our collective dreams of sunny blue skies, sparkling waters, orange trees in blossom, snow-covered peaks in the background shatter. The shards of disappointment pile up in an almost palpable heap, but we have no time to regroup and sweep up. Just "Move it" out of the red tile–roofed station to the waiting Navy gray buses, trying not to skid on the muddy marble floor, hauling our suitcases, and not looking very shipshape at all.

Well, Treasure Island at first glance certainly belies its name. I read somewhere that the name came from the gold supposedly washed into the muck at the bottom of San Francisco Bay during the gold rush days; the glittering black muck had been dredged from the bottom to create an island, like some returned Atlantis, for the World's Fair before the war. The flat pancake of land is connected by a causeway to the natural island of Yerba Buena, usually called Goat Island after its first inhabitants. Rocky and eucalyptus-covered (the trees having been planted long ago by some diligent Girl Scouts inventing Arbor Day), Yerba Buena supports the two halves of the Oakland Bay Bridge, offering a tunnel blasted through its rocky cone to travelers who wish to move from San Francisco to the East Bay. The eastern part of the bridge looks like it's been fastened together by Finn Mc-Cool and his giant children playing with an oversize erector set. The western part, the half that goes over to "The City" (as though there were only one city in the world, the one that hates being called 'Frisco), is suspended from giant cables whose graceful curves are

90

laced with harp strings of steel. The winds could possibly play Aeo-
lian melodies on the overhead harp, but if it ever happened we
couldn't hear it from Treasure Island, what with the noise of the foghorns, the bosun's pipes, the ship's whistles, and the never-ending
shrieking of the seagulls.

"So this is it? Our home away from home. A fantasy island of
magic display and delight—that's what the brochures said when I
read about the fair." I am discombobulated.

"You ain't just whistling Dixie, Dermody," Corman agrees. "It hasn't
been the same since Pearl Harbor."

Wet, cold, crabby, and disappointed—and the spirit of adventure
is leaking right out through the toes of my soppy GI Cuban-heeled
shoes. The bus lets us out in front of the administration building, a
curved stucco building that looks like it's been salvaged from the fair.
The flags droop disconsolately in the downpour, a few palm trees by
the chapel are sorrier than the flags, their fronds heavy with the wet.
A huddle of young sailors hunched in their peacoats wait on a bench
with their seabags. Shipping out? One of them has a harmonica. He's
playing "Shenandoah." Such a melancholy sound.

In the personnel office a duty officer takes our orders from Corman, checks us off some list, says, not unexpectedly, "Welcome
aboard," and sends us off to find the Waves barracks.

Inside the double door of the wooden building a tall, square-faced
Waves MAA greets us. "Welcome aboard," she says, not moving her
lips much. "We run a real tight ship here." My heart sinks right down
to my squishy shoes. "Here's where you log in and out. This is where
you get your mail. Inspection every Saturday. It's your responsibility
to keep this barracks shipshape at all times. No gear adrift. *Ever.*
There can be a surprise inspection at any time. Do you understand?
No men beyond the quarterdeck here. I'll show you where to stow
your gear. Linen exchange on Fridays." She clacks down the corridor
with our raggedy, soggy file behind her.

"Under that starched shirt beats a heart of stone," Tolliver cracks.
"You'd think she could smile and brighten her corner just a little."

"They never smile. They go on report if they smile." Atkinson snif-
fles and sneezes, but is trying to keep up our morale. Have to hand it
to her. Jokes don't come easy to her.

The dour MAA leads us to the very end of the barracks on the first
deck where there are two empty cubicles with the striped mattresses

folded back on the bunks. "You can leave your gear here until later. There's java in the lounge upstairs. The Navy runs on coffee, you know." A faint, almost invisible smile touches the corner of her mouth. "Mess hall opens for chow at 1130. Topside is off limits to male personnel. You meet your dates in the front lounge 'side the quarterdeck."

"Dates? When do we start?" Bedraggled Tolliver brightens up a little at the thought.

Our mentor continues, after giving Tolliver a frosty glare, "It is my understanding that you girls are assigned to Armed Guard. Most of our personnel get port or starboard liberty, liberty every other night. However, since you would have to stand duty in the gunsheds in the men's area, you are exempt."

Corman looks puzzled and opens her mouth to ask a question, but the MAA ignores her. "In other words you are entitled to liberty every night. You will, of course, have to take your rotation of duty in the barracks. It doesn't seem fair to the other girls that you should be so privileged. I would advise you not to abuse it. There are some hard feelings. One other thing, remember, as Navy personnel you are responsible for everything that is posted on any official bulletin board. I would advise you to check it several times a day." She turns on her heel and strides away, her back ramrod straight, her red hair resolutely curling above her collar.

"A real sweetheart," Tolliver says. "Let's go topside to the off-limits-to-men lounge and get some java. I'm freezing." For once she doesn't get an argument from any of us.

At 1130 we have changed into dry uniforms, wrung out our hair, stuffed our wet shoes with toilet paper, made up our bunks, and stowed our gear . . . not perfectly, but well enough so that nothing is adrift for a surprise inspection to end up in the so-called lucky bag storeroom, where it can only be redeemed by extra duty. God forfend, we have enough to do without extra duty. Reasonably shipshape, reasonably agreeable, but famished, we line up for the opening of the mess hall. This building makes up one side of the Waves compound, which is brand-new, actually not quite finished. If the war lasts as long as people think it might, the unseasoned green wood will probably warp and twist the whole place into a spiral, but right now it is sound, watertight, and warm. The familiar mess-hall steamy warmth, the smell of old soup, beans, and warm bread, a couple of mugs of scalding coffee each revive us somewhat. Jamoke is what they call it, not coffee, for java and mocha. Do you suppose it could really come from Java now that the Japs have it?

Nothing keeps Tolliver down for long. "Hallelujah! Jesus loves us. We've drawn good duty. We can go to 'Frisco every night of the week if we want to. Wow-ee."

"Standing watch is such a big bore, anyway, nothing to do but stay someplace and not fall asleep. Won't miss it, you betcha." Atkinson sneezes and snuffles into her paper napkin. She looks uncomfortable and feverish. Miserable, actually.

"You don't look so good, Atkinson. Better put in for sick bay." Corman looks concerned.

"Can't. All those guys will say I'm goldbricking. I just got here." She's doing her darndest to look sturdy and steadfast, but I see Corman's face over the salt and pepper shakers between us on the long trestle tables. Poor Atkinson doesn't have a chance, soon as chow is over, Corman will deliver her to sick bay.

Tolliver, as usual, is busting her buttons shoveling in the chow, meatloaf and gravy, mashed potatoes, peas, cherry pie, not paying attention to what's going on with Corman and Atkinson, who's coughing something awful. To cover the coughs, she asks, "What's Armed Guard, anyway?" If I've only learned one thing since I have been in this man's Navy it's that you never have to ask the really dumb questions. Just wait long enough and somebody else will.

"You'll find out," Tolliver says, between forkfuls. She doesn't know either. She stops eating with her USN-marked fork poised halfway to her mouth. Just about every single object around us is marked with USN or anchors, sometimes both. "What do you wanna bet when the dish ran away with the spoon, somebody saluted?"

"C'mon," Corman stands and picks up her tray. "We have to report to Armed Guard, wherever that is, whatever that is."

Anybody could have figured it out from the name, I suppose, but you never can tell with the Navy. Sailors don't talk like landlubbers. Once they put on their Donald Duck suits or their spiffy officers' uniforms they inhabit a different world. Maybe Poseidon with his trident had a different vocabulary than Zeus and Athena and that crowd on Mount Parnassus. Who would know? Naval tradition goes way far back and they still study the Battle of Salamis, where the Greeks beat the Persians, I think. It's like something has loosened in my head and I can't remember what I remember. Anyway, some clever naval person designed a secret weapon, a brazen ram on the prow of his ships, which sank all the enemy ships and his side won. You're never going to make ensign this way, megirl. Who cares? Sometimes I wonder if people who will be alive a long time from now will be studying our great battles, like Midway.

The little pancake of artificial land is jam-packed with barracks, mess halls, a brig (just a little one—the big brig is fenced in, over on Yerba Buena), a multifaith chapel with interchangeable altar hangings, more barracks, a hospital, gunsheds, a tiny airfield, supply depots, ammunition storage areas (way at the farthest end), embarkation areas surrounded by high cyclone fences, athletic fields, and even a prisoner of war camp. Three theaters. Berths around the shoreline for ships and water-taxis and even a couple of sailing ships, looking nautical but odd among all the gray painted steel ships. The Navy paints everything it can battleship gray. Almost the only things Navy blue around are our uniforms. The weather since we have been here is gray, too, the water in the greasy, oil-slicked bay the color of slate, the lowering skies only slightly lighter in tone. Fog and gray damp roll in, tumbling through the Golden Gate, pulled under the magnificent red bridge by some inexorable suction, climbing the hills of distant San Francisco. The fog settles in the low spots, spills over the tops of the lower hills, till only the tops of Coit Tower and the higher buildings can be seen floating magically. Ships anchored in that fog look like ghost ships out of some old seafarer's tale, eerily appearing and disappearing to the rise and fall of the foghorns' sound.

We find the Armed Guard building and guess what? Armed Guard is exactly what it sounds like: the guards, the Navy guncrews that ride along on the cargo ships, the clunky Liberty ships and the clipper-bowed Victory ships, in the convoys to protect them from the Bandits. That's the politest things they call the Japs and their planes, the dive bombers and the torpedo attack planes, as well as the even worse submarines, that harry the convoys criss-crossing the long, lonely sea lanes. The Armed Guard is something of a stepchild, perpetually short of men and materiel, so we find an added touch of warmth to the ritual "Welcome aboard" when we arrive. We Waves would take over the shore jobs and the guys could go to sea. On the freighters they while away their time, standing watch, chipping paint, playing acey-deucy, sometimes reading, always grousing—until an attack, when they whang away with their antiquated ack-ack guns with the old-fashioned ring sights at the incoming planes, Japanese in the Pacific, Axis in the others. Sometimes they splash an enemy plane or two, occasionally they connect with an enemy sub with one of their ashcan depth charges. Sometimes the enemy plane or sub gets them, and they go down, just as dead, but somewhat less gloried in song and story than if they had gone down on one of the big warships like the *Northampton* or the old *Lexington*. Mostly they are just bored. War is mostly hurry up and wait, they tell us.

We aren't bored, not at first. It isn't hard. Easier than Great Lakes. Groups of sailors are shepherded into the stark gunsheds all day long. Double rows of Oerlikons, 20-millimeter antiaircraft guns, are bolted to the deck. Mounted on top of the guns, where the cylindrical magazines of shells would ordinarily be, are suitcase-shaped metal boxes containing the projectors. A GI imitation of an arcade shooting range. Our job is to thread the projectors with a large reel of film of incoming Japanese planes, know how to turn the machine on, encourage the reluctant boys in blue to use the ringsight to hit the planes. Then we must write the score on each sailor's hand-carried scorecard.

Corman is spokesman—our head teacher. As each group arrives she stands in front and explains the drill. She doesn't look much like a recruiting poster Wave. They always have their full dress blues on, including hats, no matter what they are doing. Corman is as pretty as a recruiting poster Wave, but she is wearing exactly what the rest of us are wearing, neat blue wool slacks, dark-blue rayon long-sleeved shirt, and a sky-blue butterfly tie, exactly the color of her eyes. No hat, no jewelry—none that shows, anyway. She stands by the charts of the silhouettes of the planes. She always amazes me, with her way of batting her eyelashes and using her honey-toned voice so disarmingly. She never lets on that she notices the guys are unhappy about a girl instructing them. Especially instructing them to shoot guns. A girl who never would see combat.

"The most important thing is to estimate how far you must lead him," she says. "Calculate how fast he is probably going, allow for the angle, and use the farthest ring you can."

A sullen, square-faced sailor in the front row raises his hand and says mincingly, "Miss, how can we tell how fast the little bugger's going?" I had seen the sailor behind him give him a shove; looks like Square-face lost the draw today about who's going to give the Waves a hard time. Usually they have a bet they can fluster her or make her mad before the petty officer knocks them off. Dumb broads don't know nothin' is what they want to prove. Corman is unflappable.

"Simple." She gives him her homecoming queen smile and continues, "You know, I assume, that the top speed of a Zero is approximately 300 knots, a Betty 250 knots, and so on. A dive bomber usually comes in at an angle of 70 degrees." She waves her hand at the charts on the walls.

He isn't through. "But mate," he says, looking all boyish and earnest like he really cares, "sometimes they mush the planes, pull back at an angle to fly slower, and fool the gunners." He looks around at his sniggering buddies with satisfaction.

"I'm sure they wouldn't fool you, Seaman," she says, pulling a little rank on him. She looks at the rest of the class, "Remember, they're most likely to be coming in fast and dirty. If you aim right at them, by the time the shell gets there it will be behind him. Never, never aim right at him. Just remember that and you'll be okay." She smiles encouragingly and flies her left hand gracefully in a glide pattern and uses her right hand to demonstrate a shell passing way aft.

"What kind of frigging way is that to shoot?" the blue-jawed guy who had shoved Mr. Interlocutor before ventures impatiently. "We din't do it that way at Guadalcanal."

Corman pauses for just a minute, letting the "frigging" sort of hang in the air, then ignores it. With a tiny little frown she says, "Nobody here needs to be told, I am sure, just how close we came to losing Guadalcanal. Man your guns."

Poor Atkinson missed the first two weeks because she was in sick bay. She did have pneumonia after all. When she comes back to the gunshed, pale and thinner, we have to fill her in on everything we learned; how to thread the projectors, how to splice the film when it breaks, how to strap a sailor into the leather shoulder harness that enables the gun to move at one with his body. One of us is assigned to each gun station. When we turn the projector on, the sailor can see wave after wave of gray plane silhouettes coming toward him, simulating an attack on a ship. If the gunner aims sufficiently forward of the dark image of the incoming plane and pulls the trigger at the right time he's rewarded with a flash of red and a DING for a hit. The Zekes and Bettys never splash in these movies, just keep coming, but there is a counter on each machine that adds up the hits, which we duly record on each guy's scorecard.

Amid the DINGs I hear myself shouting. "Short burst. Short bursts."

"Lead him." At the gun next to me Tolliver is waving her hands and leaning like she's trying to make a pool ball fall into a pocket. She's yelling over the noise, "Lead him, lead him, Lordy, you gotta lead him." It's as though we had all swallowed Gunny back there at Great Lakes, although we mostly don't swear like he did. The Navy doesn't like it.

There had been a lot of hullabaloo about letting women serve their country in the Navy; after all, the British had their Wrens, the Russians their women's divisions and even pilots, even the Army had their WAACS, so finally in 1942 the admirals capitulated. Eleanor Roosevelt probably would have gotten them if they hadn't given in, but when the admirals reluctantly struck their colors they exacted the proviso that all Navy women would be *ladies*. Naturally, what did they expect? Don't think about that. Anyway, we aren't supposed to swear, and the sailors can get into trouble for swearing around us. So all we have to do is pat each wool blue shoulder encouragingly, mark his card, unhook him, and say in our best, firm, ladylike voices, "Next."

A month of this and it really begins to get old. The rain never stops, the sameness of the job is tiring. Same thing every blessed day; reveille in the dank dawn, get dressed, pile on guys' skivvy shirts we bought at Small Stores under our thin rayon shirts (Mainbocher, bless him, had neglected to design us Waves an elegant designer sweater), stumble to the mess hall, pour down a couple of mugs of jamoke, try to wake up, eat breakfast with fritters and syrup and bacon or eggs and sausage, sometimes both. Squabble with Tolliver about nothing. She's got it into her head that my disposition would improve if only I'd fall in love. If she thinks I'm ever going to trust another sailor she's got another think coming. I keep telling her to knock it off, but now she knows she can get my goat anytime she wants to and she won't let up.

We walk through the foggy damp to the unheated gunshed, which has been accumulating cold and damp all night, borrow a sand-flea-infested foul-weather jacket to wear while threading the machines, a choice between freezing to death or being bitten to death. Avoid the Chief, he's not so bad, but I like to maintain invisibility. Joke with the guys, there are still a few around, waiting for the full complement of Waves to relieve them for the supposedly more desirable sea duty. We read the *Chronicle* before the classes clump in. "Hey, Dermody, is your brother the one that's in France?" one of the guys asks. I grab the front page away from him to look. The war news doesn't seem all that good, the Germans are regrouping in France. The papers have little maps with arrows pointing here and there.

Which arrow is pointed at my Michael? Which at Arvid, even if I don't care about him anymore?

Every 45 minutes another class. Same thing over and over again. Chow down at noon. Secure at 1630 (by now I don't have to subtract twelve every time to deal with the military 24-hour clock). Chow down again. Corman usually has a date. The rest of us usually try to decide if the weather is too foul to go into 'Frisco, or if we've seen what's on at the movies. I can go to the library instead, or to the Rec Center and play chess, or try to. Tolliver and a couple of the other girls in the barracks are raring to go bowling tonight.

"Aw, c'mon, don't be such a mope. C'mon with us."

"No thanks, I'm in no mood to watch that stupid ball wobble down the gutters every time for me." Instead I go back to the barracks and write to Sheila on my neat blue stationery with the anchors on it:

Dear Sheila,
Thank you for sending me the pictures of your wedding. You made a beautiful bride. I wish you and Owen all the happiness in the world. You know how sorry I am that I wasn't able to be there. Duty calls, you know. Sunny California isn't all that sunny. Nobody said when you join the Navy and see the world that it wouldn't be raining all the time. There are some compensations though, like two hundred thousand guys coming and going on this island and only a few hundred Waves. Ha ha. Say hello to everyone for me.
Love,
Josie

I must have been out of my ever-loving blue-eyed mind to join up, but I'll die if I'll let anybody know it. The recruiting posters made it all sound so glamorous. Dear God, don't think I am ungrateful for answering my prayers to make Daddy sign for me. I fling my stationery kit into my drawer and get into the sack. Boredom may be a terminal military disease, but who can I talk to about it?

CHAPTER 12

Survivors

A line of sailors, a couple of dozen of them, is standing in a raggedy queue outside the hospital; I almost bump into them as I hurry along, head down against the icy-pointed drizzle. It had actually sunnied up, a pale wintry sun, for a couple of days around Thanksgiving, but it was too good to last and today the usual dreary, dreadful weather is back. I'm hurrying because Chief will kill me if I'm late again. I had gone back to sleep for just a minute after reveille, bad mistake. I missed breakfast and need coffee, but I notice the guys in the line don't say "Hubba hubba" or anything, like you would expect. They look strange in their assortment of ill-fitting foul-weather gear, not the most shipshape bunch of guys you ever saw. More like dejected-looking. No wonder. I can't believe my eyes. They are all standing there in the cold drizzle without any shoes on. They'll catch their death. How 'bout that? I don't have time to stop and ask any questions.

Sliding into the gunshed I begin threading the reel onto the projector, acting like I had been there all along. Judy Jenson, the pale new girl with the long oval face and long white fingers, who had been transferred from New Orleans to complete our roster after Atkinson got sick, gives me a thumbs-up signal.

"Chief's not down yet."

Even so, my hands shake and I snap the narrow film. I take the big reel off, slap the broken pieces onto the splicing gizmo, and tape them together. I put the whole shebang on the machine again; at last, it's ready to roll. Five minutes until the first group will clump in out of the cold and wet. Tolliver and the rest are over by the coffeepot having a loud, stupid argument about General MacArthur. Nobody in the Navy likes the general a-tall, a-tall, everybody insistently passes the time yelling about him every time they see his name in the paper; they are like the rich people back in the Midwest who can never say

"That Man in the White House" without sputtering. Jackson, our pink-cheeked striker whose main job is to make coffee and sometimes fix our machines, hands me my life-saving java in a mug he had made out of a 40mm shell casing. He makes awful coffee, hot as the devil and sludgy with sugar, but he makes neat things out of shell casings in the metalworking shop in his spare time.

"Thanks, Jackson." I cradle my hands on the mug and inhale the steam—it always smells so much better than it tastes. "Say, did you see those sailors standing on line by the dispensary without any shoes? What gives? They looked awful foolish."

Jackson turns quickly from where he is brewing some more of his awful muck. His freckled face and cowlick remind me of Buddy for a minute, he's not all that much older. "They ain't foolish. They're survivors."

"Sorry, didn't mean it." My mouth is hanging open. I shut it and try to look copacetic. "Survivors of what?"

Jackson swells up with importance. He knows something we don't and we are the teachers. "We lost a Liberty ship a couple days ago outside the Golden Gate. They was on their way to Pearl. Never caught up with their convoy. Bam."

"No kidding?" I say, just as cool as can be. "Did we lose anybody?"

"Dunno," Jackson answers. "Probably."

"The Japs are that close?" I feel my heart racing. There really is a real war out there. I hope Mother, the world's biggest worrier, doesn't hear about it. That's what censors are for, aren't they?

"Military secret, pal," Tolliver reaches around me for a refill. "Why do you suppose they've got those submarine nets across the Golden Gate?"

"Antisubmarine nets, you dumb broad," Jackson mutters, but she chooses to ignore him. Me too.

"Holy Mother of God, what's with the shoes?" I persist.

"C'mon, sailor." Jackson grins his aggravating grin. He's such a baby, really. Why did his mother let him out? "First thing you gotta do is shuck off your shoes if you go in the drink. Remember that iffn you fall off the water-taxi."

Gruesome Gus comes up behind Jackson and butts in, like he usually does. He's a big, blond farm kid turned seaman from North Dakota, his name is really Gustavus Adolphus Mortenssen, but everybody calls him Gruesome. "She better not fall off the water-taxi.

Buddy of mine, he was there when they pulled a body out of the water last week. Said the sea bass had chewed him up pretty bad." His voice is casual like he had just said, "It looks like rain."

Fighting nausea, I say, "You and your buddy stories, Gus, you all make me sick. Will somebody please tell me why those guys don't have any shoes *now?*" Aunt Geraldine has been telling me since my fourth birthday that my besetting sin is never being able to leave anything alone. I can't help myself.

"You been in the Navy so long, sister, you forgot already about ration points? Most of them guys are merchant marine, civilians. You gotta get ration points for shoes." Jackson is in his glory, explaining.

"What's gonna happen to them now?"

"Who knows? They'll probably get another ship. Maybe go to Rotterdam and draw hazard pay. Maybe Murmansk? Get torpedoed again. How should I know? I only work here."

"If you can call it work," Tolliver cracks.

"Stop picking on me, all of you. You broads got me outnumbered. If you keep on not appreciating me, I'll put in for sea duty and then where will you be? Standing around with your hair growing over your collars and your frigging machines not working. Oops, 'scuse the French. Morning, Chief."

None of us had noticed the Chief appear like a line squall the lookout didn't see. He's a huge man with ham hands, the belt holding up his uniform gray pants must be 46 inches around, but I would never accept a challenge to punch him in the stomach. A person could break a hand that way, I mean, even if you're a guy. Regular Navy all the way. If it wasn't for the war he would be retired in a nice little place with a rose garden near San Diego. We adore him but we can never resist the temptation to give him a hard time. He doesn't treat us worse than anybody else, he doesn't treat us better than anybody else. He treats us Waves like anybody else. He makes us feel like real Navy. Do your job. Do it right. Memorize the Rocks and Shoals— Navy regulations. Keep your nose clean. Keep your language clean around ladies. That's his one thing.

"Jackson, you're on report," he barks. "No foul language."

I know I must have been behind the door when they passed out the gift of gab, but Corman certainly wasn't. She was right there in the front row.

"What foul language?" she asks, merrily, turning to us, clustered around the coffee station. "Did any of you hear any foul language? Dermody? Tolliver? Atkinson? Jenson?" We take her cue, widening our eyes to look innocent. The Chief looks from one to the other, shrugs. We hear a faint underbreath "Kee-rist-on-a-raft," which we actively ignore. "Man your stations," he says, his gravelly voice weary. He leaves, probably to retire to his office and open the bottom left-hand drawer of his battered desk, even though the sun is by no means over the yardarm yet. How many regular Navy guys have the Waves driven to drink?

Jackson revives and starts chattering again. "Buddy of mine . . ."

Tolliver snaps, "Knock it off, Jackson. Me and my friends have had it up to here with you and your gruesome buddy stories. You and Gus." Her pearly face gets pink with exasperation.

Jackson looks hurt. "This ain't no gruesome story. Just that a buddy of mine, see, he was in Panama berthed next to this Russian ship that had to lay over, see, while the captain had her baby. They got women in their services, too."

It's too much. Even as the first class comes clumping in, we whack our blue woolen thighs in laughing frustration. Every sailor we know has a buddy who had laid up next to a Russian ship that had been held up for the captain's lying-in. It's one of those stories like Lorelei and mermaids that sailors tell over and over. Always it's a buddy, always a different part of the world, but never the guy who's telling the story.

Maybe someday, when the history of this war is told, they will tell of the Russian fighter pilot squadron, lady pilots all, who shot down dozens of German planes. Jenson squeaks through her giggles, "I wonder how 'If you're nervous in the service, and don't know what to do, have a ba-bee' sounds in Russian?" Our giggles turn into hiccups. The first couple of classes are a little strange. We keep catching each other's eyes and bursting into subdued giggles. Guys don't like it when you do that, they always think you are laughing at them. They keep giving us "Dames is nuts" looks but we get through the morning somehow.

After lunch, I'm feeling logy—every day I say to myself that I am just going to have a salad and maybe an orange, every day I pile my tray with enough food to feed all the starving Armenians in the world for a week (can I help it if the Navy chow is good?)—and at first I don't notice the bosun's mate with his arms folded leaning

against one of the gunmounts. The bosuns and coxswains who bring
the guys in don't have to take a go and strap themselves into the
guns, but most of them do so they can show off. While Corman does
her spiel about angles of attack for the millionth time, I realize he is
watching me. There is a certain kind of man, he should be young,
that the Navy enlisted man's uniform is made for. Guys with pot bellies look silly. Short stocky guys look okay but no better than they
look in Army khaki, but this guy is made for it; wide shoulders and
skinny middle, long legs, supple and sure of himself, really good-
looking, like Errol Flynn if Flynn were dark and had no mustache.
He keeps staring at me from under his white cap—which is bosun-
style resolutely aligned with his straight black eyebrows. I look away.
Corman finishes her arabesques with her graceful hands, the class
begins. I keep busy encouraging, "Short burst, short bursts. Lead
him. Lead him." I can feel the bosun never take his eyes off me until
he leads his platoon out. Tolliver, who never misses anything, gives
me a wink and I make a face at her. Forget it, he's probably just a guy
been at sea too long.

We initial little white scorecards for the sailors all afternoon like
we always do. We secure at 1630 like we always do. When I walk out
of the gunshed two things are different; the sun is shining, the
clouds scudding before the wind to disappear behind the Berkeley
hills, and he is waiting for me. He's leaning lazily against a white
painted anchor from some Spanish-American War battleship, one leg
crossed in front of the other, his uniform cuffs folded back from his
strong wrists. He disengages his back from the huge anchor, grins,
and falls into step with me. His teeth make a reverse arch and one
tooth in front is chipped, which gives him a rakehell air. All in all he
looks dangerous, but not too dangerous, and exciting.

"You got a steady boyfriend?" he asks, without saying hello or anything.

"Why would you want to know?"

"C'mon, you engaged, or married, or anything?"

"Well, I was, sort of." No sense in letting him think nobody ever
asked me, but honesty compels me to add, "Nope, I don't have anybody, not at the moment."

He lopes along beside me, keeping in step in that rolling way
sailors walk, sea legs, they call it. "That's good." His white gob hat, no
longer regulation over his eyebrows, perches precariously behind his

mop of black curls. He has black eyes and when I look I see they are laughing at me. I never met anybody with black eyes before, not really black. He looks like he has just shaved. He walks along beside me, not touching but confidently, like I'm his girl or something. "What's your name?"

Witlessly, I tell him. I feel a proper fool. What am I doing here, walking past the athletic field, the dispensary, the tailor shop, the post office with this guy? This cute guy? Corman has her look-like-a-movie-star fiancés, Tolliver her ensigns (so far not succeeding in catching herself a lieutenant but Tollivers never give up), Atkinson and Jackson hit it off, seems like everybody has somebody, 'cept me. Now here is this cute bosun's mate rolling along beside me acting more than interested. What vagary of Saint Catherine's attention had brought this about? I haven't asked her to send me a man in a long time, that's high school girl stuff, and besides she probably recognizes me as a hopeless case. "What's yours?" I asked him.

"Blackie."

"Blackie, is that all?"

"Yep, just Blackie. You sure you ain't got a boyfriend?"

"No, I haven't got a boyfriend." Not so sure I want one either, Buster. For all the movies I have seen you'd think I'd come up with something clever, wouldn't you?

"You do now."

"That's what you think." Indeed, he has a nerve.

"That's what I know." He grins his lopsided grin. "Lissen. I gotta go to Pearl tonight." Automatically I look around apprehensively at the empty air between the laundry building and the gym. A slip of the lip can sink a ship—even the walls have ears. He's unconcerned. "When I get back, I'll look you up. Okay?" His black eyes look directly into mine.

"Okay," I say. For some reason I'm not breathing very well. "Here's where I get off."

"See ya around, Toots." He wheels and is gone. Wouldn't you know Tolliver is waiting for me at the door of the mess hall.

"Who's that? Hubba hubba." She rolls her eyes and pirouettes like a hippo dancing.

"Just a guy. Haven't you ever seen a guy before? What's for chow? I'm starved." No point in letting on that I don't really know his name or his ship or anything. Doggone. Good thing Jenson's friend works

in Personnel, if I want to I can ask her to pull his file jacket in case I
want to find out if he's married or anything. Blackie is cuter than
Culligan. Calm down, megirl. He's shipping out. Tolliver is being in-
sufferable, chanting "Josie's got a fella," just as if we are still in grade
school. Keep calm, don't let her get your goat.

I stop on the minuscule quarterdeck to pick up my mail. Behind
the counter is a new MAA, her white shirt crackling with starch and
the ends of her black tie perfectly even.

"Dermody, J. P.," I say, indicating the mail slots. "You new here?"

"Just transferred from San Diego," she says, all business. She hands
me a fistful of letters and a package addressed in Mother's handwriting. She looks like a nice girl, but she probably took hard-hearted-
ness classes back at Specialist (S) school, wherever that is, so that she
could refuse to let anyone go on liberty if her skirt is too short or
pressed with creases or if her hair is half an inch too long. They must
have classes in breathing fire if anyone comes in at 0001 instead of
2359. She's perfectly pleasant now as she asks, "Is it always this cold
and damp here? I've been freezing in my bones ever since I got here
last Tuesday."

"Oh no, this is nothing, practically balmy. It gets much worse
sometimes." I say wickedly. Can't help myself.

When I get to our cubicle I kick off my shoes and sit on my bunk.
I sort out the letters, laying them out on the blue bedspread atop the
woven anchor like a game of solitaire. Keep the best for last. One
from Mrs. Owen R. Murphy, that'd be Sheila, nee Rafferty. How odd,
we did everything together, Brownies, Girl Scouts, Legion of Mary,
Sodality, Catholic Worker Hospitality House, and now I might as well
be in Mars and Sheila back home in Detroit. Who's better off? Who
knows? I know. I never would have seen New York and San Francisco
if I had stayed. So there. I'll read her letter later. The next one is
from my cousin Consuelo, I'll never get used to calling her Sister
Laurette, although she's not really a real Sister yet, just a novice. She
always sends me spiritual bouquets, what do I send her? I wonder, is
she happy? She must be homesick, she must be lonesome. She's
been gone for two years already, she can't write much, and she must
miss us all. Funny, I never thought of that before.

A letter from Petrelli. I haven't heard from her but once since
Hunter. Wonder how she got my TI address? She's in Washington,
D.C., where, as we used to say, many are called but few choose to go.

Not so, she writes. She's living in the Waves barracks on Nebraska, she's working as the yeoman for someone big who's working something so-so secret—and best of all, she's got a fella, he's Eye-tal-i-an like her. He's in the Air Force. Good for you, Petrelli. I can see another wedding present buying trip coming up soon, a wonderful excuse to go to Gumps, that expensive Oriental wonderland store in the city.

A postcard from Buddy has the news that his Scout troop has come in second in the countywide scrap drive. Who would think that an old postcard of some trees on Belle Isle would make me feel this way? We always have picnics on Belle Isle every summer. There must not be a stray nail or old cooking pot left in Wayne County with those little guys scouring every bit of it for their war effort.

Mother's tiny round handwriting slants down on the paper. She's worried that maybe I'm not getting enough to eat so she sent me some cookies—hadn't I received them? Yes, Mother, but they only just got here . . . that must be what's in the squashed package, cookie crumbs. She's making a novena to St. Jude. Aunt Geraldine was beaten out as president of the Altar Guild by that common Mrs. Delahanty. Cousin Little Theodosia is expecting and sick every morn-ing so she quit her job at the plant. Cecelia knitted Michael a muffler for Christmas but didn't think Josette needed one in California. Does she? Your father can't seem to shake his cough, Dr. Wax wants him to stay in bed longer, but you know your father.

What's going on here, I rattle the paper to shake more information out of it. I should try to get a long-distance call through on Sunday—if I go early enough to the Rec Center, maybe the lines won't be too long. My whole family, Lord love 'em, thinks if you don't talk about something it doesn't happen. They probably won't tell me if anything is wrong, but you'd think if it was really just bronchitis he would be better by now.

Michael's V-mail didn't say much—usual Somewhere in Europe heading, usual black spaces where the censors have blanked out the interesting parts. He hadn't had any mail in weeks, he hoped folks back home hadn't forgotten about him. His buddies, Deke and some name I couldn't read, had bet him fifty bucks he couldn't chug-a-lug a whole bottle of Calvados. He won, but his head felt like it had been kicked by a mule. (Ha-ha.) His ankles are completely well and he's fit for duty. Take it easy, Sis, don't do anything I wouldn't do. He signed it with his Kilroy drawing of the sad little man with the big nose look-ing over a fence that has written on it *"Dermody was here."*

Oh, Michael, what's happening to you? You didn't used to write me such flat, ordinary letters. Is it very bad where you are? Do you still have nightmares and walk in your sleep? The papers keep talking about "fierce fighting," and then to be encouraging they go on about places like Geilenkirchen (that nobody I know ever heard of) that are surrounded on three sides by British and American troops. I better write him right away. What can I say? He isn't getting his mail anyway, but maybe he will get a whole bunch at once. I look in my stationery kit to see if I have a V-mail flimsy left, goody, just one. At-kinson comes bursting in, rips off her tie, and hangs up her uniform jacket. "Wanna go bowling?"

"No, thanks. I have to write to my brother. Thanks for asking, though." Atkinson is so hard to like because she's so sarcastic, but she's really good at sports. Jenson is, too, and she found out some of Atkinson's story. Her parents died when she was little, she lived around with reluctant relatives on one hardscrabble farm or another in South Dakota. Nobody really wanted her, treated her like a hired girl, Jenson told us. No wonder she's negative so much of the time. Finally she ran away to a grandmother in Nebraska and finished high school there. She wanted to be a teacher, the war came along, she joined the Waves, and here she is.

"Mother sent some cookies." I tear off the tattered brown paper and open the box. Mother had sent hermits full of currants and nuts, which smell of our kitchen back home, not smashed up after all. I offer the box to Atkinson, who's ready to go in her Armed Guard bowling shirt, slacks, and bowling shoes. "Take two," I say, waiting to see what kind of sarcastic thing she will say this time.

"Thank you. You're okay, Dermody. You know that?"

I'm glad somebody thinks so. All I want to do is be a survivor. Should I wonder if Blackie will be back?

CHAPTER 13

Christmas

"Happy is the day when a sailor gets her pay," we are singing, Jenson, Tolliver, and I, as we roam the steep streets of Chinatown doing our Christmas shopping. We are not singing it very loud because there had been another one of those eternal directives stating that naval personnel who create public disturbances will be arrested by the shore patrol, or worse, the MPs. Military Police. We would just die of mortification if that happened, and so would the Navy, apparently. People sure worry about how we behave, mostly they worry about whether we will get caught misbehaving. If we do, they have to do something about it, write reports in seven carbon copies on multicolored onionskin paper, all that filing, and then they have to keep it out of the newspapers. Better to scare us into behaving, so we will be on our best behavior, keeping an eye out for officers and the shore patrol, keeping our white gloves on at all times, keeping our white gloves clean.

Christmas is coming, even if it seems funny with the palm trees and all. Why is that so strange? Our Christmas hymnbook back home had pictures of the Little Town of Bethlehem and it had palm trees. No snowflakes. No sleighs. Maybe Baby Jesus was born in a place like California and all the snow and stuff is just a story. Does it matter?

"Lordhamercy, look at that, willya?" Tolliver is peering in disbelief through the dusty panes of what appears to be a drugstore. We can recognize dried seahorses, dried frogs, and all sorts of little alligators and other creepy things pickled in bottles. Jenson squirms squeamishly. I'm fascinated.

"If you only had the recipe you could buy stuff to cook up a real witch's brew, I bet. 'When shall we three meet again?'"

"Stow it, Dermody. Your mind's adrift again. Corman said to find the Shanghai Bazaar, they got the best bargains." Tolliver pushes her way through the crowd like a tug, towing us like barges behind her, till she finds it.

109

So many choices in the bazaar, I feel myself getting dizzy. Fragrant camphorwood chests, wall plaques cut out of tin depicting the Golden Gate Bridge (Mother will love one of those), cinnabar boxes carved with flowers the color of the Chinese flag are so pretty I buy one for myself and one for Sheila. Tolliver buys a pair of little slippers with tiger's faces embroidered on the toes for Randall Junior. Jenson takes the easy way out and buys everybody she knows a brass incense burner in the shape of a fat laughing Buddha or a pagoda. I buy a pair of fake ivory fangs for Buddy, embroidered handkerchiefs for the aunts. Nothing in Chinatown for Daddy, I can get him a Zippo lighter with an anchor at Ship's Stores.

Poor Daddy. When I finally got through on the telephone last Sunday after a long wait—first you wait in line, then you wait while lines go click, click, click, and people with different accents move your call along by way of odd places like Boise, Idaho, and Tallahassee, Florida—he just harrumphed like he does, said he was fine, and what was I wasting good money for? Sometimes you make me so mad, Daddy. Is it all right to waste bad money? Sometimes I think nothing makes any sense.

World weary, as though we really had been to Shanghai and back, we take our poor burning feet to the park in front of old St. Mary's Church. We plop on the benches with our overflowing shopping bags next to us, all the purchases wrapped exotically in Chinese newspapers, and just feel the sunshine in our bones. Somewhere a radio is crooning, "I'll be home for Christmas." All of us, even Jenson, who never, never talks about it, are thinking of home. Do they miss us? Do they keep a candle in the window under the red, white, and blue service flag? The guys could complain because they had to go but we couldn't so much. After all we had joined up out of our own stubborn free will. We had to lie in the beds we had made for ourselves or never hear the last of it.

It's probably snowing back home in Detroit now, but here the sunshine blazes off the huge steel statue of Sun Yat Sen in the square in front of us. I don't know much Chinese history but Sun Yat Sen is right up there with George Washington and Benjamin Franklin, good revolutionaries. The Chinese have been fighting the Japanese since I was Buddy's age. How awful. Madame Chiang Kai-shek is a friend of Mrs. Roosevelt's and now we are all in this fight together. I keep staring at the statue, trying to discern the source of its power, which

seems to be more than just its size. I can't help but wonder what
Saint Aloysius might look like if a sculptor like Buffano—whose
name is on the base—made a statue of him, instead of all those simpering plaster statues with the sickening green and burnt umber
draperies for clothes we have at home. Never know.

Tolliver pops awake from her little sun-induced snooze. She
straightens her wrinkled rayon stockings and says, "Let's go to the
canteen."

"Dummy, they won't let you in." I say. Everybody knows the Stage
Door Canteen won't let servicewomen in. We like to think it is because the guys would talk knots and trajectories with the Waves, leaving the civilian girls sitting there in their ruffles. Who knows?

"Smile when you call me Dummy, podner." Shopping has put Tolliver in a good mood. "I mean St. Mary's Canteen right here." She
waves her hand at the red-brick facade, the most un-Chinese-looking
building you could ever imagine. "I have a mad urge to play ping-
pong. I may even play a coupla games of pool. Then I may just dance
all night." She stands up and pirouettes in one of her Sugar Plum
Fairy routines. "All the people in this town turning themselves out to
provide wholesome recreation for our brave service girls and boys—
well, here I am."

I have to laugh. St. Mary's Canteen in the basement of the church
closed at eleven. When we say wholesome, we mean wholesome. I
always found St. Mary's intimidating somehow. It's pretty in an old-
fashioned way with its square bell tower. Halfway up the tower is a
white statue of the Virgin, with her hands extended at her sides in
that welcoming, enveloping way. In the space between the clock and
the statue is an oblong square of white stone with the words "Son Ob-
serve the Time and Flee from Evil" carved on it. Flee where? The
Barbary Coast? Forget it.

I jump up, gather my purchases in the bursting shopping bags.
Jenson picks hers up, too, but says, "I'll see you later, back at the
base. I gotta meet some friends at Mona's." She stuffs her bag into
my hands and whooshes away. Tolliver raises her pale eyebrows, starts
to say something, and shuts her mouth. She tags me and hurries
across the square.

"Wait up, Tolliver," I huff, feeling an emerging blister on my left
foot. "I can beat you at ping-pong anytime. Maybe I can even protect
you from catching something from the Catholics in there."

"You're on."

I skunk her at ping-pong, as I knew I would, but she beats me at pool. She never gets rattled like I do at the guys standing around and hooting. They seem to think it as odd as a whistling hen to see girls playing pool, especially playing it well. 'Spose you can't blame them, back home in Chitlin' Switch where they come from, or even Detroit, for that matter, ladies don't go to pool halls. Nuts. Here we are in the wholesome basement of wholesome St. Mary's Canteen and a vector is a vector, a game is a game, and winning is winning. Some of these guys are a pain in the neck. Thank you, God, for making some nice ones.

The war news is just awful. Shopping for the family and hearing all the songs about Joy to the World makes it seem so much worse, but this is a gloomy December for everyone. The Germans are counter-attacking in the Ardennes Forest by a dinky country called Luxembourg. It's hard to find on the maps in the papers, it's near Belgium. They caught our guys by surprise and surrounded them. Not good. The papers said that the 82nd Airborne was moved up—Michael's in the thick of it for sure, and Corman's Jack, too. In all that snow. Surrounded. JesusMaryandJoseph. The news that the censors let the papers print is bad enough, but the scuttlebutt is worse. There's talk about the Germans massacring unarmed prisoners at some place called Malmedy in Belgium. They wouldn't do that, would they? Would they? It's hard to know what to believe, the guys hear stories from their buddies who are radiomen on ships who can listen to the Armed Forces Radio. There are different versions, the guys say; one for the folks at home and another for the guys overseas who are doing the fighting. Dear God, after all this the Germans aren't going to beat us now, are they?

Sometimes I really wish I were old-fashioned like my mother and my aunts. However insurmountable any problem seems, they know exactly what to do; they take off their aprons, put their hats four-square on top of their marcelled hair, and march straight to church. There they light a few candles and turn the whole thing over to Higher Powers. It doesn't make Uncle Louie, Cecelia's feckless husband, stop gambling his paycheck away, but it seems to give them strength to keep going. Better start another novena, Mother. How can I say that when I need to keep up the morale of the homefront?

In the gunsheds every morning we pore over the papers, trying to read between the lines and make mental maps of where people we know are. Brothers, fiancés, buddies, cousins, sisters' husbands, the gap-toothed fat boy who carried our books in the second grade, ex-lovers, each of us has somebody there to make our heart stop when the papers report such and such division is surrounded. Each of us confronts the fear differently, but we each try to present an air of confidence and serenity—we are the best and we are going to win in the long run. It just seems to be taking a long, long time, and it's harder than we ever thought it was going to be. So we do what we can, after all, we did enlist to help. Maybe if we are really strict and conscientious, keep the DINGs going, maybe our guys could actually *hit something*. Sometimes I get so mad that I can't take a direct crack at those illegitimate sons of Satan myself. No way for a lady, even the most patriotic of ladies, to feel, I suppose they would say if they knew. So what about Molly Pitcher? She should be the patron saint of Waves gunners. In the pictures in our history books she stands stalwart with her sleeves rolled up and her far-seeing eyes looking across the body of her luckless dead husband, calculating the wind drift and the rotation of the earth before setting her match to the touch hole of her cannon aimed at the distant British in New Jersey or somewhere. Dummy, I sez to meself, sez I, how can you have a Prod patron saint? Bad sign, Josette megirl. You're starting to think in brogue again. This is 1944—sure and I'll be that glad to see the back of it, that I will.

Some mornings in the gunshed we get silly. The Navy guys, even Gruesome Gus, who is getting sea duty at last, prefer to laugh at disaster. If you are going down, you might as well die dancing, or taking a nice hot shower, or baking a cake with double chocolate frosting, or playing acey-deucy—at least cracking a joke. I don't know and don't intend to find out if Death would enjoy a quip as much as a Camel, but we try not to let our worry show. We give blood as often as the medics will take it, we increase our war bond allotment a little, and try to show up for work every day, colds or no, cramps or no.

Even when everything seems out of control there's always jitterbugging. Jackson's devoted widowed mother is a strict Hard Shell Baptist and doesn't hold with dancing and cards. Poor Calvin, he has the grace of a Junebug and the soul of Fred Astaire. Since I have the effervescence of an airplane hangar in the fog we are a natural cou-

ple, lumbering around the gunshed in empty moments, joints cracking and popping as we swirl, dipping and laughing. I figure it will be
a nice thing to know in case Blackie comes back. Calvin figures, he
told me in confidence, that in case his dear mother is right, he will at
least roast forever knowing how to dance and win at cards. His innocent face is perfect for poker and he's piling up quite an impressive
nest egg with which to buy his own chicken farm back in Arkansas
when the war is over. That's what everybody thinks about, when the
war is over, when the war is over. This is now and Jackson throws me
away and twirls me back to him without either of us losing our balance. We really are getting better.

"A winner at cards and a dancing dervish to boot, eh, Jackson? A
good thing when you're 2,000 miles from home you don't have to
tell your mother *everything*." Here I am turning into a Miss Occasion
of Sin, but I'm not sure that even counts anymore.

"That's for damsure," he says. "Hey, Dermody, you think Atkinson would go the Snowball Dance at the Rec Center with me Friday
night?"

"She'd love to, just ask her and see."

What a disgrace. I have burst into tears right in the gunshed, right
in front of God and everybody. Sailors don't cry, Waves mustn't. It's
just that the sailor I was strapping into his gun, one of the Russian
ones who've been coming through our shed lately, is so young; his
name is Mischa, Russian for Michael, or Mickey, and it suddenly
comes over me that he is going to die—I'm teaching a doomed
child; the whole thing opens up and I can't stop crying. The Chief is
being very good about it, I must say that for him. He scurries me into
his office before Lieutenant MacIntosh's arrival, our Ladykiller Lieutenant would just chalk up another one in his war against the Waves.
Chief gives me a clean handkerchief and a glass of water. He just sits
there like a great stone statue until I finally run out of water and hic-
cup to a stop like a one-cylinder outboard sputtering out of gas.

"You in trouble, Dermody? You wanna see the medics?" His homely,
pockmarked face is swollen with concern. "You want I should send
you to see the Waves representative?"

"No thanks, Chief. I don't know what came over me. I'm okay,
now honest. Can I go back to work now?"

"Suit yourself." He shrugs. I know he thinks I'm getting the Curse,
but I'm not.

***

I have to go see the Waves representative after all. Lieutenant MacIntosh heard how I couldn't stop crying and told the Chief to send me, hoping, I believe, that they would find me unacceptable for the service. Kenneth MacIntosh is one of those guys who is frantic because he can't get sea duty. He hates what he's doing and makes everybody's life miserable, including Waves under his command. He might, nevertheless, kiss any Wave junior grade officer who would arrive, kit in hand, to relieve him of his hated duties running the gunshed school. Washington in its wisdom is slow to send her. He only has us, enlisted girls who giggle at him behind his back and refuse to see him as God's gift to the ladies and the cause of the Allies. We only add to the cross he has to bear, and we learned early to keep out of his way. Whenever he gives an order we have to say, "Aye, aye, sir," which we do, politely, snappily, by the books, looking him straight in the eye and giving him the time of day. He can feel the sneer but there's nothing so overt he can do anything about it. He's a real pain. Anticipating a breakdown of hysterical women, which would make his command record look bad, he tells the Chief, who tells me, to go and see Lieutenant Kaufman over in Personnel, in that semicircular airport-looking administration building I haven't been in since that rainy day I arrived.

I find her in her little office with a single rose in a vase on her desk. She's blonde and pretty, neither old nor young, maybe 35. Calm and competent, she looks up from her typewriter as the yeoman striker ushers me in and indicates I should sit down. I tell her who I am, I tell her I don't know why they made me come.

"Tell me about it," she says, her Midwestern voice noncommittal. I watch her hand, with her perfectly manicured nails in their pale polish, brush a wisp of pale hair back in place. I curl my bitten fingernails into fists and rest my chin on them. The clacking of the typewriters and teletype machines comes through the door, why am I taking up valuable officer time when the war is clacketying importantly? She waits.

"Lieutenant MacIntosh hates us. Hates me." I bite my cuticle.

"You want out of the Navy." It's a statement, not a question.

Startled, I straighten up and look her in the eye. Her eyes are blue and have a laugh way in the background, although in the foreground they are all business, like an officer's should be. She waits silently. She should be saying something, shouldn't she?

"It's just that everybody's gonna die. Everybody says I'm such a ninny. I don't know what I'm doing here. I'm afraid my daddy will get sicker and die and I won't be there."

She waits. I can't stand the silence. "I just don't know where I should be."

"And it's Christmastime and you're dying of homesickness. Me too." She moves the crystal bud vase to the side and the pink tea rose silently drops a single petal to the surface of the impeccably ship-shape desk. She flicks a speck off the blue braid on her uniform arm with her forefinger. "Tell me about what you think is going on at home."

"I don't know. All I get is hints. He's failing. He's not well. He's pining for me."

"And you feel you should be there. Your family expects you to be there." She doesn't say anything for several minutes. "Tell me," she says, looking straight at me, "do you have a special fellow? Somebody who might be wanting you to prove your love or something?"

I shake my head. Blackie had just laughed when I told him right away I didn't like wrestling. "Suit yourself," he said. I look at Lieutenant Kaufman. She's already married. Had she ever felt this confusion of falling apart? I hate it. I don't know what to do. She makes some notes on a pad.

"You should check with the Red Cross to find out what the real story is about your father." She looks up from her notepad. "Come back and see me next week." I stand up, but she isn't through. "We all need to learn how to face reality. We'll talk again about what needs to be done." She hands me a tissue and returns to the papers on her desk. Comforted, some, but still confused, I leave. What does "face reality" mean, exactly?

When I get back to the gunshed it's almost chowtime. Tolliver puts her arms around me. "Buck up, the Lord is with us." She grins. I give her the V for Victory sign automatically, but I look at her quizzically. "Whilst you were gone, Skipper's yeoman told me, Lieutenant MacIntosh's orders came through. He's got his sea duty. They're sending his replacement." She punches me on the shoulder. "He's got a tincan, a dinky destroyer. He'll be seasick all of the time. How 'bout that?"

"Just shows you that clean living and brushing your teeth every day will lead you to the answer to your prayers. Tolliver, you're as pitiful as I am."

"Ain't it awful?"

"It's like the Navy is giving us a Christmas present." Just shows what the Spirit of Christmas can do. Tolliver and I aren't even fighting.

I almost don't go to Christmas mass, the Armed Guard people have a big Christmas party, and close to midnight I figure it's already three A.M. back home in Detroit, everybody asleep under the crisp December starlight, all the Christmas trees turned off and the Christmas candles extinguished. In our cubicle we have a little fake Christmas tree eighteen inches high and under it we have piled the presents that have come from home the last couple of weeks. Among the packages for me is one wrapped in pale green paper with a bunch of cellophane straws tied to make a sunburst—Mother went to a lot of trouble.

To play fair, I decide I should only open my presents after I have gone to midnight mass, whenever midnight is, wherever you are. I'm late enough that the only seat I can find in the cavernous theater is so far back that the chaplains and choirs look like dolls in a toy theater. The flowers around the altar, red poinsettias, I guess, are a blurry scarlet bank, the candle flames glimmer in the dark hazy air, so full of incense and candlelight that I feel like I'm breathing golden pollen. The music is gorgeous, no way I can pretend it would be prettier back home. It ricochets off the walls, vibrating through the floor boards and my bones—it makes me shiver with excitement and delight.

The mass should be as familiar as *Introibo ad altare Dei,* the Church Universal and all that, but for some reason it isn't. They keep adding hymns and all of the choirboys are full-grown men. They sing and we all join in "Fall on your knees, da dum, da dum, a new and glorious morn." I'm for that—any kind of new morn would be better than the ones we have been having this December.

After the Epistle a singer stands by the altar rail all by himself. It takes me a minute to realize he is singing *Adeste Fideles.* It sounds strange. We've sung that song every Christmas of my life, but this sounds different. I feel it in my bones first, not my head. The soloist with the wonderful-gift-of-God-voice is a German prisoner. Has everybody gone mad?

At first I think I will faint. The smell of wet wool crowdedness fades in favor of the invading smell of incense. The golden voice makes me think of angels, fallen angels, so far from heaven and home. Do you suppose Lucifer ever gets homesick? German prisoners of war must. Nearly everybody here is lonesome and sad, looking for Joy and Peace. The heat, the music, and the golden speckleness of the air make me feel like I have been drinking champagne. I try to pray. My mind swirls and the mass is over. I file out with the crowd into the soft foggy night. When I get back I open the pale green package. It contains, as I suspected, a lacy white slip. An antidote, an underpinning for the harsh military blue we cover ourselves in. *Pacem in Terris,* everybody.

CHAPTER 14

Corman is getting to be a problem. She doesn't think so, but our guncrew does. Right after Thanksgiving we started clouding up for a mutiny, not against a fat old Captain Bligh but against our own Corman. Ever since boot camp we've all been charmed by her unfazability, her sureness. We usually do what she says, at least until now. It seems to make life easier that way, but now Tolliver mutters at us in the head, "We didn't join no Navy to be no traffic cops for all of Corman's fian-*says*. No-siree-bob." Corman has five at the moment. She was already engaged to Jack, the original Boy Next Door, when she joined up. His picture on the inside of her locker door is bigger than the others. Across the bottom he had written "To Barbara—Now and Forever." She gets batches of V-mail from him somewhere in Europe. He's in the Fifth Cavalry, driving a tank. He's no problem to us. She writes him a weekly V-mail, her big handwriting scrunched as small as possible. Sometimes she sends him a package but she never knows if he gets it. Things are pretty snowy in Europe and the front "fluid." That probably means that the Germans are advancing and overrunning the depots. It's hard enough for the Army to get fuel and food through the snow, much less packages. It makes you mad, though, to think that the devil's own spawn, Germans, might get the hand-knitted mittens, wool socks, razor blades, and candy meant for our guys. Sometimes Corman sends him a filled-to-the-top-so-it-won't-gurgle bottle of bourbon in a hollowed-out loaf of bread, with no return address, of course. He'd never say he got such a package, naturally, but she keeps sending them anyway. She always wears Jack's high school ring on her dogtag chain under her shirt where it won't show.

Emmett, Chuck, Hilliard, and Raymond are the other four. The only thing they have in common is that they look a little like Glenn Ford: his grin, dimples, and dark hair make her heart melt into a puddle. She must have seen each of his movies a dozen times. Em-

mett is an AvCat, or was until they washed out his whole class when
they decided they didn't need any more flyboys. They made him
a radarman instead. He has the firm jawline and clear eyes of a born
flyer. Too bad. He's in and out of port all the time. He bought her
a ring, an aquamarine, her birthstone. He can't get enough of
Chinatown.

Chuck is the ensign she met in New York. Wouldn't you know he
would get transferred to the Twelfth Naval District? He's waiting for
his ship at Mare Island, the refitting seems to be taking longer than
expected. Fortunately, some admiral attached him as an aide, so he
has the duty a lot. He's crazy about Corman and bought her an an-
tique ring with seed pearls. He's so good-looking when he picks her
up at the barracks in his spiffy uniform to take her dancing at the
Cirque Room at the Fairmont. He seems a little la-dee-dah to me,
stuck on himself.

She never told us where she met Hilliard. Tolliver allowed it was
most likely the Pepsi-Cola Center on Market Street, the home away
from home where a person could put her feet up, take a shower, write
a letter on their free stationery, make a phone call home, also free, if
you could wait out the line. Everybody goes there when she doesn't
know what else to do with herself, a real life-saver sometimes. Hilliard
is younger than the others, hardly 18, from Texas. He doesn't have
much personality, but Corman says he's sweet. He was low when she
met him because, as he saw it, all the girls back home were already
married and his life prospects were bleak. Corman got engaged to
him and he shipped out, dreaming of future bliss. He gave her a silver
charm bracelet with little anchors and ship wheels and tiny silver destroyers clanking from it. It makes so much noise she can't wear it
much, lest she be put on report for wearing jewelry in uniform.

Raymond is the latest and the most interesting. A jazz musician
from New York, nervous and high-strung, he has absolutely no ambi-
tion about the Navy. He does as little as he can get away with and waits
for the war to be over. Corman met him when he came through the
gunshed with his platoon. He's pretty cool, with his slicked-back hair
and hooded eyes, and it's hard to tell how much he really likes Corman, but when he's here he takes her to all the clubs to hear Billie
Holliday and artists like her. He even gave her a gardenia Billie threw
at him once—her trademark is flinging the gardenia from her hair at
sailors in the audience. Whenever they jitterbug they are so good, so

magical, that everybody else on the dance floor moves to the edges to form a circle to watch them. We think Corman likes him best, but she won't say. She takes no chances wearing his ankle bracelet on the base. That girl sure loves jewelry, especially jewelry somebody gives her—not being able to wear it is the hardest part of the Navy for her.

None of these guys knows about the others. It's bad enough that Corman overloads us with complicated instructions before she goes out at night, "If Emmett calls, tell him to call me tomorrow, tell him I've got the duty tonight. If sweet old Hilliard calls, tell him I'm busy until next Thursday. If my mother calls tell her I'm in the shower and will phone her next Sunday." That's nothing. We all do that. More or less. What Corman has us doing, though, is keeping track of the ships the guys are on.

We corner her in the upstairs lounge in the barracks. She's dateless, for once, sitting sideways in an overstuffed chair, legs dangling over one arm of the chair, idly leafing through a dog-eared copy of *Life* magazine. Her hair done up in bobbypin snails, no lipstick, her face pale and shiny with cold cream, she looks a little bored and distant, almost a little ill. Fine time to pick on somebody, I think.

Tolliver is our Fletcher Christian. "We gotta bone to pick with you, Corman."

"Fair enough?" she says, looking quizzical. Jenson, paler than usual, smiles a tentative smile; Atkinson in her scruffy pink robe, her hair in curl rags, scowls behind her. I am, by nature, the mutineer with the sneer who is always in the background in the movies, grasping the marlinspike and waiting to see how it all turns out. I look as determined as I can; I have always been afraid of confrontation, but not Tolliver.

"We decided, Corman, we ain't gonna do it no more."

"You aren't going to do what?" Corman asks, raising her left eyebrow teacherishly. She knows correcting Tolliver's grammar drives her nuts, even if half the time Tolliver is just putting on.

"We," Tolliver glances around at the rest of us for confirmation, "we ain't going to make any more phone calls to Fleet Operations to ask when those ships your guys are on are coming into port. Reckon you can just handle all your fian-*says'* comings and goings without us." Electricity crackles in the air like a thunderstorm coming up. "Me and Dermody here, Jenson, Atkinson, all the others. We talked about it. We ain't going to do it no more."

"I'd do it for you all." Corman swings her legs down to the deck and leans forward, nonplused.

"C'mon, Corman. None of the rest of us would get ourselves in such a pickle." My voice, when I find it, squeaks a little. "Here you've gone and got yourself engaged to five different guys who don't know about each other. How could you?"

"How could I what?" Corman reaches into the pocket of her robe and pulls out a pack of Luckies, takes one out, lights it, and puts the pack back. She puts her head back and blows the smoke out of her nostrils like Barbara Stanwyck in a crisis situation. We have all practiced that one, but Corman is best at it.

Atkinson, who is okay sometimes, says in her raspy voice, "I hate it, calling up, saying I'm Commodore Zeinberger's yeoman, needing to know when the *Seabass Victory* is due back from Pearl. Why don't you do it yourself?"

"Why, honeychile, they'd recognize my voice."

"So," I say, indignation rising, "you get us to do it. It's probably illegal. There's all kinds of war secrets acts, you know. They most likely have some kind of secret device that can trace where the calls are coming from, in case we are Japanese spies. Besides, how can you string a baby like Hilliard along like that, anyway?"

"That ain't no worry of mine," Tolliver brushes me aside. "If he's old enough to be in the Navy, he's old enough to take care of hisself. What I wanna know is what's going to happen when the war's over and they all want to marry you? Wow-ee, that's going to be some wedding with five bridegrooms. Don't they have laws about bigamy back in Kentucky? We shore do back home in West Virginia." She's so puffed up with self-righteousness that I almost laugh, but mutineers need to keep the seriousness of the situation intact. Otherwise they hang you or make you walk the plank. We've all seen the same movies.

"We got the same laws back home, you betcha." Atkinson is catching the piousness, too.

Corman pulls out her cigarettes, lights a new one from the old, and absentmindedly puts the pack on the table. "You all are just jealous. Just positively green-eyed. You ought to be ashamed. I can't help it if they ask me. The war is going to last a long time. I can't bear it if they die thinking nobody loves them or cares if they die."

"What I don't understand is how you can be in love with so many different guys at the same time." Jenson's voice is deep for such a wispy girl. Tolliver leans over and helps herself to one of Corman's cigs without even asking.

"Whichever one I'm with, I think he's the nicest and the best," Corman says, like she is explaining things to kindergartners. "I just want to make them happy." She sighs. "My grandmother always said the highest virtue for a woman is kindness. I can't help it. It would be so unkind to turn them down." She stands up and retrieves her cigarettes. "Fine friends you all turned out to be." She stalks out. In high dudgeon, you can say.

"Now I s'pose she won't talk to us anymore. Too bad." Tolliver reaches over and turns on the lamp. The lounge looks cozy in the lamplight. "She'll find a way. There's lotsa ways. I met a signalman t'other night told me he knows of a Wave lieutenant who uses the signal tower on top of Yerba Buena to signal the ships in the 'road' whenever her husband is in port. Special kind of Keep Clear."

"Tolliver, you're as bad as the guys with your sea stories." I don't know if she's funning me again.

"Betcha it ain't no sea story. Didn't you learn anything at that school you went to, Dermody? Betcha you think you were an Immaculate Conception." She's still laughing when I leave, one more minute there and I might kill that girl.

Just about the time I am convinced I am growing gills it stops raining for a while and the sun comes out. The water around our little island turns blue and sparkles playfully. The orange and green hills that rim the bay appear from behind their modest fog draperies. California hills are so strange, are they naturally green with mangy tan patches or naturally tan with a green fungus of shrubs and trees? I'm so unaccountably happy with the sunshine as I hurry back from mass that I am almost skipping.

"Hey, hey, baby. What a tomato. What are you doing tonight, honey?" I ignore the guy hanging out of the window, only way. After I am past him I realize it is one of the German prisoners of war who work in the laundry, first time I ever heard one of them speak. He must be learning English from the sailors. Mostly, they just strut around the island, grim-jawed, in their perfectly aligned formations, disdainfully arrogant about the happy-go-lucky chaos around them. It must be hard for them to see what beat them. They're always in step, always correct, yet they lost. Our sailors don't like to keep in step—sometimes they count the cadence by Hip-Hop, Hip-Hop, just to be larky. Big overgrown kids mostly. If I were a German it would drive me nuts. So much for International Understanding, but you've got the wrong Girl Scout, *Übermensch*, if you think I'm going to flirt with you. When we finally beat you guys there won't be any more wars. *Dona nobis pacem.* Give us peace, O Lord.

It's funny about the Germans, I think, as I head toward the Wave compound. Look at all the trouble they cause. First they give Caesar a hard time, although maybe he didn't have any business going there. Then they had Martin Luther, who made all that trouble for Holy Mother Church. It must have been really funny, though, when he threw his inkpot at the devil—that would be something to see. Then they got the Kaiser and my Uncle D'Arcy died in that war. When I was in high school they started another one and this war has been going on for five years.

Those movies of those German planes, those Stukas, machine-gunning the people with the baby buggies by the side of the roads in Poland are burned into my brain forever. The planes were so beautiful, like the Siamese fighting fish Uncle Buddy raised in separate tanks back home. I had never thought of beautiful and deadly before—it makes my bones shiver like a horrible ghost story.

The strangest thing about the Germans is that they look like everybody else, not like the Japs, who don't look like anybody I know. It's easier to believe the Nips doing all those nasty things people say they did and being sneaky—like attacking Pearl Harbor before anybody was awake. I don't understand about the Germans. Lots of them are even Catholic. I wish I could say, "Explain that one to me, please, God, if being Catholic is supposed to make people better." I'd never have the nerve. I don't think God likes questions much. Certainly Monsignor O'Callaghan never did.

"Hi, Toots."

I jump like a scalded cat, thinking maybe it's some vengeful German Catholic after me, yelling, *"Gott mit uns,"* but it's Blackie, blocking the way to the barracks door. He's grinning devilishly, his rake-hell grin, just like he'd never been away. It's a good thing for him I don't have an inkpot handy. Not a word for six weeks, after all that blarney. I look at him like I never saw him before in my life. He just laughs.

"Ship put into Peedro 'stead of here," he says, reading my mind. "First chance I got to get up here." He whips his left hand from behind his back with a flourish and hands me a lavender tin box. How could he know, how could he possibly know that the one thing that would disarm me is Almond Roca? Best candy in the whole world, chocolate and toffee brittle, wrapped in elegant little gold foil papers. Expensive, too, this guy must be serious. Uncannily, like he's still reading my mind, he says, "Cargo net broke when we was loading. Tins was rolling all over the dock. I saved this one for you."

"Accidentally on purpose, I suppose." I wasn't born yesterday. He shrugs.

"They do allus seem to slip when we're loading candy, cigarettes, or nylons." He spreads his hands, palms outward, in a what-can-you-expect gesture.

"Nylons?" I gasp involuntarily. "I haven't seen a legal pair of nylons since they started making parachutes."

"Next time. Next time I'll bring you some. There's usually nylons in Ship's Stores. You can get anything you want with nylons. Broads in Australia would sell their grandmother for some."

"Thanks for the information." I try to push my way past him. This isn't going well at all, although he is even cuter than I remember. I feel a perfect fool standing here with my missal, my elegant leather missal with the thin pages and narrow red ribbons, clutching a purloined tin of Almond Roca, getting a lesson I don't need on the seduction of Australian girls. Next thing I will be referring to them as broads. What am I doing here? Why am I not a Discalced Carmelite somewhere—all I would have to do is get up early and pray for the world. Live in silence and not have any of these dumb conversations with a cute guy standing in front of me blocking my way like he's Clark Gable playing Rhett Butler. I can't stand here forever, my missal like a shield across my tailored bosom. I say, not totally sincerely, "Glad you're back. I gotta go now. Thanks for the candy."

He reaches out his arm across the doorway. "You din't get engaged or married or anything whilst I was away, didja?"

"Nope." Who did he think I was, a twin of Corman, with half the sailors in the U.S. Navy queuing up for a chance to give her an engagement ring? What a flatterer. I like it.

"Good." He grunts with satisfaction. "Let's you and me go to the city. We could go to Golden Gate Park and take a walk. I ain't had a

walk in a while." His black eyes lock on mine, I find I have no de-
fense against black eyes. Six weeks on a metal platform a block long
and a third wide. Makes sense. I see in my mind's eye a blackboard
with a list of to-do's for today: wash hair, mend stockings, write letters,
polish shoes. The whole list erases itself in a second. They'll keep.

"Can do," I say, cool as you please. "Be right back. Wait while I
stow this gear and pick up my pass."

Something must show in my face. Tolliver sits scrunched up, cutting her toenails, her radio blaring out the Sons of the Pioneers
singing "Cool Waters" for the twenty-seven-millionth time. "Lordy,
what's with you," she says. "You get *saved* at this morning's service, or
what?"

"Catholics don't get saved. You should know that, hanging around
with me all this time." I stow my missal on the top shelf of my locker,
shove the candy under the neatly folded slips in the third drawer,
run a comb through my hair, insert a forbidden barrette. "Gotta
date, gotta run."

"Glory Hallelujah. High time. Love comes to the Ice Maiden. Who
is it?"

"None of your beeswax." I slam the locker door shut and skedaddle before she can come out to the quarterdeck for a looksee.

Just an ordinary date, another sailor and another Wave taking the
A train to 'Frisco and the cable car up California Street, just walking
through the lovely park, which is looking green and lush after all the
rain, smelling of eucalyptus and pepper trees, the furry little squir-
rels chattering merrily as they race away from our approach. Even
though it's winter, pink flowering bushes line the curved paths—
it's not exactly the Garden of Eden; Adam and Eve never heard the
clanging of the cable cars and the drone of the lumbering PBYs overhead—but on such a beautiful Sunday it seems close, even if most of
the people enjoying the day are in uniform.

By the Tea House bridge we find a bench and sit down. The Tea
House has a sign with the first word painted out by some patriotic
park person, but the letters J-A-P-A-N-E-S-E still show. The iridescent
ducks, oblivious to a world gone mad, paddle serenely, upending
themselves to find their dinner under the water. It's so peaceful.
Blackie has one arm stretched along the bench behind me, the other
hand holds mine. I can see the tattoo on his forearm, a blue dagger

dripping blood. Above it the word DEATH, underneath BEFORE DIS-HONOR. Now's my chance.

"Does it hurt to get tattooed, Blackie? I've always wondered."

"Dunno. Don't remember. Me and some buddies got drunk in Pearl one night." He shows me his other arm, which has a red heart with MOTHER skirling on it, blue letters on a purple ribbon. "Got this one in New Orleans."

"Does your mother like it?"

"Dunno. Never asked her. All my brothers and my dad are sailors, so I guess she's used to it. You could get used to it, too. Easy." He tickled my chin with his knuckles. "Wanna walk some more? I'm getting hungry. Ever been to the Cliff House?"

An ordinary date and I never want it to end. The sea lions bark on the rocks outside the window where we eat our scampi and talk, talk, talk. The sea swallows up the scarlet sun with a sizzle, the full moon rises, and makes a silver path on the water.

"We gotta get you back," he says. "Don't want my girl in no brig."

"Holy Toledo." I look at my watch for the first time all evening. We race for the streetcar and collapse laughing. He holds my hand all the way back to the island.

"Gotta get back to Peedro tonight. Ship's leaving soon," he says as the cattlecar truck they use instead of buses on TI lets us off by the Waves compound. I can't keep the disappointment off my face. "I'll be back. I shouldna come today but I wanted to see you." He puts his index finger under my chin and tilts it up toward him. I feel my knees turning to goo. If this keeps up another minute, my whole self will be goo. He kisses me quickly, drops his finger, and says, "See you around, Toots." He wheels and is gone, giving me a wave as he turns the corner. Here I am, standing in the moon-washed compound. How can you do this to me, God? First he comes and then he goes. It's not fair. Thank the good Lord for small favors, though. Tolliver is fast asleep as I creep to my bunk in the darkened barracks. Now I'll have to call Fleet Operations to track a ship for myself.

CHAPTER 15

Russians and Rescue

Tolliver yells across the arcade noise of all the guns dinging in the gunshed, "Hey, Boris, on the double, I need you to tell this guy what to do." Boris has an easy job, detached duty, all he has to do is show up when a Russian freighter is in port and interpret. He's usually three sheets to the wind whatever time of the day it is, teetering between despair and jollity; he apparently spends the days he's not on duty in his apartment on Russian Hill, drinking vodka, lots of vodka, and singing sad songs. Russians are as bad as Irish in the sad-song department. Today is no exception—he balances his big stomach carefully as he caroms from gun station to gun station in his linty Donald Duck uniform, being helpful. I have never gotten around to asking him how he ended up in the U.S. Navy.

We didn't know any Russians back in Detroit, except one red-headed girl in high school whose name was Romana Romanovna Something—she didn't have any time for friends because she had to practice her ballet at four in the morning and after school. She told me once that the only thing she wanted in the whole world was to be a prima ballerina. She had long, glorious red-gold hair and long limbs, but she was shy and hard to be friends with. I do wish I had tried harder, to be friends, I mean, but she was only there for a year. I think her family, she only had a mother, I did learn that much, were White Russians, not so happy with the Russian government. When the war came and Hitler invaded, you had to admit that the Russians were remarkably tough people; we heard about them in the film series the Navy showed us called "Why We Fight" and we see them in the newsreels holding out against the Germans so stubbornly in Leningrad and Stalingrad and those other "-grad" towns—the pictures of all those bodies in the snow are unforgettable. Starving to death isn't something I want to think about much, and freezing wouldn't be much better. These weatherbeaten old guys with their leathery sunburned faces and the green really young ones are here on TI waiting for their ships to load up so they can get the ammo and stuff back to Mother Russia through the U-boat and air attacks. We hear that almost half of them never get through. Daddy would just die if he knew I'm consorting with Godless atheists, Communists, but he doesn't understand. They are on our side.

This time I really need Boris; I've drawn a Russian guy I can't do anything with. He's young, like our ninety-day wonders who get their commissions before they are 19. He's all white and pink and gold, pink cheeks, golden hair, and gold braid on his spotless white uniform. A profile like a collar ad. I would think the Russians wouldn't have any more like him, what with that Revolution of the Proletariat and all that *tovarisch* stuff, but here he is, handsome and intransigent as any Prince Alexei or André I ever read about in those big, fat Russian novels I used to get from the public library back home. Not my type, actually. Stuck on himself. He stands on his rank and refuses to get into his gun. "Boris," I call, my revolutionary fervor rising, "come and tell this guy he has to take his turn, whoever he is." Boris balances over and straps the icy princeling into the Oerlikon, whereupon the blond god dings the requisite number of DINGs.

"*Spasebo,* Boris." Thank you.

Usually he would just say, "You're velcome, Miss-s-s Sailor Girl," like he calls all of us, but this time he says something back to me that I don't understand. I don't know all that much Russian. It sounds like *dusha.* The Russian sailors laugh and wink when he says it. Tolliver really likes Boris a lot, but she told me once she thinks he's sweet on me. I don't know why.

Corman got over her mad eventually, as we knew she would. She made friends with one of the commodore's yeoman, Littlejohn, a pop-eyed girl with a space between her front teeth and a quirky sense of humor, who pretty much knows everything that goes on around the base, heck, the whole Pacific Theater, even if she doesn't let on much. Corman has sweet-talked Littlejohn into keeping track of the important ships for her so she's not surprised when Hilliard calls and asks her to go to the movies. He's got a buddy with him and she should get a date for the buddy, too. Nobody is around below so she tracks me down to the topside lounge where I'm reading *Mary, Queen of Scots* by my lonesome.

"What's with you? You look like a month of rainy Sundays. You been fighting with Tolliver again?" How does she know?

"I can't stand that dumb hillbilly music she always has on her dumb radio."

"You two are a case. Why do you make such a big thing out of it, anyway? I came up to ask you to double-date with Hilliard and me tonight. Movies?"

Why not, I think. Blackie's on his way to Ulithi, probably to dally with the dusky damsels, with his supply of purloined chocolate and nylons. "Okay. What time?"

"1900."

"Will do."

At precisely 1900 Hilliard and his friend, a pudgy, short guy wearing glasses, are waiting on the quarterdeck all spruced up. They exude showers and shaves, haircuts and shoeshines, for all the world like two little boys dressed up in their best sailor suits for a birthday party. Hilliard's buddy is a radioman third class, like Hilliard. His name is Specs. "Hi, Specs," I say, when we are introduced. Such heavy glasses in such a young, untried face with such an engaging dimple in his chin. I feel my face color as I realize he is looking me over with an equally appraising eye. "Let's go," I say.

We feel the full force of the gale when we leave the shelter of the Waves compound. Corman and Hilliard, in step ahead of us, are bent almost double, Corman holding on to her hat. "Windy tonight," I begin, straining for conversation.

"This ain't nothin'," I think I hear Specs say in his raspy New Jersey voice; the wind blows his words away.

When we are in the lee of Theater No. 3, he repeats, "This ain't nothin'. Didja hear about the typhoon off'n Okinawa right before Christmas?"

"What typhoon?"

"Heard about it on the ship's radio when we was on our way to Pearl. Third Fleet got caught in the great-granddaddy of all storms. Winds went to 110 knots. Waves 70 feet tall. Ain't that something?"

"One hundred ten knots," I calculate rapidly, "that's almost 132 miles per hour. I don't believe you. No winds get that high."

"Suit yourself." Specs shrugs, then looks to Hilliard for corroboration. "You heard it, too, din'tja, Buddy?"

Hilliard turns. "Sure enough. We lost a whole frigging bunch of ships, more than the Japs ever sank in the whole war. Those old tin-cans just capsized and went down with all hands."

"All hands?" Corman picks up the conversation, almost in tears. "You mean they couldn't pick up *anybody?* What about all the other ships?"

"They was all busy trying to keep upright themselves. They had come in to refuel and were caught dead in the water with no ballast. Airplanes busted loose on the carriers and racketed all over the place, going over the side. Lost 150 planes right there. Honest to God."

"Sure am glad I ain't with the Third Fleet. I don't wanna see Davy Jones' locker just yet," Specs makes his voice casual.

"I think you're maybe just feeding us sea stories," I say.

"Wish I was fibbin'," Hilliard says. "Got me some buddies on those destroyers over there but nobody's saying which ones' numbers came up yet."

"Geest, can you imagine that? One hundred and ten knots? Radio says the fleet's tore up worse than if they'd been in a major battle." Specs's raspy voice is full of awe.

"Whose side is God on, that's what I'd like to know." I really would.

"Maybe it din't have nothing to do with God, sweetheart. Maybe some of them fatheads with the gold braid were so busy chasing Japs and glory that they din't pay attention to the weather reports. They shoulda listened to their radiomen. Most important person on the ship. I keep telling them, but nobody listens." Specs is funny, even if a little pudgy and rough-voiced. Holy Toledo, Blackie's ship couldn't have gotten that far, could it? Nope. Hear us when we cry to Thee, for those in peril on the sea . . .

To change the subject I say, "There's nothing like a good patriotic movie to perk up the homefolks. Let's go on in and watch Betty Grable sing and dance her way to Victory. Is Van Johnson in this one?"

"Dunno," says Hilliard, cozily sticking Corman's hand in his pea-coat pocket. "Life should be more like the movies."

"That's for damsure," I slip. Corman's eyebrows shoot up when she hears me get too close to the forbidden "foul language." "I mean wars certainly should."

Blackie's Christmas card comes, three weeks late, in a flat package of three embroidered linen handkerchiefs, each with a green and black palm tree in one corner and "Hawaii" stitched in red. Good, he hasn't forgotten me after all. The card has a picture of a hula dancer on it and inside he has written in a square hand—

Hi Toots,
Don't get marryed or enything until I get back. Good ship, good trip, good buddies. Have a good Christmas.

xxxx Blackie

He's okay. Thank you, Fleet Post Office. Slow, but he's okay. Thank you, God. I write Blackie a letter, full of leading questions for him to answer. I like to write letters; thanks to the Sisters in various English classes I got lots of practice, but when I get out my stationery kit to write to him I am struck dumb. I want to write poetry, I want to make the words sing, I want to make them zing, like touching his hand makes me feel, all pink buzziness and short of breath. No way I can do it, so I write a conventional letter full of inventions and evasions, full of jokes and larkiness. You'll never know, Blackie, how much I wish I were standing watch with you, watching the constellations wheel in the velvet tropical sky like you described it. In my imagination I can feel the deck rise and fall rhythmically under our feet, I can feel how we would hold hands and tell each other secrets. Is this love? I keep a straight face and cool demeanor around Tolliver and the roommates, but they sense something and they extend their arms, not really, but now they act like I know something they have known all along and have an "ain't it wonderful?" attitude. Maybe so. Watch yourself, megirl.

We always read the papers in the mornings after the machines are threaded and we run out of lies to tell each other. The guys and some of the gals are usually hung over from last night on the town and at least once a week someone gets a Dear John letter. The worst are the ones that close with "I hope we can continue to remain friends"; we all have to rally around to protect the recipient of one of those, and protect ourselves, because the poor guy or gal is scattering enough gloom to envelop the whole Pacific Theater in heavy black clouds. Another day in a boring job, stuck with people you don't even like very much, in a war that seems to be taking an awful long time to win. The rain and the fog never let up. Even Tolliver is

never her ebullient self on these dreary mornings, slurping Jackson's
sludgy hot coffee and heaving great sighs. She spots the story first in
the Berkeley paper.

"Lord hamercy, Dermody. Look at this. Here's your survivors."

What's she talking about? I lean over her shoulder to see where
she is pointing. The *Berkeley Gazette* has a page full of pictures, one of
them of a bunch of guys on a broken-up raft, and another of some
guys, some in lifejackets, some not, standing up in a whale boat. (One
thing about the good old U.S. Navy, whatever happens, someone is
right there with a camera loaded and ready-o. Any day now I expect
some bearded Navy frogman to emerge from the briny with some
splendid official shots of Davy Jones' locker.) At the bottom of the
page is a picture of a bunch of sailors looking exactly like the guys I
had almost run into in the barefooted line in the drizzle that morning, but here they are on the deck of the Navy rescue ship. Some of
them are clasping each other's hands, others with their arms around
each other's shoulders, dirty-faced and happy to be alive. I hear
Gunny's grating voice in my memory's ear, "We ain't playing beanbag, ya know." Under the picture of the guys standing on the raft
waiting to be rescued is the heading:

Victims of Jap Torpedoing Tell of Fanatical Attacks
    Men Swimming Are Machine Gunned: Sub Rams Raft: Planes
Guide Rescue
    Murmuring the Lord's prayer and clinging to floating sacks of
flour while the Japanese submarine that had sunk their Liberty
ship shelled and tried to ram their life rafts, a group of merchant
seamen weathered the fanatical fury of the Nipponese and came
back to Treasure Island to tell their story.

Jackson was reading over our shoulders, his lips moving as he followed the words. "So where was our good old Armed Guard? Sighted
Sub, Glub Glub is our motto."

"For God's sake, Jackson, knock it off and let me read. Here it is,"
I said, scanning down the page. I read aloud:

Lt. (jg) Kent Van Zanburger, commander of the Navy crew of the
SS *John A. Johnson,* was the man who flashed the help signal to the
airplane. He told one of the first first-person survivor stories to be
approved by the Navy:

"The torpedo struck amidships," he said, "I was in the officer's
wardroom. The impact slammed me up against the ceiling. I
rushed to the bridge to order my men to the guns.

"The sea was rough, there were heavy swells. We saw the ship
was beginning to break apart. We went aft. The after part of the
ship was about two feet under water. The skipper told us to aban-
don ship."

Jackson howls gleefully, "Into the drink, all you sinners." Anybody
can tell he's never been baptized by fire.

"Shut up, 'fore I shut you up for good," Gus says, most unnauti-
cally. "Keep reading, Dermody. What happened next?" Sometimes I
thought old Gruesome wasn't as eager for sea duty as he let on. You
can't always tell, all of the guys all swear they are pining for sea duty.

Corman impatiently takes over the reading aloud from me.

"We went to the after gun. Water was breaking over. I had one of
my men cut down a doughnut raft and lower it. The three of us
went over the side, into the water. It was thick with oil.

"The seventeen of my men whom I'd ordered off were on a raft.
I called to them to drift down the ship's port side, intending to re-
board the ship if it stayed up.

"We thought it was going to tip over on us, instead it broke exactly in half. We went on swimming down the starboard side, still
pushing our raft."

"Don't give up the raft," Jackson the irrepressible says. Tolliver
cuffs him one on the cowlick. Corman resumes, still reading the lieutenant's first-person account.

"We spotted a shape ahead. It was too big for a lifeboat. It was the
sub, swooshing to the surface about 300 yards dead ahead. It got
under way and began bearing down on us. The sub passed us by
about 25 feet on the starboard side. I could hear the men yelling
'BANZAI, BANZAI, you American ——.' They opened up with their
machine guns dead ahead, several times, thirty or forty shells at a
time."

"I don't understand how bags of flour can float," Atkinson says, her
broad forehead creased in a frown. "Morning, Chief." He had lumbered unseen into the shed to see what was holding up the war, since

he wasn't hearing any DINGs. He just stands there with his arms folded across his massive chest, listening along with the rest of the rapt audience. The sailors who had arrived for the first class are listening, too. Wonder if the Chief's ever been torpedoed? Corman reads a little faster, her words tumbling over one another, with the Chief wheezing a little in back of her.

"There must have been twenty miles of oilslick on the water and we were afraid it would catch fire. Later a plane flew over us and let us know that we had been seen. We quit worrying about the sub and started bailing, each man taking turns.

"About 3 p.m. on the next afternoon we sighted a ship on the horizon and were soon taken aboard. It was the Motor yacht 'Argus.' It rescued all the survivors, but the raft which had seventeen men aboard had been rammed by the submarine.

"One man was caught in the sub's propeller and killed. Another man swam too far away and couldn't get back. I guess he drowned.

"When the ship picked us up we all had a solid coat of grease all over our bodies. None of us had any shoes. I had gotten my men to take off most of their clothing and few of them had on more than their underwear."

There's more, lots more, but it's getting repetitious what with the captain telling his version and interviews with several others. The Chief breaks the spell. "Man your stations," he says in his usual loquacious way. We move right into the drill, the lecture, the strapping into the guns. DING, DING, DING. No joking around today. Had any of the guys drowned or machine-gunned or rammed in the oil-slicked Pacific been in any of the platoons run through our gunshed when we first came? Most likely. I don't recognize any of the faces, the guys in the pictures look like anybody under all that grease. Like everybody we see every day. Ten men dead out of a whole warful of thousands. Millions. Still, I stop off in the chapel on the way to chow to say a prayer for the repose of their souls.

Sister Euphemia, where are you when I need you? Didn't you always have a wise Latin proverb for every circumstance? I've forgotten most of my Latin anyway. Pretty soon I'll forget English, too. All I can speak is Navy. Sister Christina Martine made us memorize a poem a week in English class, I know lots of short ones:

I seek a garden
 shade dappled and breezy
where my life can flow gently
 to a quiet end.

No gales or wild storms there
 nor nettles nor tiger sign
no new wounds to bleed and bind
 no apples of despair.

Pretty, but never happen. When is this war going to be over?

CHAPTER 16

Captain's Mast

We might have known, things were going too well. Thank the good Lord it wasn't me who ran afoul when the brass decided to make an example of somebody. Now Tolliver has to go up before the skipper tomorrow, our whole reputation as Waves in Armed Guard riding on the outcome. It's sure taking the wind out of Tolliver's sails, let me tell you. Ol' Coralee, who's not afraid of anything (she says) is just as patriotically unwilling to be sent home in disgrace as any of us.

Our skipper is old, older than my father, more like a grandfather. We had all heard sea stories about how he was with Admiral Dewey's Great White Fleet in the Spanish-American War. Could it be possible? Subtract 1898 from 1945. Barely. Hard to believe he was ever young and beautiful like Blackie. Commander Macklin has a whiskey-red face, little veins tracking across his dew-lapped cheeks, his triangular ice-blue eyes almost hidden by puffs of flesh. He is portly, but holds himself so rigid in his double-breasted uniform it almost looks like (perish the thought) he is wearing a girdle. He leans backwards as he walks to counterbalance the weight in front of him, and rocks on his heels a little when he's standing still, like a dinghy bobbing at a mooring.

Toward us Waves he's usually affable enough. Sometimes when we cross his path as he is waddling around Armed Guard headquarters, he greets us as "fellas" because we are wearing our uniform slacks. You can tell by his voice he means it as a little joke. During inspections on Saturdays we hold our breath, our necks rigid, feeling our hair uncurl down past regulation length in the fog, our stomachs knotted with anxiety, trying to be as anonymous and nonprotuberant as possible. Jackson and his buddies keep telling us terrible tales of the skipper's rages when something doesn't please him at inspection. Maybe Jackson is telling lies again, maybe not. No sense in taking chances.

Prudently, I keep out of his way, but sometimes I wish that he was my great-uncle or something, who would tell me stories about Admiral Dewey and the old days. He could tell about what it was like to be an ordinary sailor who came up through the "hawse hole"—through the ranks. Our U.S. Navy really believes that officers and gentlemen are born and not made—that doesn't seem very American to me, not very democratic. There are always some, especially during wartime, when there never seem to be enough birthright gentlemen to go around, who are lucky enough, tough enough, and smart enough to rise from the ranks. Did anybody take time to certify John Paul Jones' pedigree? Nowadays the Navy calls the ones who rise up "Mustangs." The sailors tell us Mustangs are the worst. They have Rocks and Shoals (Navy regs) for brains, they are sticklers for rules, prone to expect more from people, and give everybody a hard time. Ninety-day wonders or once-upon-a-time ratings with hash marks to their shoulders, drawn back from retirement by the exigencies of this global war, all our Mustangs are doing their damndest to prove they are as good as any gentleman born and bred. Nobody seems to know why they named them after wild horses, though.

Our Old Man, as they call him, not too fondly, puffs around his Armed Guard in his weighty gold braid, competing with all the other demands for men and materiel to keep his command manned and supplied. Stories abound about how the first Armed Guard crews to leave TI after Pearl Harbor were sent out with "only" two gallons of gray paint and ten pounds of cleaning rags. Helluva way to run a war, or a Navy, they say. If you can't salute it, you have to clean it or paint it. The Old Man sent telegram after telex to BuPers for more personnel. When they sent him his first Waves you could hear his roar all the way to Mare Island, but pretty soon he began to think of them as "hands." He needed all the hands he could get. "Send me more Waves," he telegraphed. Everything's 4.0, he runs his command, enjoys his reputation for a "tight ship," and we keep out of his way. Until now.

"Damn those Marines anyway." Tolliver is pretty hung over and pretty mad this morning. The guys at the main gate are trigger-happy and scary, rotated from the Pacific, given easy duty while they recover from their wounds, their jungle rot, and their Section-Eightedness, what Daddy and Uncle Bud call shellshock. They're sure jumpy, you can tell why, but we aren't the Jap sniper who had creased this one's skull, or the Japs that yelled day and night, "Marine you die—Marine you die," while keeping their company pinned down on the coral. Tolliver just happened to be the one they chose to pick on last night. They said she was falling down drunk and put her on report, just because she crashed to her knees when Corman let go of her arm for a minute to get out her pass; she tore her last pair of nylons and bloodied her knee, which made her swear something awful. I helped Corman haul her up, brush her off, and try to shush her, but by then it was too late.

"'Fraid they got you, pal." Corman holds out a handful of aspirin. We are in the head to splash ourselves awake. "How can we expect to force back the powers of darkness if people go falling down on the ground shredding one of the last pairs of intact nylons on the island?"

"I ain't in no mood for jokes. My daddy'll whomp me iff'n he finds out. Us Tollivers always serve . . . honor-ab*lee*. My great-granddaddy, he . . ."

"Was with Stonewall Jackson. Tell it to the Marines." I immediately realize it's the wrong thing to say. "Too bad old Lieutenant Mac hasn't actually gone yet. He's just trying to look important, putting you in for a Captain's Mast. Maybe you should go see Lieutenant Kaufman."

"Stow it, Dermody. Why aren't you out lighting candles or something?" She grimaces at her image in the mirror.

"Sorry, pal, I used up all my candlepower at Christmastime." Fine friend, but she is upset.

"You really should go see Lieutenant Kaufman, sugah," Corman says. "She's on our side."

Corman is right about Lieutenant Kaufman being on our side. We learned from Littlejohn, our favorite gossipy yeoman, who has the scuttlebutt about everybody on the whole island, that the lieutenant had been a teacher (surprise, surprise), who enlisted when her husband was called up early in the war. She was a super yeoman in Florida for a year or so, then her skipper persuaded her to fill out all the forms for Officer's Training. She went to Midshipmen's School in Northampton with the wire-jaw ladies and made ensign. When she hit Treasure Island, her blue braid and enthusiasm spanking new, her boss in Personnel told her she had to be the Waves representative. Every installation with women has to have a counselor/mother-hen representative. Littlejohn heard him tick off the reasons why she was chosen and told us. "You're a woman," he said, "you're married, you're 33. You just volunteered." She didn't have any choice, but she did fight him for an office with a door that would close.

"Surely," Littlejohn said she told the commander, "you don't expect me to discuss my girls' problems in the middle of the open office with a hundred ears perking up, do you? In front of all those men?" Overmanned by her persistence, he liberated an office for her, the same glass-walled one with the desk with the rose in the bud vase that I was beginning to know so well. She and I hadn't come to any agreement about what "facing reality" means, but since I had been talking to her occasionally I hadn't had any more crying fits in the gunsheds.

When she told us about it later, Tolliver said she felt pretty ragged talking to the lieutenant. "She sure wasn't very sympathetic. I told her they were picking on me. I hadn't had any more Pink Ladies and French 75s than anybody else. 'French 75s—brandy and champagne on an empty stomach?' she asked me. All us gunners drink French 75s—you think she'd know that. Besides, I told her, we went to Chinatown and had some sweet and sour pork at the Mandarin Palace. There sure were lotsa toasts at the Top last night." We nodded in unison. We had been there. Everyone in San Francisco knows about the toasts at the Top of the Mark for the guys who are shipping out the next day. Drinks all around and lots of spit-in-the-devil's-eye bonhomie. It could spook a person into a melancholy fit if she let herself dwell on the idea that the gigantic flag over the Mark Hopkins, lit all night by spotlights, was the last sight of the United States that so many guys saw—we never talked about that part at all.

"Betcha the lieutenant has been there drinking toasts, too," Corman said. "Then what did she say?"

"She said I had too much of a night on the town and too much to drink—not supposed to do that, but since it's done, it's done—get a good night's sleep, brush your uniform, and above all, don't lie." Tolliver sighed. "She said she'd be there."

We do what we can for Tolliver to get her ready for her judicial ordeal next morning. Corman cuts her hair into a smooth gold helmet,

Jenson spits on her shoes and shines the hated clodhoppers until a Marine could see his face in them, I iron her dress white blouse like a Chinese laundryman does, twice. Atkinson takes Coralee's clean uniform and hangs it in the shower room to steam. The skirt comes off the hanger but doesn't fall into a puddle, maybe the Lord is on our side after all.

It's chow time before we hear what happened to her. We had been on pins and needles all day, but we had a war to run, as the saying goes. She's pretty full of herself. We all ask her at once, "Are they going to send you home? Will they cut the buttons off your uniform with a sword and play the drums backward? How do they play drums backward anyway? Were you scared . . . ?" Tolliver's sense of drama takes over. She pushes us away, saying, "Stop crowding me. You all took those movies they showed us at boot camp *too* seriously."

"What happened? What happened? No fair driving us crazy. What's a Captain's Mast like?"

"We-ull, you'd never believe it. I'm starved. I'll tell you during chow."

Honestly, you have to admire that girl. We would have to draw straws to see who would strangle her if she didn't hurry up and tell us. She sashays into the line, chooses her knife and fork, a pat of butter, her roll, just as if we weren't all about to scream in her ear, "Tell us, tell us . . ."

"There was the skipper, of course, all dressed up in full dress uniform. You know how the skipper looks like Captain Bligh if you squint a little? He was all blown up like Charles Laughton. That skinny rat-faced Marine who put me on report was there. Said I was falling down drunk."

"You were." I couldn't resist.

"Who's telling this story anyway, Miss Priss? You had just as much to drink as I did that night. Lieutenant Kaufman was there, said I'd never been in trouble before. She should only know.

"The skipper, he fair growled. He harrumphed so much I thought he was fixing to growl, 'Come down from that mast, Miz Tolliver.' I almost burst out laughing, all that gold braid sitting there blinding everybody, like they ain't never been drunk."

"Coralee, you didn't." I couldn't breathe.

"Nope. I just stood there straight as a Tolliver and thought of my granddaddy. I looked the skipper straight in the eye. He said, 'This is very serious business, young lady. You realize your country is at war, fighting for its very survival. We really cannot tolerate this dereliction of duty. Do you have anything to say for yourself, young lady?'

"'Nossir,' I told him, sweet as pie. 'No excuses, sir. I've learned my lesson, sir.' Then he said he was going to put a notation in the record but he was going to let me off with a warning. Never again was I to do anything to disgrace the service. That was all."

"So it turned out all right after all," Corman says, to get everybody calmed down.

"No, it ain't over. I'm gonna get me one rat-faced Marine, just you see." Tolliver's face is getting red.

"C'mon, pal, let it go. Those sad-sack Marines are so jumpy since Saipan—you gotta make allowances." I'm catching Corman's look-on-the-brightsidedness somehow.

"Yeah," Atkinson chimes in, "just make sure that you aren't in their way when they shoot the tires of your taxi." Oh c'mon, Atkinson, you know that only happened once, but it sure scared the bejabbers out of all of us.

Blackie thinks it's the funniest thing he ever heard when he turns up in that spooky way he has. For a minute I can't tell if I am dreaming or not, he's standing there by the Waves compound with his crooked-tooth grin like he's never been away. Dreams are funny, you can see things, hear things, even fly over things, but you never smell things. At least I never do. Blackie smells of Aqua Velva, Lifebuoy soap, salt, fresh air, wool, and a guy smell I can't quite identify. I know I'm not dreaming when he gets close enough to brush my cheek and the Aqua Velva kicks in. "Hi, Toots," he says, "got back as soon as I could, here's your nylons." I take the two envelopes from him, thank him casually, like guys bring me nylons all the time. He acts like he does it all the time and he probably does. "Glad to see me?"

"You know I've been pining for you all this time," I say, joking to still the racing in my chest where my heart is reacting like an out-of-control motorboat.

"You gotta be kidding," he says when I answer his question about what's been happening since he's been away. "You ain't telling me they gave your best buddy a Captain's Mast just for being drunk?

Hell, me and my captain been blind drunk together more times than you can count."

As we lean together watching the white spray at the front of the water-taxi on our way to the city, he says, "Ain't nothin' to a Captain's Mast. You shoulda ast me. Or do they have a special Captain's Mast for you dames?"

"No, silly. We are Navy, too. You guys don't care much about Captain's Masts but we do. None of us wants to make the Waves look bad."

"So what happened to your pal? She get busted?"

"Nope. Skipper just gave her a reprimand and said never, ever, never disgrace the uniform again. After all our heart attacks and worry, nothing much happened except Tolliver says she is going to get one skin-headed Marine."

"You want I should do something about him for you?" Blackie asks.

"Thanks a heap, but I think Tolliver will get over it soon. She was pretty scared though."

"Dames is diff'runt, that's for damsure. Not like bein' with guys all the time. You should sail with me on our ship—then you'd see what it's really like—see some action.

"Silly boy, you know the Navy will never change its blue-eyed mind about women on ships. We're shore-based personnel and that's that. The very idea."

"Too bad. We'd have a good time. Where'dya wanna go for dinner?"

Around us, as we amble our way along the sidewalks of what some people like to call Baghdad-on-the-Bay, the fresh-faced young sailors in their pristine white hats, who will man those great gray ships all too soon, are tumbling in and out of the arcades and neon-signed bars under the fog-haloed streets of the old infamous Barbary Coast, which had been cleaned up and renamed the International Settlement. Uniforms from the whole Free World mingle and bump into each other: guys who have been rotated and feel that they have a lot of catching up to do alongside the gawky green recruits who feel they have to live a little before they go into action. Combat—that is the real action. "Seen any action?" they ask each other. The streets around us are pulsing with people feverishly looking for something that would match their internal excitation. Looking for what? A fight? A drink? A monumental, memorable binge? A meal? A tattoo? A connection? Anything you want is here for the taking, particularly if you have the sea pay for it. Tonight we are on our way to Tadich's for a steak.

When we get to Tadich's the line is too long, you could starve to death, so we try Omar Khayyam's, which is better. Waiting for the waiter, Blackie says casually, "Got my sea pay."

Sea pay has a way of piling up in the far reaches of the Pacific without any way to spend it unless you are into blowing it by gambling. Sea pay makes a date with a sailor just like Christmas every day. You might as well help him spend it for something enjoyable, otherwise he might get rolled for it in some dive and it would all go for naught. There aren't that many Calvin Jacksons saving for a postwar chicken farm in Arkansas in the Navy I know.

"How long you in for this time?" I ask after the waiter takes our order.

"Dunno." He knows. He always knows things like that, but he isn't saying. "A while. We gotta load up." He seems remote, distant. I'm glad to see him, but his world seems so much larger than mine; he still has the untrammeled look of those who travel to distant places, and here I am living on a confined island, working in even more confining gunsheds, tangled in confining rules. It looks to me like Blackie has the whole world to soar in, like it's his private balloon.

I search for conversation, having used up my small talk with Tolliver's encounter with the captain. "How was Ulithi?"

"Ulithi is a hellhole," he bursts out. "So's the whole damn Pacific. So's the whole frigging war." He sucks on his knuckle absentmindedly. He looks so vulnerable, so angry, despairing, so little-boy-lost that I long to hold him in my arms and croon comfort. Watch yourself, megirl, or you'll find yourself standing on the end of a dock, waving goodbye for the rest of your life. I reach out to take his hand. He winces.

"What happened to your hand?"

"Nothin'. Me and some buddies got into a fight with some Aussies. Three of them jumped me, worked me over good. I went back to the ship, got my buddies. We found them and tore their asses up good. 'Scuse the French." His face reddens under his tan. I make my face expressionless, speak no evil, see no evil, especially hear no evil, as we have all learned to do when the sailors swear around us. "Got busted to Coxswain, but it was worth it. You want any dessert?" Anything to change the subject. He resurrects his devil-may-care smile.

I rub his poor swollen hand lightly. My heart pounds, for a minute I feel a pull, like I am whirling down a corridor of nothingness, lined with babies with black hair, bubbles, and black eyes. I blink and it goes away. "Baklava, coffee, no cream," I say in my worldly sophisticated way.

"Whaddya wanna do then?" He signals the waiter and leans toward me, puts his arm along the back of the booth. He is wearing his skin-tight illegal tailor-mades, the creases on his collar sharp enough to cut.

"Let's go dancing." Lurching around the gunshed all those times with Jackson, Boy-Baptist-Junebug, was preparation for just such a moment. "We can go to the Cirque Room." I feel just like a golddigger in the movies when I think of all that sea pay, but it is so wonderful there—it's really like being in a movie, with all those tiny tables arranged around the dance floor and the big band playing swing and jazz, but mostly swing.

When we emerge into the drizzly evening, we hail a spare-no-expense cab to take us to the Fairmont. It really is heaven. Blackie is a hundred times better dancer than Jackson will ever be. Thousand times better. Sometimes he twirls me so energetically the others back off to the edge of the dance floor to watch us and cheer. The band plays "In the Mood" a couple of times, but the one I really like is "Dancing in the Dark." I want it never to stop. Maybe Tolliver is right. Maybe I am in love.

CHAPTER 17

Vodka Victory

Darn the war, darn Duty-Honor-Country. Just when I get used to Blackie being around, solid and comforting like a good wicker basket attached to a balloon in which we can soar together, like the whole sparkling bay is some sort of magic playground, he's got to go again.

"Ship's loaded." He kisses me again, right on the corner of my mouth. "Don't do nothin' I wouldn't do. Don't forget to write. Keep a weather eye out for gyrenes. Don't get engaged or nothin' while I'm gone, Toots."

"Who me?" My heart plummets to my shoes. "Maybe I will, maybe I won't." I can't ask him when he will be back. I can't do anything, really, except wave him off bravely with my eyes glistening like some kind of sappy heroine in some war movie standing on the dock with little drops of glycerin on her false eyelashes. This is getting old, saying goodbye to him. I don't need glycerin. Remember, sailors don't cry, megirl. I never knew I could miss anybody so much. There are plenty of guys around to joke with, to dance with, play chess with, to go to the movies or the craft shop or even the ballet with, cute guys to hold hands and neck with if you're so inclined (they always are), but they are all so ordinary and boring compared to Blackie. "Take care of yourself." I give him a thumbs-up signal as he turns and goes.

At least the war news is a little better. Our guys finally threw the Germans back in Belgium and Holland, but the casualty news is not so good. The papers report things like "The U.S. War Department revealed that American casualties for the Western Front between December 15 and January 7 totaled 52,594—these figures are subject to revision—of the 40,000 Ardennes casualties, 18,000 are listed as missing and presumed prisoners." It's not over yet, either. Numbers like that don't make any sense to me, even if I believe them. What I want to know is how is, where is Michael Francis Dermody, and for that

146

matter, Arvid Axel Lundgren? Don't give me numbers, just send letters. Mother finally got a bunch of V-mails from Michael last month. Most had been written a while back. He didn't say much except it was rugged and he was okay, thank the good Lord and all those novenas. Corman got word from her tank jockey fiancé, Jack, that he was okay. That's old news, like Michael's V-mails to Mother; today there is what the papers call "fierce fighting" on every front. That probably means somebody is getting clobbered. Hope it's not our guys. On the other side of the world things are heating up on Iwo Jima. If it's this bad now, what will it be like when our guys hit Japan? I hope the bottom falls out of Blackie's beloved Victory ship in the harbor at Ulithi so he can't go anywhere near old "Iowa Jima."

Tolliver is picking on me again. She has some sort of secret weapon radar she uses on me. "You're moping again," she says. "I thought you'd cheer up after you fell in love, but you just mope around all the time. You ought to stop reading the papers. Don't do no good, moping."
I know she's right. "I'm not in love." She makes me cross.
"Sez you. Grow up, pal. You only live once. Even if you're Irish."
"You make me sick."

Corman pokes me awake. "You okay, honeybunch? I brought you some aspirin."
"*Go* away, let me die in peace."
"You're not going to die yet. Here sit up and swallow these." Obediently I do. "You go back to sleep and you'll be right as rain before long." What's so right about rain, I think, but all I can do is groan and fall back into my sodden pillow. She pulls the pillow out to plump it and lets my poor baseball head fall back on it. "See you later." She smiles her bright, reassuring smile and leaves, trilling something about going rowing with Hilliard. Rowing, when I'm dying?
All I want to do is go back to sleep and wake up to find it's all a bad dream, like you do sometimes when you are running down Main Street without any clothes. Fat chance. I can hear gypsy violins dancing inside my head. When I shut my eyes I see a set of stainless steel teeth gleaming at me. Whatever would they say at home? Why had I been so stupid? Boris lied to me, him and his Roosian secrets of so-

briety. Now I know what to die of mortification really means. There is only one thing to do, just die and face the Day of Judgment early.

It all started because Boris likes to cheer us all up, calling us Russian names that mean things like "little dove" or "dumpling," he said. He asked me out a couple of times, but I said no. I didn't feel bad about turning him down because he asked all the girls, he should have known we would talk among ourselves. Tolliver went out with him one time to the Balalaika Tea Room, where he broke down and sobbed from the sadness of the music. He wanted her to go back to his apartment with him, but she didn't. So she said.

Somewhere he got this big idea. We must have been mad to consider it, but at the time it just sounded like fun. He invited all of us Miss Sailor Girls to a party on one of the Russian ships in port. He was buddy-buddy with the Exec or whatever they call them in Russian. Next Choosday, he said.

"Miss Priss won't go," Tolliver said, as we lounged around the empty gunshed waiting for the next class, which was late.

"Whaddya mean, I won't go?" I retorted, my sense of adventure challenged. Talk about taking leave of your senses.

"How will we get back?" Corman may get engaged a lot, but she's basically practical.

"That iss no problem. We will trans-sport you personally back by the captain's gig at precisely 2300." Boris was vibrating all over with the intensity of his plans. "We will have some good Russian food. We will sing and dance. We will see how we live the good Russian life." His moist black eyes shone as he strummed an imaginary balalaika. He twirled around and around, singing, *"Kalinka, Kalinka, dum de dum."* He really is funny.

"Count me in," Jackson piped up, appearing with fresh mugs of java, steaming and sludgy as usual. The word "dancing" sent Jackson's feet tapping and his little old Baptist heart pounding.

"We haff enuff sailors on the *Vladivostok Victory,* thank you. This invitation is for Miss Sailor Girls, thank you very much," Boris puffed importantly at poor Jackson, who slunk away.

Tuesday wouldn't do, but on the next Saturday the Russian sailors, some of them very young, rosy-cheeked farmboys, and some old hands who looked sort of sneery, like the mutineers in *Mutiny on the Bounty,* watched as Boris handed us gallantly up the swaying ladder to the deck in the soft, pearly twilight. We had come on the water-taxi, so much for the captain's gig. Boris was the last aboard. His buddy-buddy, the Exec, was standing stolidly by the ladder as we came aboard. Boris kissed him on both cheeks and, raising his arms like a football coach, shouted, "Victory!"

Our hosts had laid on a feast on long tables set up on the deck: platters heaped with pork chops and piroshkis mostly. More vodka than anybody had ever seen in her whole life, all colors. They must use vodka for ballast in those Russian ships.

Russian music is usually sad, but that night they were playing the lively kind; sound carries so over the water, all the ships in Alameda must have heard "Moscow Nights" played so energetically on the concertinas, accordions, and guitars and wondered what was going on. The music started out at about the same rate as a heartbeat and then went faster and faster, so I felt like my heart was beating faster and my feet wouldn't keep still, and when the song was over all I could do was shout just like the Russians do—"do-HUH." The stars came out and the dark ships around us made ours seem brighter in contrast.

It was all the toasts that did it. Boris said it was a big Russian secret he was telling us in the spirit of international amity. "You will neffer get trunk," he said, raising his tumbler of pink vodka, "if you do like we Russians do. Eat something every time you toast. Have a pork chop. To *Victory!*" He tossed off the pink vodka and reached for a re-fill of amber vodka. Who ever knew that vodka came in so many colors? Not me. Back home in Detroit we have mostly brown whiskey and beer. Lotsa things I never knew before. Another toast. Boris was getting into the spirit of things. Or the spirits of things.

"To Undying Friendship between the Hew Hess Hess Ar and the Hew Hess of Ay."

Have another piroshki—half-moon pastries full of spicy meat, heavy in the hand, leaden in the stomach. There must have been a whole crew in the galley frying pork chops and piroshkis in buckets of lard because unending platters of them were heaped on the long trestle tables. The water glasses of vodka were always full, too.

I remember Corman writing down her address for a handsome, black-haired Russian guy with a cleft in his chin, I think his name was Anatole. I remember Tolliver falling on her fanny as she tried to do that Russian dance where you squat down and kick your legs out. Everybody was laughing. The other Waves in our guncrew were catching on to some of the dances the guys were showing us. Very merry, this international friendship.

The next time I lift my head from my pillow I hear Tolliver tunelessly humming "Moscow Nights" as she rummages in her drawer. I groan. "You okay?" she asks, her mouth full of bobbypins.

"I think I'm gonna die."

"Nah, never happen. You'll be okay tomorrow." She slams her locker door shut and puts her hands on her hips. "You ain't the only one ever had a headache, don't make such a big deal out of it." She sashays down the corridor, her heels clicking on the linoleum. Fine friend. Why did I have this odd feeling that I owed her one? Oh migod, it's coming back to me now. I bury my head in the pillow but I remember. Holy Mother, I don't want to remember.

I was awake, but somewhere strange. It was a different bed, a bunk. On a ship. I could tell it was on a ship, something about the bobbing and creaking, the close below-decks air smelling of fuel oil. My head hurt. I tried to figure it out. O migod, I thought, I've been shanghaied. People are always being shanghaied in books . . . there would be a trap door in front of the bar in those sailors' dives and the luckless fellow would wake up with a monstrous headache at sea. A Mickey Finn, did anybody give me a Mickey Finn? There's a long-ago saint who was the patron of galley slaves and generally press-ganged nautical persons. Saint . . . Saint . . . how could I call on him when I couldn't even remember his name? I closed my eyes to try to remember.

I sensed a presence and opened my eyes just a little. A gray-haired man hovered over me, looking concerned. His hair was very short, his ears flat against his head, which was, you might say, square. He was wearing a uniform jacket with stiff shoulder boards. When he noticed my stirring he smiled at me. He had a mouth full of aluminum teeth. Maybe stainless steel? They were exactly the color and shininess of a torpedo. I winced and shrank into myself. Nobody has steel teeth. You must be having a nightmare, megirl. I pretended to swoon.

I peeked through my eyelashes again. The man, who looked harmless enough but how could you tell, had turned away and was looking at some charts on his desk. He turned and strode out of the cabin. I tried to think. My head was full of little cartoon figures peering over a wall saying "Wot 'appened?"

I felt like I was inside a drum. The whole metal structure of the ship reverberated with the noise of music and fast dancing. I recognized "Meadowland" among the thumps.

The Russian ship. Boris's party. They must have invited us aboard so they could shanghai us. Why? We can't type Russian. But what else could I be doing on this bed/bunk in the chart-strewn room? This is 1945. Holy Mother, that must have been the Russian captain. I felt like I was going to throw up, but I didn't dare throw up there—why was I flaked out, fully dressed, in the captain's bunk, apparently intact, not taken advantage of as far as I could tell? My stomach was roiling and threatening to overflow any minute, but I mustn't throw up, better to die first. I lay motionless, but the dancing pounding on the deck overhead made everything in the tiny cabin bounce around sickeningly. I was angry. Why was I missing all the fun? Where are your buddies when you need them most? Why had I gotten into this mess in the first place? Holy Mother, just get me out of this one. Just one more time, please, I beseeched.

Like an answer to my prayer, Tolliver appeared through the oval doorway. Her purply lipstick was smeary and her strawy hair disarranged, but she looked like a guardian angel to me. "You awake, Dermody? Shake a leg. We gotta move it outta here. Last water-taxi in ten minutes."

"What happened?" I groaned, half knowing and hating the whole thing.

"You passed out. Right in the middle of a toast. Slid right under the table. Boris picked you up and carried you into the captain's quarters. You know Boris, nothing is too good for Miss Sailor Girl. I gathered he indicated he would kill anybody who touched his *dusha,* but I don't speak Russian."

"I can't move. I'll throw up."

"No time for lollygagging. Move it. Head's right over here." She helped me up and led me to the tiny cubicle. Twenty-seven varieties of vodka and pork chops came spewing up. She held my forehead firmly in her cool fingers. When there wasn't any more she helped me wipe off my spattered stockings and led me topside. The fresh air felt good. A breeze had sprung up and the water was choppy, little white caps winking in the darkness. I thought I was going to be sick again, looking at them, but Corman shook my elbow in warning. I took a deep breath of salty air and clamped my mouth shut.

The captain was standing by the ladder, but I averted my eyes. How was I supposed to make my manners? Thank you for letting me pass out on your bunk? I ignored him as majestically as Aunt Geraldine sailing by the bishop when she was unhappy with him and allowed myself to be handed down the swaying ladder into the bobbing boat with as much grace as possible. Boris was nowhere to be seen. Just as well.

It's dark in the barracks when I wake up again. Corman is shaking me to see if I want some chow. She has brought me a sandwich and a container of milk, which surprisingly tastes good. Atkinson's with her. She and Atkinson act like doctor and nurse, nodding to each other.

"Sitting up and taking nourishment," Corman burbles.

"Looks like she's going to live." Atkinson holds my wrist, feeling my pulse. Think they can make me laugh, do they?

"Dermody, you've got to learn to use some common sense. You could have been in big trouble if we hadn't been there with you."

"*Mea culpa, mea culpa.* How'd we all get by the Marines this time?"

"Just lucky. You were walking pretty good, but you got feisty with the taxi driver. You owe me a dollar because we had to give him an extra tip."

"JesusMaryandJoseph. Never again. Never again. I swear. My life as an International Adventuress is o-v-e-r."

"All of ours."

"So?"

"We weren't supposed to be on that *Vodka Victory* at all. Boris just did it on his own, without any permission or anything."

"You're kidding."

"Nope." Corman looks unusually serious for her. "Big International Incident brewing, who knows?"

"Holy Toledo, I can see the headlines now. TI WAVES SPIRITED ABOARD RUSS SHIP FOR WILD PARTY. NAVY INVESTIGATING."

"You were out for most of it," Atkinson said. "You don't know how wild it got. What the Navy doesn't know won't hurt it, I figure. Mum's the word, you betcha."

"You bet."

Lucky for me. Thank you, whatever saint had the duty that night to look after Irish drunks. Word went out that there was no word, as far as anybody was concerned there had been no *Vodka Victory* party. Jackson was a little sulky for a while, but he was a sport and didn't say anything. We knew the Chief knew, he always knew everything that went on, but he was as mum as a portrait of rectitude. Even Tolliver was restrained, for her. Every once in a while she would say, "Have another piroshki, Dermody," and double up laughing. Boris must have gotten transferred, I don't think they fire you in the Navy with a war on. We got another Russian interpreter, a skinny guy with a big bush of curly hair in front and wire-rimmed glasses. He wasn't any fun a-tall.

So now it's the Saturday afterward, my poor head and stomach have recovered. I am convinced I must have a friend upstairs, but I don't think I'll mention it in confession. I'll just make a private Act of Contrition. Racking my brain, I can't figure out which category of the Seven Deadly Sins it would come under, anyway. Catechism classes back home had gone into quite a lot of detail about a lot of different sins and things—all those questions and answers to memorize—but vodka was never mentioned; not even *poteen*, which is the same thing, only Irish.

There doesn't seem to be any point in mentioning it to the chaplain, either. Everybody knows he likes his little nip. Those who were a little less diplomatic or kind say he likes to get roaring drunk with his boys. Monsignor O'Callaghan, the terror of my life back home, lived most of his life, as I can see it now, at least two sheets to the wind. Daddy always gets snockered at the American Legion meetings. I have a feeling that it's supposed to be different for girls, but there isn't anybody I want to ask about it. So why worry? Holy Mother, you've got to explain it for me to those recordkeepers up there. Please do it toot sweet.

There are plenty of other things to worry about, even if Lieutenant Mac has finally left and we have a nervous, pretty little Wave, Ensign Bauzer, in his place. She's still learning her job, so we don't see much of her, except at inspections; she's okay, but like anybody new, nitpicky on regulations like how long hair is. Corman is kept busy on Friday nights giving people a trim or helping them curl their hair up as tight as possible. That's just a nuisance.

This week the big worry was that Corman is late. When Tolliver first heard about it, she said we were going to have to look back on the entire Fleet Operations to find out who the father is, but then when she saw that Corman was really upset she let up. It turned out to be a false alarm, Corman was so happy this morning to find out. I never saw anybody so happy to get the Curse in my life, cramps and all. I would think Corman would have more sense, but who am I to talk? Sometimes I think being everybody's Miss Priss means I miss out on all the fun, but then I think maybe it is better to wait till you're married to find out what it's all about. I wouldn't want to be Edith Shaughnessy leaving her baby in St. Louis for some strangers, I wouldn't want to have to leave the Navy. Not yet, anyway.

CHAPTER 18

Springtime

"Oops," I say as I hurry across the quarterdeck of the Armed Guard Center (Pacific). Bixby has his eye on me and he isn't flirting either. He's a big guy, a bosun, leaning on the pillar that has the ship's bell and the Honor Roll on it. I'm hardly ever on the quarterdeck, but whenever I am there to pick up my pay or something, he's there, frowning, with his white gob hat obscuring his eyebrows, his meaty arms crossed on his chest. He's supposed to oversee the decorum of the personnel that come and go across the busy lobby. He's not any-body to mess with, meaner than a snake, he'll put a person on report faster than you could say "drunken sailor." He unwinds himself and moves toward me languidly with a "gotcha" look on his face. I decide to check on my war bond allotment another day—this calls for eva-sive action. I swerve toward the ladder leading to the Chief's office, quicken my pace as much as I dare, make it, barely. I turn to look at Bixby, who has skidded to a stop. He shrugs, the stairs are out of his jurisdiction, he can't do anything to me now. He lumbers back to his post. What does he care? You would think, though, that as long as there have been Waves on this base, the guys would get tired of giv-ing us a hard time, but some guys just don't give up.

I make my way topside, thinking of home, parties, green beer, and green shamrock candies, a whole bellyache full, when I bump right into a heavyset lieutenant coming down. He's almost middle-aged and preoccupied. Nobody I ever saw before. We back away from each other, he starts to apologize and suddenly freezes. The incipient wat-tles on his jaw quiver with indignation. "Young lady," he sputters, "you, you, YOU ARE OUT OF UNIFORM." He's one of those officers who always sound like they're talking in capital letters. His eyes bug out at the little green hairbow affixed to a bobbypin on my head.

"Oh no, sir," I say, figuring he's transient. "It's seventeen March and this is the uniform of the day. The skipper's Irish, don't you

155

know?" This baldfaced lie Bixby would never buy, but I skedaddle past the stunned officer before he can think what to say next. I can hear him muttering as he stomps on down, "THIS 1945 NAVY! THIS 1945 NAVY!" You probably think you're Admiral Nelson reincarnated, Bub, I think wickedly. I bet before Pearl Harbor the only water you ever saw was in your bathtub.

I compose my face and walk into the Chief's office, plunking the papers I have for him onto his scarred desk. "Morning, Chief. Howsabout my leave, huh?"

"Dermody, you're out of uniform." He sighs. "You ain't eligible for leave yet. One of these days you're gonna get put on report."

"You wouldn't put me on report just for a bit of wearing o' the green on St. Paddy's Day, you're much too kind-hearted. You wouldn't be able to sleep a wink, thinking of me in the brig on bread and water, no sir."

"Knock it off, Dermody. One of these days you're gonna push me too far. You got a smart mouth sometimes. If you was a fella, you'da hadda fat lip before this."

"Nossir, never, sir, I mean no, Chief."

"I gotta good mind to put in for your leave myself. Things would be a lot more peaceful around here if you was back again in Michigan where you belong. You shoulda stayed there. Kee-rist." He leans back in his swivel chair and rubs his huge hand across his scarred brow.

"No can do," I reach for the return papers he holds out, "gotta serve my country in her hour of dire need. I just want my home leave as soon as I can get it. Thank you kindly, sir." I duck out the door before he can throw something. I can hear him swell up like a bullfrog likely to explode.

"DON'T CALL ME SIR. I toldja a thousand times, I'm a Chief."

"Sure, Chief." Nicest guy in the whole Navy. I sure hope he survives us Waves.

I pick up my mail at the barracks. You have to be in the service to realize what mail means. That's why we spend so much time writing letters on our stationery marked with anchors, trying to keep the fragile spiderweb silk of connections going. You can imagine the world like a picture in the geography book, criss-crossed with gossamer lines of mail routes. Hundreds of Waves and I suppose WACS sort thousands of letters into canvas bags and send them on their way.

It's no fun thinking of people you care about being only a Fleet Post
Office or APO number. I flip through the pack of letters quickly.
None from Michael. Again. Where are you, boyo? The letter from
Mother is inside a card—one of those that has the Old Irish Blessing
on it, printed in that fancy script the old Irish monks used. It
certainly wishes me well, even though I have heard it a million times.
"May the road rise up to meet you / May the wind be always at your
back / . . . and until we meet again / May God hold you in the palm
of his hand." I wish I could believe He was that interested. The letter
says that Buddy was ready for his confirmation, nobody knows if the
bishop will have the gas to come for the ceremony. (Come on now,
Mother. Bishops always get the gas.) She closes with "Be careful,
Angel," like she always does. A P.S. says, "Daddy sends his love."

Mrs. Lundgren's card is one of those silly ones with a leprechaun
and a pot o' gold—it hopes that I will be in heaven an hour before
the devil knows I'm dead. Thanks a lot. I throw the rest of the letters
unread into my locker and flake out, sometimes that's the only rem-
edy for homesickness.

After the *Vodka Victory* fiasco, I swore to give up parties for the rest
of my natural life, but when Judy Jenson invited us to one in town, it
did sound like a nice change. Judy, a pale quiet girl, so pale her skin
looked translucent, had arrived after us and always seemed like the
"new girl." She had been spending most of her time in the city with
her friend, Ens. Beverly Woodley. Most of us kept out of the way of
officers pretty much, but Judy told us Beverly was someone she knew
before. When the rest of us would sit around the topside lounge
telling lies and gossiping, Judy would sit quietly, listening, chain-
smoking Pall Malls or Lucky Strikes; she smokes so much her index
finger has a permanent yellow stain on it. You could borrow change
for the phone or use her shoe brush anytime, count on her to cover
for you when the need arose, a real nice girl. Not so Ensign Woodley,
when we finally got to meet her one day outside the Twelfth Naval
District headquarters. She's not the sort of person I would take to
right away—well, to put it truthfully, I hated her on sight. She's short,
chunky, and bossy, and she talks in short bursts, like she's spitting wa-
termelon seeds. She has a job at the Twelfth Naval District and an
apartment on Telegraph Hill near the Shadows Restaurant. That's

where we are going to the party, Atkinson, Tolliver, and I, climbing
the rickety wooden staircase, nailed together like a kid's playhouse,
with an even more rickety handrail.

The climb is worth it. We arrive, a little breathless, at the stoop
by the kitchen door of Woodley's apartment and turn back to see a
bird's-eye view of the San Francisco Bay and pancake-flat Treasure
Island. Beyond it we can see the other side of the Bay Bridge and the
white campanile of the University of California against the hills of
Berkeley; to our right we can see the Oakland Naval Yard and Alameda, a steel forest of radar posts and masts on all the carriers. Back
in November, when I first came to Treasure Island, TI everybody calls
it, smack in the middle of San Francisco Bay, I would fantasize that I
could put on seven-league boots and jump from the Island, ship to
ship, all around the bay and never get my feet wet. I would hop from
rust-buckety Liberty ships riding high in the water waiting to pick up
cargo to the riveted steel decks of the delicate, bouncing destroyers
all the way to Hunter's Point where the carrier *Intrepid* lay up for re-
pairs and refitting. Careful landing, though. Her deck was all torn
and jagged where she took another kamikaze at Leyte. It made me
sick in the stomach to see her all torn up like that. Then I could leap,
like a manic angel observer, over the Bay Bridge along the Embarcadero where the clipper-bowed Victory ships with names like *Willard
A. Johnston* were being outfitted or repaired. From so high up I could
see the long antlike lines of men carrying their barracks bags strug-
gling up the gangways at the Port of Embarkation. I could jump high
over Alcatraz and Angel Island to Sausalito where more ships were
waiting to take on loads of ammunition or Almond Roca or C-rations.
Hip-hopping across the mouth of San Pablo Bay where I could spy
Mare Island farther up, I could skip, still dryshod, down the East Bay
side where the hospital ships unloaded the wounded for Oak Knoll
Hospital or that other big hospital the Army had. Easy hopping
across ships crowding the Oakland Navy Yard over to Alameda Air
Base. More ships in "the road" on the other side of the Bay Bridge,
sometimes aircraft carriers or a fat cruiser, sometimes a stubby ferry
chuffing along. Jump right on back to Treasure Island before anybody knew I was gone.

"What a wonderful spot for a Japanese spy," I say to Atkinson as we
wait for Tolliver to catch up. All of the ships—both freighters and
men-of-war—are jockeying for position to move with the tide out

through the Golden Gate as soon as the guys at the net station at
Tiburon open the way.

"Fair enough," Atkinson agrees with me, for once. "From up here
all those ships look just like those bathtub-toy models they had at
boot camp, don't they? Suppose that's the *New Jersey* over there?" She
is pointing to the distant gray shape with the characteristic long,
upward-sloping foredeck.

"Can't be. Must be the *Iowa*. Hey, Tolliver, hurry up, you could see
everything from up here if you were a spy."

Tolliver overhauls us, trying to hide her puffing. When she gets
her breath back, she wraps her lips around so her teeth buck out and
says, "Ah so, Honable Emperor and Admirl Tojo require much information." She folds her hands into her sleeves and bows at us and at
the ship-laden bay. She drops her fake Japanese accent and continues, "It's a good thing for us all those Nip spies are all rounded up
and far, far away, ain't no more Japs left in California. Where's this
here party?"

As if she can't hear it. Someone is playing "Tuxedo Junction" on
the victrola, *loud*. Inside the tiny little apartment (in what back home
we might call a shack perched precariously on the side of the hill),
we can hardly see anything through the cigarette smoke but we make
out Jenson dancing with Ensign Woodley in the middle of the room.
You wouldn't know she's an ensign in her beige slacks and brown
and orange Hawaiian shirt.

Jenson pumps her arm up and down to acknowledge us and
points with her head to the kitchen. She goes right on pumping to
"Tuxedo Junction" with the other dozen couples dancing in the living room. We push our way to the tiny kitchen where the chow is
higgley-piggley laid out on the table and sink: Chinese takeout boxes,
crackers, potato chips, bread, cheese, peanut butter, FFV cookies in
tins, baked beans, potato salad from the deli, canned sardines. A corner of a counter has a forest of bottles: tequila, rum, wine, vodka (I
never ever in my whole life will be able to look at a bottle of vodka
again), coke and beer crowd the fridge. Our contribution is a flat
gingerbread cake with white frosting Jackson had gotten from a
friend in the galley and given to Atkinson as a small token of his af-
fection. He's really sweet on her, even if she is more than a foot taller.

I lose track of time at parties. By the time people are down to
drinking muscatel because everything else is gone, all the records in

the stack have been played two or three times, and we are back to
"Tuxedo Junction," I go outside to sit down on the little stoop to get
some cigarette smoke–free air and a little quiet. Most of the people
at this party we never saw before; they seem to be gals stationed in
San Francisco, some of them at the Waves barracks on Jones Street,
others on subsistence and quarters, especially the officers, who have
their own apartments here and there, wherever they can find them
in war-crowded San Francisco. These gals don't talk about any of the
places we like to go to, like the Fairmont or Omar Khayyam's or the
Balalaika. I wonder why there aren't any guys around to crash the
party; most of the guys we work with can smell a party twenty miles
downwind. Here there's just girls with their shoes off, dancing with
each other, like we did back in high school. Some of them are really
good dancers.

I go back in to sit on the couch next to Jenson, who's chain-smoking
everybody else's cigs. Ensign Woodley emerges from the back with a
bosomy yeoman from Operations. "Who's Simone Simone?" she asks
us. She pours herself a jelly glass of muscatel and raises it, sloshing
just a little. "I'm Beverly, Beverly. I'm an officer and a gentleman,
even if it took an act of Congress to do it." Everybody laughs, everybody but Jenson, that is. She is biting her lip and straightening the
lampshade and has the same look on her face that my aunts get
whenever they're anxious to get their husband home before the old
boy makes a complete fool out of himself. That's funny. Jenson doesn't
have a husband.

Ensign Beverly Beverly waves Jenson aside like a mosquito and
shouts above the noise from the scratchy Victrola like she's on a parade ground, "Let's all go out and show this town how to have a good
time, everybody. Let's move on out." Gals are laughing, putting on
their shoes and looking for their purses. Atkinson heads for the
kitchen to put the cheese back in the refrigerator. Tolliver grabs my
arm so hard it hurts. She's got a tight look on her face.

"Let's get outta here. Go get Atkinson." I must look bewildered, at
least puzzled, because she snaps, "Step on it." Who does she think
she is, anyway? She herds us out the door and down the rickety staircase ahead of the main group, who are still getting ready to leave.

"Hold up, wait a minute, Tolliver. What are you being so strange
about? Everybody was just having a good time and now you're acting
like a scalded cat, like maybe the devil is chasing you or something.

Wait up." I have to stop to extricate a heel from a hole in one of the
steps.

"What's your rush?" Atkinson is huffing along behind us. "You
look like you got a burr in your saddle, Tolliver, you know that?"

She does look upset and she doesn't stop pell-melling down the
staircase. "We gotta get back to the base. Go sommers. Any place but
here."

"You crazy? You're getting on my nerves, and besides I don't think
we will do the war effort any good ending up a pile of broken bones
at the bottom of these confounded stairs. Slow down, willya?"

"Dintcha notice they was all gals? We ain't going out with that
bunch anymore. It's not for me, nohow." When Tolliver gets upset
her face gets red under the pearly skin and little beads of perspira-
tion bead her upper lip. That's how she looks now.

"So what? It's all girls back in the barracks, too. What's gotten into
you, anyhow?"

Tolliver sighs, raises her shoulders, and lets them sink. She stops
on the next-to-last flight and says, "Dermody, you are so dumb. Didn't
they teach you anything at that St. Alley Oop School you went to?"

I will not get my Irish up, sez I to myself, sez I. "Of course they did,
dummy. I know all the exports of Java, the date of the Missouri Com-
promise, and how to do square root. Lots more, like making my
manners to my hostess. You are such a pain, Tolliver, you really are."

Atkinson may not be the swiftest person in the world, but sometimes she surprises even herself. "I get it. I don't care. Those gals can
do what they want. It leaves all the guys for us."

"Whatever are you talking about?"

Atkinson just goes on without acknowledging my question. "Nobody made a pass at me. Anybody make a pass at you?"

"Jesusgod, I don't understand you two at all." I'm full as a gunny-
sack with feelings I don't understand and knowledge I have no notebook room for. "I'm going back to TI, see you later." I stalk off toward
the Embarcadero. They let me go. Some shipmates.

When I get back to the barracks there are two letters in my box,
actually three, if I count the monthly Spiritual Bouquet sent by Consuelo, the world's most pious cousin. She may be right, you know, all
those Hail Marys and Our Fathers she and her buddies in the convent at Adrian have said for me all this long time may be responsible

for my being here, intact and hearty and unbusted. Who knows?
'Ray, Consuelo.

Michael's letter gives no indication that the war in Europe appears
to be coming to a climax, what with the Allies bombing Germany on
one side and the Russians advancing on the other. It must be horrible to be bombed night and day like they are, but as everybody says,
they started it. Bet they wished they hadn't. You can't tell any of that
from Michael's month-old letter, which contains a snapshot of him
and three paratrooper buddies standing stalwartly in front of some
fat palm trees. That seems strange, but I gather from his censor-fooling
play on words that they are, for some reason, in Nice. Which is nice,
he says. He looks thinner than ever, but okay. He wonders why I
haven't written to him. Hey, I write you every week, brotherdear. Are
you absolutely sure the U.S. Army knows you and those buddies of
yours are in Nice? Better check it out.

Blackie's war, according to his letters, is a lark. He sends me a fort-
nightly SWAK letter written on his tablet with the blue lines:

> Somewhere in the Pacific, Sometime
>
> Hi Toots,
>
> How are you? You should have bin here with us last week when
> we overhalled the ice-cream barge. They got this ship made out of
> ciment that just goes around making icecream for the fleet. Me
> and my buddies liberated 2 gallons of black walnut and 3 fresh
> peach gedunk and had a party. It was sposed to go to some carriers
> but those carrier guys got it too easy anyway.
>
> We got a new exec. He's okay, not too much chikenshit from
> him so far. Write me some more letters. Dont do anything I
> wouldnt do. (Ha Ha)
>
> > Your Friend,
> > Blackie xxx ooo

Well, at least he's okay, probably with a bellyache. The censors
won't let anybody say anything, but things are not all that peaceful in
our Pacific, cement ice-cream ships like sea-going Good Humor men
or not. We hear from the radiomen guys that Iwo Jima is pretty well
mopped up but there's still Okinawa in the way.

Today's mail call brings everybody good news, for a change. Atkinson, who hardly ever gets any mail, got a package of cookies and

some religious tracts from her grandmother, the only one in her family that ever cared for her. She fair glows with pleasure and passes them around. When Tolliver gets back, she has a letter from her mama that tells her errant sister Rosalee has turned up in Newport News, when everybody was so worried and didn't know where she was after she ran off. Rosalee's fine, the letter says, working in the shipyard, engaged to a foreman, and planning to come and get Randall Junior just as soon as they find a place and get married. Mama sent pictures, too, the fat and sassy baby nephew sucking his thumb, his jug ears not nearly so noticeable as they were at first. "That's a load off my mind, let me tell you," Tolliver says. "I was so worried Rosalee would do something real foolish, without me being there to straighten her out."

I look at her. She looks at me. She looks a little sheepish, since she puts down sentimentality with her wisecracks all the time. I am in awe at how much her hayseed facade covers up. I know how she feels. "Families," I say, mixing all the Scanlons and the Dermodys and McSweeneys and Cuchulains and the Tollivers and the rest into one violent swirl like a kid's fingerpainting, "they get on your nerves when you have to live with them, but when you are away you worry all the time. Is it just us? You should come to Detroit sometime and meet my Aunt Geraldine. Your family will get on fine without you. Ain't it awful?" I wish I were as confident as I sound.

"Maybe I will, someday. Who knows what will happen when the war is over?" She thumbtacks the snapshot of Randall Junior on the inside of her locker door right next to her autographed glossy of the Sons of the Pioneers and slams the locker door shut. "Let's go to the Rec Center and see what they have put on for our morale tonight."

"Why not? Who knows, we might meet the love of our lives, our destiny's soulmate, the answer to our prayers, in one single encounter at the Treasure Island Rec Center. You have noticed, I assume, that it is located right next to the chapel; maybe there is a secret communication network that goes right up to heaven for maidens' petitions." I swing my feet off the bunk and shrug on my uniform jacket. "Let's go, mate."

"I always knew you was crazy, pal," she answers, looking for her shoes. How were we to know I was right? Not for me, but for her!

CHAPTER 19

Sorrow

Franklin D. Roosevelt is dead. The president is dead. The radio said so last night. It's like all the losses and deaths in the world rolled up into a ball, squashing my chest and pressing all the air out. How can he be dead? He's been president practically all of my life. We had a mock election when I was in second grade, just like the grownups' election and Roosevelt won, just like my daddy said he would.

Only a couple of months ago the president had been in the Crimea somewhere, someplace called Yalta, with those other big guys, Churchill and Stalin. We saw it on the "March of Time" at one of the base theaters; there he was with his cigarette holder and his cape, smiling encouragement that the "Wah Against Tyranny" would soon be over and everybody could go home. Maybe it would be over soon, but FDR would never see it, not now.

When I was a kid, we listened to him on the radio. His voice was kind of stagy, to our Detroit ears a little la-dee-dah, but when he said everything would be all right you believed him. He had a way of making you believe him, especially after the war began. When he called Pearl Harbor a "date of infamy" the words ran like an electric charge through the whole country. We couldn't be scared, not when the president was in charge. Now he's dead. Gone. All the flags are drooping at half-mast, will be for a month. The radio plays nothing but sad music, classical sometimes, but mostly "Goin' Home." Now *there* is one sad song. No way to get away from the melancholy music, wherever you go on the base you can hear it, even Tolliver's hillbilly station is broadcasting organ music. She snapped it off. I know how she feels, it's like losing a big part of yourself, like your rudder or your steering wheel. He was always there, don't you know, to tell people what to do and now he isn't. What will become of us?

***

Everybody says she can remember exactly where she was when she heard about Pearl Harbor. I know I can. Arvid and I had gone to see *Snow White and the Seven Dwarfs* one snowy Sunday afternoon that December. It seems such a long time ago now.

We were laughing and Hi-Ho-ing as we came out of the Fox when we heard the newsboys yelling, "WUXTRY, WUXTRY, read all about it."

Arvid hailed a kid and gave him a nickel; we stood under the marquee, our breath congealing in clouds in front of us as we read the headlines aloud. "HARBOR BOMBED. TWO U.S. WARSHIPS LOST IN HAWAII ATTACK." Without another word we folded the newspaper and drove home through the swirling snowflakes. My family was in the living room, huddled around the Philco listening to Hans Kaltenborn. Daddy made a shushing motion with his beer bottle as we came in noisily, stamping the snow off our galoshes.

"It don't look good," he muttered as he bent forward to hear better. Mother looked tearful and stricken, like she couldn't draw a whole breath. She had her hand in front of her mouth and kept looking at Michael like he was a stranger. Daddy was getting all red in the face. "Those sonsabitches got us when we weren't ready, wish I was a young man, I'd show them a thing or three." Arvid and Michael just looked at each other, they didn't need to nod. Mother got the salmon loaf out of the oven and put it on the table along with the Harvard beets and the lettuce salad. She forgot the scalloped potatoes, so I went to get them out of the oven.

"Set another place, Angel, for Arvid." Shows you how upset she was.

The next morning was worse. Much worse. The Japs were attacking Guam and there were reports of Japanese paratroopers in the Philippines. The Red Cross had gone on alert. In spite of the repeated injunctions over the radio to Stay on the Job, nearly everyone stayed home from work or school to listen to the radio, to listen to President Roosevelt.

"Yesterday," he said, talking to Congress and all of us within reach of a radio, "Yesterday, December 7, 1941—a date which will live in infamy—the United States of America was suddenly and deliberately attacked by naval and air forces of the Empire of Japan."

Buddy, who was only nine, paled. He looked to the adults around him for reassurance, but who could give him any? Here we were smack in the middle of the continental United States, but who knew what would happen? I passed him the cornflakes and pushed the milk pitcher over to him. Michael took two bananas, I knew without his telling me that he was thinking of enlisting and was making weight. Poor skinny Michael had to eat a lot of bananas before the Army would take him.

But I am not in Detroit, but in the gunshed on Treasure Island with all the mopey mourning people. The guys aren't crying, but Jackson looks like he is almost; generally, the guys put on a stone face like they are biting on a pipe and being stoic, like the movies where the ship is going down. The girls' eyes are red, their hair sort of straggly, but there's no sense in howling anymore, all you would hear is an echo. It's awful. We secure the gunsheds to stand down early, go to get some chow, but the food is tasteless. Who has any appetite?

It's a relief when they finally turn off the sad music for a while and the new president, Harry S Truman, a man nobody ever heard of, comes on the radio to talk to the Armed Forces. He sounds pretty good, sort of like a school principal taking charge. He tells us the war will go on just the same . . . we will finish up in Europe and turn our full attention to the Pacific. So look out, all you bastards out there. He doesn't really say "bastard," you'd hardly expect the president to talk like that in public, but we get his message. He goes on to say, "Franklin Roosevelt never faltered and neither shall we." That's right. We shall not falter. Someone is in charge again.

Even so, the sad feelings don't go away. My arms and legs are so heavy I can barely move them, the air feels like syrup I have to swim through. I have to get up, put on my uniform, and go to work in the leaden atmosphere by the guns. Every time I see the Stars and Stripes flapping forlornly halfway down the flagpole I feel like crying. I'm not the only one. Corman bursts out in tears when *Life* magazine comes out with the pictures of the funeral, all the mourners, and especially the picture of the Negro man who had served Roosevelt all those years with tears just running down his face. Seems like we are all cried out and there is still a war to win. We have to get on with it.

The Germans continue to surrender all over the place. We hear that when General Patton liberated a concentration camp he vomited when he saw what the Germans had done, all those prisoners looking like skeletons with big eyes, and the piles of dead bodies in those striped pajamas. He made all the German townspeople come and bury the dead. Incredible. I can't imagine the stories Michael will have when he gets home. Maybe it will be so bad he won't want to talk about it. Michael can clam up when he wants to and nothing will make him talk. If the war in Europe really is almost over, he should be coming home soon, but then they will probably send him to the Pacific. The Nips are dug into those damned caves on Okinawa —digging them out one by one will be an overwhelming job. All the sixteen-inch guns in the world can't touch them under all that rock, although our salty, colorful Admiral Halsey says he wishes his battle-wagons had wheels so he could drive right up to Tokyo and crush the enemy once and for all. Jackson, like the other guys, really likes Halsey. "You know, that old Bull, he's got a saddle with silver things on it right in his quarters."

"Whatever for?"

"He's gonna ride ol' Hirohito's white horse right through the Imperial palace. No kidding. Hee hee, ain't that something? Won't be long now."

You never can tell if the guys are snowing you with sea stories like that. Jackson is getting so jumpy that the war will be over before he sees any action, he actually has us help him study so he can pass the exam for gunner third. There is so much blood flowing, so much gunpowder going off, it makes me wonder what all you blessed saints are doing up there in heaven? Playing mumblety-peg? Practicing some heavenly chorus? Making lists of who didn't make his Easter duty? Seems like nobody up there is really paying any attention to us down here a-tall.

A small pink envelope arrives in my mailbox to announce the arrival of Deirdre Eileen Murphy, 6 pounds, 3 ounces, 19 inches long. Good girl, Deirdre, not too big for a seven-month baby. That's from Sheila, of course. I wonder if Owen knows yet—he's somewhere in Germany, last I heard. Deirdre is Irish enough, but it's not a saint's name. What are you going to do when Monsignor O'Callaghan carries on at the baptism, like he usually does when it's not a sanctified name? Too bad I'm not there, I could be a godmother. I'm not really sure I want the responsibility of overseeing someone's religious upbringing. It seems strange that Sheila got to do something before me, how 'bout that?

After all the sadness, it's exhilarating to feel the expectation in the

air, covering the streets and hills of San Francisco like a white cloud
of hope instead of the usual pearly fog, when the United Nations
conference arrives in the city. The whole free world is gathering to
work out a way to ensure that what the world just went through the
last eight years won't be repeated ever again. The League of Nations
after the first world war didn't work out somehow; we were supposed
to learn about it in American history in high school, but it seemed
vague and shadowy and I never understood much about it or why it
didn't work. Now we have a chance to do it over and do it right.
UNO, they are calling it, the United Nations Organization. Four
Freedoms, fifty nations, what a show.

In the bustle on Market Street near the fancy War Memorial
Opera House we can stand and gawk to our hearts' content; wherever we turn there's a famous person. What an assortment. Lots of
uniforms, of course, with the military police in spanking white helmets everywhere. Lots of Arabs with their white headdresses held on
by gold squares like pasture fences; most of them have little pointed
beards and sweep along like they are princes, maybe they are. Chinese delegates are in gray military uniforms, the Russians are in dark
civvies. We see Molotov getting out of a big black car, he's the one
they named the cocktail for after they ran out of ammunition but not
gasoline. We pore over the pictures in the *Chronicle* every morning,
memorizing faces, that's how we knew it was Molotov. He's got a real
cookie-duster mustache. Lots of the foreigner guys have mustaches.
Funny, Yanks don't wear them much. Anthony Eden, who's English,
wears one, a little tailored one. It's not his mustache that makes the
crowds murmur when he goes by. It's not that he's tall, his civvie suit
more tailored than any uniform, his hair silvering into distinction at
the temples. It's his hat. A homburg, they call it. So distinguished,
so-o-o European. Corman and I are wedged into the crowd standing
by the curb near the striped marquee/awning when he goes by, and
we can hear the collective whoosh of under-breath from the guys
nearby; if they had such a hat, could they look that great? It's kind of
funny, their being so envious, but everybody is getting sick of uniforms by now, that's for sure. Peace is in the air.

Corman is the one most interested in going to the city with me to
watch the show, but we all go as much as we can. When we can't get
into town we pore over the papers and cut out pictures and articles
for our scrapbooks. Corman has the best scrapbook, she saves and

mounts everything: programs, theater ticket stubs, menus, letters, clippings, her old ratings, she even has all the cards people gave her at her going-away party, all the mushy Valentines her fiancés sent, pictures of practically everybody she has met in the Navy, every group picture ever taken, lots of pictures of each fiancé, with his arm around her shoulder and her laughing into the camera, all properly pasted into her big leatherette-bound scrapbook. "I'm saving this for my grandchildren," she kids. Or is she kidding? "I want them to know that old Grandma was right there in the front row in history."

"You're just about due to start another one, you're running out of pages." I hand her the mucilage and she curls her tongue out of the corner of her mouth in concentration as she adds a picture of the president speaking in front of the Honor Guard of guys and gals in uniform.

I'm cutting for her, all our newspapers spread out on the big table in the topside lounge. The newspapers, which love the eyes and ears of the world being on San Francisco, keep putting out special editions and we have to hump it to keep up. "Here's a good one of Molotov."

"He's hard to miss with that mustache. I've never kissed a man with a mustache, have you?" She wipes up a bit of errant glue with the corner of her tissue. I'm flattered.

"No, can't say as I have. We're young yet, maybe it's all there waiting for us in our interesting future."

"Speaking of future, what do you hear from Blackie?"

"Oh, the usual. Ulithi is a hellhole. The guys are so bored they fight with each other all the time. The captain is full of chickenshit, but he had that old bucket standing right out of the water when he poured on the steam to zigzag. Twenty-eight knots. What a liar. He wishes I was there. I bet. At least the sub that must have been chasing them missed."

"You serious about him?"

"I'm not serious about anybody, really."

"You should play the field more, honeychile. Don't let yourself wither on the vine."

"Too late." Do I believe it? She just looks at me and shrugs, knotting her pretty eyebrows in her what-am-I-going-to-do-with-you look.

One day I see Dean Gildersleeve going into the meeting at the

Opera House. She's wearing a kind of black tricorn hat tied on with a veil with black spots. I feel like rushing up to shake her hand; she had been one of President Roosevelt's advisors when he and Eleanor were putting the arm on the Navy to let women in to show what they can do, but one look at all the MPs and I think better of it. If it wasn't for Virginia Gildersleeve, who used to be a dean at Columbia University, I would still be at Meekin Brothers Plumbing and Heating Supplies, really withering on the vine, instead of here where all the action is. Even if I'm only watching it, I'm here. I wave my white gloved hand at her as she goes in, flanked by senators Vandenberg and Connally. I don't know if she saw me. I'd like to be like her some day.

When we get inside to the visitors' gallery to watch history being made, it's Czechoslovakia's day. Jan Masaryk, escaped from the Germans, is speaking from a podium in front of the stage. Along the back of the stage is a row of fifty flagpoles, one for each nation. Every color in the world, but it's hard to distinguish one from another because the flags just drape triangularly around their poles. Old Glory is far over on the right, they must have lined them up alphabetically. In front of the flags the Honor Guard stands. And stands and stands. 'Twoulda been an honor, but I'm glad they didn't ask me. Like statues they stand there in full dress uniform, Wave, sailor, Woman Marine, Marine, WAC, soldier, SPAR, Coast Guardsman, Wave, sailor . . . all the way across the huge stage. I suppose they must rotate them because these meetings go on for days.

I can't hear what Masaryk is saying very well, but he seems to be full of "Never Again" sentiments like everybody else, not hard to understand after what happened to his little Czechoslovakia after Munich. Hitler just gobbled it up. When he puts on his glasses, he looks just like the pictures of Benjamin Franklin. How odd.

It's really sad that President Roosevelt isn't around to see all this, something he'd been working on since the Atlantic Charter. It's a bit spooky, him being not so long gone and people quoting him like he's still with us. "This time we shall not make the mistake of waiting . . . as we fight together to get the war over quickly, we work together to keep it from happening again." Can't quarrel with that. People say that the president was really sick before he died—maybe he wouldn't have had the strength to last through all the discussions and arguments that are going on. And on and on. Still, if it brings lasting peace, it's worth it.

President Truman has everything under control. He addressed the conference, but nobody we know got into that one. When we saw it on the "Eyes and Ears of the World" at the newsreel theater on Post Street, his gold-rimmed glasses glinted in the lights. He's not striking-looking, like Franklin Roosevelt, but he's sure of himself. You wouldn't catch me trying to cross that one.

It's exhilarating walking down the streets looking for famous people, exotic people from faraway places. Flags and bunting give a festival excitement everywhere, activities everywhere are mostly for the delegates, but we can wander through the outdoor sculpture show in St. Mary's Square on a sunny day. Jenson's lieutenant gets us tickets for recitals in the opera house, Rise Stevens last week and Ezio Pinza this. Can you believe it? Tolliver went with me to the opera house just to hear him sing some opera stuff from Russian operas. We were pretty far back but we could hear his wonderful voice.

"Hey, he's good-looking. He can put his shoes under my bed anytime," Miss Irrepressible said as we emerged from the dazzling red and goldness into the soft night.

"Tolliver, you're impossible. You're going to lose your hillbilly credentials if you don't watch out."

"Stow it, Dermody. I can prove I've got more royal blood in me than the king of England. My ancestors lived in palaces bigger'n this, 'stead of some broken-down old straw-roof shanties."

"What a liar you are. Shall I call your carriage, your majesty?" She gives me a dirty look. Oh c'mon, we're in America, aren't we?

Late as usual, I race through the quarterdeck, trying to get to work before the Chief, when I almost run into Lieutenant Kaufman.

"Watch yourself. Have you heard the news, Josette?"

"What news, Lieutenant?" Lieutenant Kaufman is just about the only person in this whole Navy who acts like I have a first name.

"Hitler's dead. Killed himself and that Eva Braun person." She rattles the *Chronicle* she's holding for emphasis.

"No kidding." I bend to read the report. Inside I am exulting, Glory Be to God, the devil must have been waiting for that one, but

where can they find a place bad enough for the likes of him? People
go to hell just for eating meat on Friday or having a baby too soon.
I straighten up and look at her. "When do you think we can all go
home, Lieutenant?" Suddenly for a brief moment it all seems possible.

"God only knows."

"And He's not telling. Anyway, good riddance to bad rubbish." I
turn to go, but she holds out her arm restrainingly.

"Are you all right, Josette? How are things?"

"I'm 4.0, I guess. Everything seems okay at home for now."

"Good. You look a little pale though. Maybe you need more recreation and fresh air?"

"Maybe I do. Gotta run now." Do I need a mother to tell me I look
a little pale? Maybe I do.

Hitler's dead. We won. Hitler's dead. We beat him. Hitler's dead.
We won. Hitler's dead. Shouldn't I be happier? I feel yucky and sick
to my stomach. So many deaths. Will it never stop?

After a while I discover that being in the middle of history-making
events can get tedious. The history-making war drags on forever, it
seems, even with Roosevelt and Hitler dead, and so does the conference. The delegates talk and talk and talk. They argue and argue and
argue. They start making compromises. They let Guatemala in even
if it does have a dictator. Things are as murky, raggedy, and confused
as ever. We all, even Corman, the demon scrapbooker, get tired of
trying to read everything about it in the paper, tired of trying to col-
lect every word and picture in our scrapbooks, and we go back to our
usual grousing, working, daydreaming, as we wait for the war to be
over, wait for everybody to go home.

CHAPTER 20

Fly Away Home

The sky is bright blue and filled with puffy white clouds for all the world like a flock of celestial sheep, but even the pretty day can't lift my spirits. I have to fly home, all my fears and worries suddenly coming true when the Red Cross sends a telegram to say that my daddy is real sick and I have to go home toot sweet. I only talked to my folks last week, things seemed okay then. Now I don't have time to get to a phone, I have my orders in my hand, but nobody has told me any details.

I always wanted to be Amelia Earhart the Second, not sadly dead like her but free to soar and play hide and seek among the cloud sheep, but now that I am flying it isn't any fun at all. This plane isn't a nifty little two-seater that allows your white silk scarf to stream out behind romantically, nor is it even a regular airliner, but a new DC-3 put into service so quickly by NATS, Naval Air Transport, that the inside is just a cavernous hollow space with upturned buckets for seats. I always thought the guys were kidding when they talked about bucket seats. There isn't anything to look at except the printing on the bare ribs of the plane. Over and over again the letters spell out ALUMINUM COMPANY OF AMERICA ALUMINUM COMPANY OF AMERICA ALUMINUM COMPANY OF AMERICA marching around the curved bulkheads till I get dizzy following the words. I wish I had my rosary with me. Grandmother Scanlon was never without hers, you really need one at a time like this. I put my folded-up raincoat between me and the window for a pillow and try to say the rosary by counting on my fingers. I keep losing count, I'm so worried something terrible is happening. I haven't been going to mass every Sunday like I should. To be honest, I haven't been since I made my Easter duty last month. Daddy won't die just to punish me for being a sinner, will he? I try to make a sincere Act of Contrition, promise to do better. I hope it's not too late.

The next thing I know we are at Olathe, someplace in Kansas. The flat fields seem to undulate like a sea until I get my land legs again and walk to the mess hall for some chow. I shovel scrambled eggs, biscuits, and bacon in but don't taste it. Some of the other passengers, sailors mostly, are larking around, but I sit moody as a statue. They leave me alone.

We sprawl waiting until the shiny plane is gassed up and ready to go. We file up the ladder and I notice a petty officer with a clipboard check off a name, look at a colonel apparently asking for transport, look at me, and shake his head. The colonel shrugs and walks away. Holy Toledo, that's scary. It must be serious when a lowly Specialist Third Class can have a higher priority than a bird colonel. What is the Red Cross not telling me? *Deus meus, adjuva me*, O God, help me. I settle myself against the dark, cold window and fall asleep.

Daddy has bought us a toboggan gleaming with varnish and the smell of brand-new. He loads it onto the top of the old blue Hudson and takes us to the snowy hills of Rouge Park. Bundled up so much I can hardly move, I clutch Michael's waist and bury my scarf-wrapped face into his sheepskin collar as we hurtle down the baby slope, spraying snow all the way. Michael couldn't stop it so we tip off at the end, rolling in the snow and laughing. We trudge back up to the very top of the hill, dragging the toboggan by its rope, our breath steaming and snow on our eyelashes. Daddy positions the toboggan again and shoves us off. Faster and faster we hurtle, the skinny barebranched trees blurring as we whip by. There's no way to stop. "Daddy, Daddy," I scream.

The cessation of motion wakes me. The baby-faced sailor next to me says, "You okay, mate?" I nod. "Plane's down for refueling. You prob'ly want to get off and use the can." Trust a sailor to put things delicately, but he's right. I do want to use the can. My face looks strange in the mirror in the head, puffy and streaked from where it pressed into the raincoat wrinkles. I splash cold water on it and comb my hair. Corman will kill me . . . after all her manicures and lectures, my fingernails are all bitten to the ugly quick again. Doggone.

One thing about emergency leave, you don't have to do anything, you just thrust out your papers and others make the arrangements. In a fog I hitch a ride in a Navy bus from the airport to the Book-Cadillac Hotel recruiting station to find Aunt Geraldine, looking grim but firmly in charge, waiting for me in her ancient Buick. "How's Daddy?"

"We're hoping for the best. It's his heart. He collapsed at the plant. I told Bernadette that he's been working too hard, not feeling well as he's been, but Joe's stubborn. I think men named Joseph tend to be. Stubborn as mules, all of them. You'll rue the day, I told Bernadette, you'll regret the day you marry a Joseph. Especially a Joseph Dermody. She was in love and wouldn't listen to me or dear Papa, God rest his soul. It almost killed her when she had Michael, but Joe insisted and she had you."

She came to with a start as she remembered me, the real live 1945 person, sagging next to her on the front seat of her Buick, half dead with fatigue and anxiety. It comes to me with a sadness, clear as a minstrel boy's lament—Aunt Geraldine is growing older, mixing up past and present just like Grandmother Scanlon had. I long to rest my droopy pageboy on her ample bosom but instead I sit up straight, my spine as perpendicular as any historical Scanlon woman and ask, "Does Michael know? Where is he, anyway?"

"He's somewhere in Europe. We couldn't reach him. The Red Cross is still trying."

Michael, where are you when I need you? You're older. You always took my hand when I was scared. Geraldine rattles on, ignoring the other drivers who honk their horns at her.

"Theodosia and Cecelia are with Bernadette at the hospital. Monsignor O'Callaghan comes often. Do you want to stop by the church first?"

"No, no, thank you." What good would that do? "No, thank you, Aunt Geraldine. I just want to wash up and to see Daddy right away." My white gloves are filthy and I automatically stuff them out of sight in my purse. I'll go to church later, maybe.

Daddy is asleep when I get to the hospital, white curtains drawn around his high white bed. The rosy-cheeked nursing sister with snow-white wimple pushes the curtains aside and whispers gently, "Mr. Dermody, Josette is here to surprise you."

He opens his eyes and says, "Kitten, where have you been?" He raises his right arm weakly, but it falls right back onto the cover and his eyes close.

"It's the medication," Mother says, squeezing my hand. "He's pleased you are here, I'm sure. How are you, Angel?"

"I'm okay, just need some sleep, that's all. What's going on? All the way here, nobody would tell me anything."

"It's his heart. Dr. Simpson says he may pull through, he has a strong constitution." What do they mean it's his heart? Did it break somehow? Wear out? Stop beating? Will it mend? How? Why doesn't anybody ever explain anything? Mother starts to weep a little just then, her spine bending like she really wants to curl up into a ball, she muffles her mouth and swollen nose with her sodden, lace-trimmed handkerchief. "Did you get anything to eat, Angel?"

"Affirmative. Yes. Aunt Geraldine made me oatmeal with maple syrup. What now?"

"We just wait. Wait and pray." She balls up her handkerchief and roots in her handbag for another. I give her mine, one of the many I have with green palm trees embroidered in the corner, Blackie must have a duffel bag full somewhere. Don't think of Blackie now. Death is a torpedo. Death is a bomb. Death is a sniper. Death is a plane crash. Death is a stillborn. Death is a heart attack. Living is waiting.

Wait we do, wait and pray for five days. The elderly, overworked doctors come and go, brushing off our questions. They keep Daddy asleep most of the time. On the sixth day we can see that Daddy has turned some sort of corner and begins to get better, his skin turning from gray to pinkish as he lies against the white pillows, but he's still asleep most of the time.

Buddy is staying with Aunt Theodosia, now that her Cornelius has joined the Coast Guard in spite of being barely old enough—there's room and ol' Buddy likes being with all the cousins. I prefer to stay at our house and try to take care of Mother. She stays at the hospital till they throw her out, then she comes home to sit in the rocker in the living room, chain-smoking Kools and staring into nothingness. I don't want to think what will happen to her if Daddy dies. All my life they have been there: Mother-n-Daddy, Bernadette-n-Joe. At least if I am there she makes an attempt to eat something—a little soup. I let Aunt Cecelia do the shopping though, I have forgotten what a pain it is with all the ration stamps and coupons.

Outside St. Joseph's Hospital who should I see but Sheila, wheeling her baby carriage toward me. I must stop and admire the miraculous Deirdre, wrapped like a slug in an ugly pink ombré crocheted coverlet. Owen's baby daughter, named for the beauteous Irish queen who captured King Conor's heart, is, if you must know, not the prettiest baby I have ever seen. A flat round face without much nose and little squinty eyes, maybe she will get prettier when she gets

older. She does have Sheila's auburn hair and her little curled fists
have dimples where the knuckles will be. Poor Sheila looks a little
the worse for wear, her lovely red hair all stringy, lint and spots all
over her royal blue dress. Sheila, how can you bear it? I'm thinking,
but she's actually glowing when she says, "Would you believe it, Josie,
this blessed child already claps her little hands when I show her the
picture of her father?"

"What do you hear from Owen, Sheila?" A shadow passes across
her delicately freckled face for a moment, but she erases it stoically.

"You know they can't write much, but his mother is sure he's in
Germany somewhere. Poor fellow, I do hope he's gotten the snapshots we sent of his child."

And his wife, I think. Dimbulb Owen is probably a big hit with the
hungry surviving ladies in Germany, with his chocolate bars and
C-rations and coffee from the PX, naturally no time to write home.
We can go to Germany after the war and see how many flat Irish
faces with little squinty eyes populate the villages of Bavaria. Stop it, I
scream to myself silently. What's happening to you? I can't intervene
between him and Sheila. I can't tell Sheila about Blackie dodging
shore patrols or torpedoes and pursuing dusky damsels in the Pacific,
I can't tell her anything anymore. She's got a husband and a baby
and I don't know anything at all about that. I want to holler.

Instead I lean over the perambulator to coo at the innocent Irish
Beauty, but just then she spits up. The smell of sour milk overwhelms
me, I almost swoon. Yipes, when and if I ever have babies they will
smell sweetly of talcum powder and warmth like Aunt Theodosia's
babies all do. I straighten up and brush off the front of my uniform,
swipe at the back of it, readjust my garrison cap, which had almost
fallen into the carriage, and say, "Nice to see you again, Sheila. If my
dad wasn't so sick I would have time to visit. That's some baby you've
got there. Bye."

When I look back from the top of the worn steps of St. Joseph's,
Sheila is adjusting the baby's blankets.

So preoccupied am I that I don't listen to the radio, it's as though
the world outside the hospital room has ceased to exist. I can even
smell hospital as I curl up in my white spool bed for fitful sleep every
night. So I am really surprised when Buddy comes whooping home
on his bicycle, yelling like an air-raid siren, "Sis, Sis, Josie, turn on the

radio." All arms and legs, he clatters across the living room and turns it on himself. "The war is over. Eisenhower says so. The Germans have surrendered. Un-con-dition-ally. Quit. We beat them. Kapow!" He throws a roundhouse in the air. "Michael will be coming home."

He's right. Not about Michael coming home, exactly, but the war in Europe is over. The announcers are almost sputtering with excitement as they describe the dancing in the streets all over the Allied world. "The lights are turned on again all over Europe!" Norman Corwin is saying. It's pretty hard to believe that it's actually over Over There but it must have been inevitable after Hitler committed suicide. I wonder where Michael is—probably dead drunk celebrating somewhere, which is lots better than dead somewhere.

Daddy is well enough that the hospital contingent of aunts can take a break and listen to the celebrations over the radio; all the cousins, uncles, and neighbors within reach gather in Aunt Geraldine's overstuffed living room around her big console. Trumpet fanfares blare out of the speaker triumphantly. "So, they've given up," the narrator says, "the rat is dead in an alley back of the Wilhelmstrasse . . . take a bow, GI . . . this is the day."

We can hear the crowds whooping it up, cheering and singing in Times Square, the Loop, Piccadilly . . . all over. Someone is singing about bluebirds in a high, trilling voice. One thing about peace, we won't have to hear that dopey song much longer. What's with me? I'm glad everybody is so happy, but don't they know the war is still going on in the Pacific? V-E Day is only the first half. We still have to get the Japs off Okinawa and invade Japan. Are you listening to the same broadcasts I am, Blackie, sitting somewhere in the tropic sun with your shirt off, drinking warm beer? I do wish you were safe and sound right next to me, grinning your crooked grin and cracking jokes.

The announcer is asking, "What have we learned? We've learned out of World War II that we learned nothing out of World War I. We've learned that freedom isn't something to be won and then forgotten . . . it must be rewound like a faithful clock . . . What do we do now? Why, the war goes on . . ." There's a lot more, a long prayer about the Lord God of Trajectory and Blast . . . Personally, it seems to me that the announcer is getting out of control, but I keep my thoughts to myself. Trajectory and Blast?

Monsignor O'Callaghan insists on having a *Te Deum* at the church, even if we do have another whole half of a war to finish. I'm glad to be there in my uniform, I thank God for keeping Michael and Arvid and Blackie safe and pray that they will be home soon. Thank you, God, for making Daddy better. Thank you, God.

I'm still in the service and my leave is up. Daddy is propped up and eating gruel when I go to say goodbye. He looks so thin and pathetic, the lines on his face so deep I could weep, but the doctors say he is going to get better. He must be getting better because he is mad at me. "Can't wait to leave your old dad," he glowers and gesticulates with his spoon. "Take off that monkey suit and stay here where you belong. Never should ha' let you go, megirl."

"Oh, Daddy, you know I've got orders. When you gotta go, you gotta go." I'm feeling more than a little guilty about leaving him, but there isn't much good I can really do by staying. He's going to be all right, the doctors say so, they should know.

"Don't get smart with me, young lady. Your mother needs you here. Tell the consarned Navy so." He flops back against the white pillows, exhausted by his outburst.

"No can do. Sorry. Duration and six months. You know that." My voice comes out in a tiny squeak. I gotta get out of here. "Goodbye, Daddy. Take care of yourself." I lean over and peck him on his stubbly cheek, flash Mother a V for Victory sign and walk quickly past the crucifixes in the lobby, out past the flowerbeds in front where the red and yellow tulips are dancing in the breeze, to where Aunt Teddy and little Victor are waiting in Geraldine's Buick to drive me to the Navy pickup station.

"Joe is so proud of you, Josette. He brags about you and Michael all the time at the war plant, I hear from Packy. Take care of yourself and don't forget to write. Victor, let go of Josette's purse strap so she can get out of the car."

I ride back in the same plane, but this time it is bucking a headwind all the way. Bucking and bucking. Some sailor I turn out to be, barfing continuously for 1,700 miles. The other passengers, sailors mostly, are airsick, too. They spend their time in between upchucks yarning about various seasick remedies that they swear work like a charm: Don't eat anything is one; don't drink anything but tea; never, never drink tea or coffee; eat only crackers; eat often, keep the stomach full; I quit listening and try to ignore the turbulence of the plane and the turbulence of my feelings. The plane bucks bravely into the storm, the propellers singing to me: 21—you will be 21 soon—soon— soon you can do what you want when you are 21. 21, 21, 21.

When I get back to Treasure Island things seem pretty much the same. The bay is full of ships, looks like they are already transferring stuff to the Pacific for the Big Push people talk about all the time. I have three letters from Blackie in my mailbox, two out-of-date V-mails from Michael. He's in Germany, there's a picture of him by the Brandenburg Gate before they blew off those awful gigantic swastikas on the top, which means that he at least passed through Berlin. A letter from Griffin, haven't heard from her since boot camp, who says she ran into Petrelli at the Waves quarters in Washington. Griffin says that she and her farmboy Marine are getting married at the VA hospital just as soon as he gets his casts off. Wonder whatever happened to Whatzizname, the rat-faced pest in New York? Do I care?

Corman is actually twittery with excitement about her Jack getting out of his stuffy battered tank at last and coming stateside right soon. Jenson is paler and quieter than ever, Atkinson says she's glad to see me, our volleyball players made the playoffs. I'm glad to see everyone. Chief grunts something about things had never been run better than when I was away. "Your dad okay?"

"Affirmative. Okay."

Coralee Tolliver is the only one who has changed. She's in love. Really in love. Besotted. I can't believe it.

CHAPTER 21

True Love

Never had Tolliver made any bones about her plans to catch herself an officer and live on Easy Street the rest of her life, but none of us, I don't think, ever believed *she* believed it would really happen. While I was home she met this guy from Maryland at a Ship's Company jitterbug contest at the Rec Center, but instead of her catching him she got caught, entrapped, pierced by Cupid's arrow herself. Not only is he a lieutenant, he's a pilot, silver wings on his chest and the golden-god posture to boot. He flies the big seaplanes in the air-sea rescue operations that fly out of Western Sea Command on our island. Dashing, that's a good word to describe Connery Caddo McLeod, naturally called C.C. by some and Mac by others.

First thing she does is show me his picture; all he needs is a white silk scarf and he can give a whole lot of handsome Hollywood heroes a run for their money. He has the pale, bony face, a movie hero's rugged face, with freckles and deep-set blue eyes under a broad smooth forehead. His large white teeth gleam in his tanned grin, his sandy reddish hair is shaved short. Skinny, but not too, just right to show off his flyer's whites. Like so many of our guys, he looks just past the gangly stage where the wristbones stick out below the sleeves. Now he's learned about tailors and his whites are dazzling, like he has been cleaned in pipe clay from head to foot.

C.C. is a nice young man, Mother would be enchanted by his manners. He spends his working days, sometimes nights, plucking the unlucky from the clutches of Davy Jones' locker and has the appropriate down-home "aw shucks, 'twasn't anything," reaction. How nice, but we have a Navyfull. Can someone tell me what kind of joke it is, by whoever is in charge of these things for Protestants (can't blame Saint Catherine for this one), to have Tolliver fall in love with a Ca-ath-o-lick, one right back there with Lord Baltimore and all those guys wearing doilies around their necks, those Cavaliers?

Right in front of our eyes, Missy Tolliver is turning from sassy to fluttery. You'd think she's Miss Melanie all over again, confronted with an Ashley Wilkes and Rhett Butler in the same human form. Let me tell you, it's not so easy to flutter in a trim and tailored Waves uniform, she should have a parasol and false eyelashes. Instead she moons around, covering endless sheets of paper with purple ink. Mrs. C. C. McLeod. Coralee McLeod. Coralee Tolliver McLeod. Lt. and Mrs. Connery Caddo McLeod. Mrs. C. C. McLeod.

"When's the wedding, pal?" I ask her on Tuesday after work. We are in the topside lounge, catching each other up on all the scuttlebutt.

"He says he's not the marrying kind." She sounds sad.

"That's what they all say." I can't believe my own ears, what they all say? Where is this knowledge coming from? Me, of all people. I forge on fearlessly, "You've got it bad, huh?"

"Who, me?"

"I can't believe it. A Catholic. A mackerel eater. Tolliver, how come? You want I should start a novena for you . . . I could write my cousin Consuelo and she can get the whole entire convent working on . . ." I stop teasing when I see her face. She's looking like she's about to tear up.

"He wants me to go to the Russian River with him this weekend."

"So?"

"So."

"So. You didn't say you would, did you? Holy Toledo, Tolliver, you know if you go, you'll never see him again."

"So, I'm no angel. I'm no baby. Get off my back, Dermody. You think you know so much."

"So. I know you like this guy a lot, for some strange reason. He won't respect you if you go to some hotel in Guerneville or somewhere with him. All the other guys will know, for one thing. How can you?"

"So he caught me in a weak moment, Miss Know-it-all Priss."

"So, tell him you changed your mind, dummy."

"I can't do that. He knows I've got liberty."

"Just don't go, whatever you tell him. Just don't go."

"You're so original, Dermody. You make me sick." She looks so pitiful instead of mad.

"This is the time to trust your old Cath'lick buddy, pal. *Don't-go-with-C. C.-to-the-Russian-River-this-weekend.* Don't go. This is a test."

Corman has walked in to borrow some bobbypins and says, "She's probably right, you know, Coralee. Maybe you need to come down with a strep throat or something, honeychile."

"You're all such a bunch of liars, I hate you all."

C.C., furious, asks an adenoidal civilian girl named Estelle, who had set her cap for him, to go instead. Navy flyboys are never known for shilly-shallying and C.C. didn't waste any time. When Tolliver finds out she is ready to kill. Estelle. Him. Me. Herself. Everybody.

"Calm down," I soothe. "He'll be back." She's lying face down on her lower bunk, sobbing and yowling, kicking her heels around, totally demolishing her perfect square corners on her blue coverlet with the woven-in fouled anchor.

"You don't know nothing, dummy. I hate you. I wanna die. How could you do this to me?"

"Trust me, trust your old Auntie Josette. He'll be back." I sound more sure of myself than I really am, but I hand her a wet washrag for her tear-swollen eyes and a tissue for her nose. Maybe someday I'll be as wise as Corman about these things, but now I have my fingers and toes crossed.

Hah. Turns out I am right for once. Three weeks after the lost weekend, right before poor Tolliver almost pines herself to death, C.C. takes her to the Palm Court at the Palace and proposes. He's so pleased with himself when she accepts, after thinking it over for about ten seconds, that he stands champagne all around. Both of them act like nobody ever was in love before, like nobody ever got engaged before, like all the soppy love songs in the world are for real.

As usual, she is mooning and sighing around the gunshed, dreamily turning her left hand this way and that so that every errant sunbeam that hits her engagement ring fractures into a rainbow, a cascade of bright sparkles, when Jackson, who has finally made Gunner's Mate Third Class and is shipping out at last, comes by to say goodbye. Tolliver hardly notices him. He comes right up to her, opening and closing his hand like he is a signal light on a ship: R-E-Q-U-E-S-T C-O-N-F-I-R-M-A-T-I-O-N Y-O-U S-I-G-N-A-L-E-D W-E H-A-V-E S-M-A-L-L-P-O-X A-B-O-A-R-D D-O Y-O-U N-E-E-D D-O-C-T-O-R Q-U-E-R-Y R-E-P-L-Y. Instead of laughing, as he expects, she bursts into tears and falls on his neck.

"Jackson, I never thought I would be this happy in my whole entire life. I'm gonna miss you, Jackson." She's blubbering all over his dress blue jumper.

He backs off and smacks her a hearty one on her plump shoulder. "You'll get used to it, mate. Folks say you can get used to anything, even happiness, I guess." He turns to shake hands with the Chief and the rest of us. He never lets on that once upon a time he had been a little sweet on her himself, he just picks up his seabag and leaves. Good luck, Jackson.

Tolliver is so happy she hardly bothers to fight with me when we go to town for my birthday. Twenty-one is such a special birthday. Now I can vote, now I can sign things for myself, now I'm a full-fledged citizen of the best country in the world. Course, ol' Tolliver continues to tease me about the shore patrol guy who almost ran me in, and she just can't seem to let me alone about Blackie, but her heart isn't in it.

When we get to Pasquale's and slide into the red artificial leather banquettes, the elderly waiter shuffles up and hands us the enormous leather-bound menus. He smiles diffidently. "Bon appetit, ladies. Nozzing iz too good for our sailor girls tonight. Maybe you know my grandson, Bronko. He iss hon the Hew Hess Hess *Phoenix*."

"Good ship," I say automatically. What other kind do we have? "I don't know anybody on her. Sorry."

Tolliver gives me a good poke on the arm. "You don't know the *Phoenix* from a hole in the water, Miss Priss." I ignore her and say, "Let's order. I'm starving." We all pick steak, even if it is $1.75. A celebration is a celebration and besides it is only three days after payday.

While we sip our French 75s from the wide-mouthed champagne glasses, Atkinson asks, "Did Blackie send you an engagement ring?"

"Negative. He sent me a pint of White Shoulders, if you must know. He got it at the Ship's Service in Pearl." I don't need to mention the mushy "To My Sweetheart" card that came with it.

"A pint. He must like the way it smells. He must like you a lot," Atkinson says, between spoonfuls of minestrone.

"I hear the Seabees use that stuff, that White Shoulders, for paint remover." Tolliver grins at me, then attacks her mashed potatoes and gravy.

"I'm going to kill you some day, Tolliver, just you wait." I know by this time that I won't, but she sure does get on my nerves.

"You gotta be sure it's true love, that's for sure." She looks so smug. "I'm not sure Blackie is the lad for windy weather. I'll let you know, pal, when I find it, if I find it."

Corman interrupts by handing me a package of notepaper with ARMED GUARD CENTER TREASURE ISLAND printed on the top. Tolliver produces a little blue leatherette manicure kit. Blue, blue, blue, everything is Navy blue nowadays.

"Thanks, Coralee. That's really sweet. Now that I'm a big girl I can stop biting my nails." She bites hers worse'n me, but I don't mention it. Atkinson gives me a pair of rayon stockings—can always use another pair. Wonder if they remember it's my birthday at home? Maybe the mail is just held up. Dontcha know there's a war on?

The lights in the restaurant go out and the waiter brings in the cake with little sparks of golden light cascading in showers. Everybody in the whole place sings the birthday song. For me. Well done, megirl. You made it to 21.

June—you'd think of a month with roses and hydrangeas and tiger lilies blooming under sunny blue skies, wouldn't you? Ha. Negative. We have clouds, we have fog, we have more clouds, we have more fog. Foghorns day and night. Treasure Island in June is like living inside a box stuffed with damp gray cotton batting. Once in a while the sun will come out and hit the fog at sunset—the Glory Hallelujah streaks of gold shoot off every which way and anyone can see why those old explorers named the opening to the bay the Golden Gate. Some days you could almost believe the Day of Judgment is at hand, so much does the world look like the mosaic in our chapel that has our Lord floating on just such a cloud of glory. No such luck, it's just an ordinary California day in a war that goes on forever. The bay fills with ships, the bay empties. Japan is out there waiting for us on the other side of the Pacific.

Here, boring is the name of it all. Same old gunsheds, same old chill, same sailors, getting younger as I get older, clumping through the gunsheds to shoot at the same old raggedy films that had been taped together a million times. Same old jokes, not funny ones, but the mean stupid kind guys make about women. We've heard them all, most of the time we don't even listen. At least we have the satisfaction of watching things fall flat when the clown fails to get any reaction from us. His joker buddies guffaw, of course. Wouldn't you think they would get tired of the jokes? You'd think they'd get tired of each other. It's easy to get tired of sailors, let me tell you. What would you do if you were one and got tired of yourself? I wonder what Blackie would say to that? I wish he would turn up so I could ask him. I don't know where he is. I don't like to think about it . . . maybe he is near Okinawa with the typhoons and the kamikazes. C'mon, megirl, he's probably safe in a brig somewhere. Why am I worrying? I just am, that's all.

There's a notice on the bulletin board at the Rec Center promising those lucky ladies who sign up in time a trip to Yosemite. Welfare and Recreation must have noticed that we are all getting more than tired of the fog and the dank gunsheds, losing enthusiasm for working with their raunchy sailors, their trigger-happy Marines, and their chickenshit officers. The only good thing that has happened in the last month, aside from Tolliver's engagement and my birthday, was that the German prisoners are gone. Just like that, one day here, strutting around in their perfect squares and squads, the next day gone. Probably they will be exchanged now that they have lost for sure. Good riddance. I can't bear to look at the pictures coming out of Europe of the skeleton-people survivors or the piles of dead bodies on carts in the concentration camps our guys are liberating from the Germans in Europe. Who can believe things like that? Worse than the illustrations in the Dante book about hell that always scared the bejabbers out of me when I was a kid.

Anyway, we can all use a change. I don't hesitate to sign my name, Tolliver's, Corman's, Atkinson's, Jenson's, Littlejohn's, even Amaretti's, that funny little radioman in Jenson's cubicle. Dispatch. That's Navy. Act with dispatch. Sort it out later. Then I go to meet Corman in the workroom behind the library.

\She looks up from the table cluttered with paper, ink, glue, and scissors. "Well, look at you, honeychile. A regular little ray of sunshine this evening. Something happen? Don't tell me. Let me guess—you drew duty in Hawaii? No? You got a letter from Blackie and he proposed."

"Negative." I look at Corman, who has a wisp of blonde hair hanging down over one eye. She blows it away. She has changed lately, gotten a lot quieter and more distracted somehow. It's as though the weight of so many fiancés in so many dangerous places is weighing

her down. We keep expecting her to perk up and be our own Corman again. This war is changing everybody.

"You know, honeychile, you'll be sor-ree if you keep on with Blackie.
You're not thinking of marrying him, are you?"

"What have you got against Blackie?" I say, surprised. "Everybody is
always giving me a hard time because I don't encourage him enough.
I thought you liked him. To answer your question, he hasn't exactly
asked me to marry him."

"Slow down. I don't have anything against him. He's one of those
sailors who has a girl in every port. They're exciting, but they never
change. You two don't have a thing in common."

"But, but . . ."

She's not finished. "You should be able to tell that, smart girl like
you. You probably just like the way he kisses or whatever." She is sitting there with her pen poised, her pink tongue poking out of the
corner of her mouth. She's India-inking cartoons for the *Masthead,*
our base paper. I crane my neck to see what she is working on.

"No whatever," I blush. "I'm saving myself for when I get married."
I change the subject. "That's not my news. I just signed us all up for a
trip to 'Yose-might.' What's that? I just saw those magic words 'weekend trip' and signed us all up. I think it's just Waves."

"Well done, Comrade. 'Yo-sem-i-tay' is a park in the mountains
south of here. Nice to see something besides greasy water for a
change. How do you like this one?" She points with her pen to a
drawing of a very fat short sailor with a halfmoon gap between his
jumper and the thirteen buttons on his trousers. She prints under it
"Turret Tummey."

"Pretty good, you can draw better'n you can spell. I like this one,
the one you call 'Glamour Boy.'" Corman has drawn him in skin-
tight blues with a zipper from his armpit to his waist and pants so
tight he couldn't sit down. He has one foot on a bar rail and his profile turned so everybody can admire it.

"Well, somebody has to do one to answer that cartoon they had in
last week about the Treasure Island Waves." She indicates the copy of
the paper turned to the page of wicked cartoons of Waves, the long
and the short and the tall, as the song goes. The homely and the
glamorous. A buck-toothed chinless Wave with sparse, spiky hair has
a balloon that says "She enlisted for love or lack of it." Another prettier Wave has her nose in the air as she strides along. The balloon

says "The hoity-toity type. If it rained, she'd drown." Another shows a
chunky Wave with her arms up like a triumphant boxer with the cap-
tion "Miss Judo, or the pride of Mud Flats Orange Juice Club." There
are about a dozen more, some of them kinda cute, drawn with the
exaggerated bosoms and tight waists you'd expect. Corman's pencil
is quickly drawing "Our Ideal" for the centerpiece, a pop-eyed, pin-
headed, jug-eared guy with a real stupid look on his face. I have to
laugh. "Corman, you really are awful, but it's funny. Now you'll be
famous, published right in there with the movie listings and the
church notices and all the terrible jokes."

"We all have to do our part," she says as she screws the top back
onto the India ink bottle and starts gathering everything up. "It just
so happens that I am both bee-yoo-ti-ful and talented." That's our
girl.

It's foggy as ever when we get back to Treasure Island, but it
doesn't seem so bad. All that fresh air, huge trees, and breathtaking
mountains, all right for a weekend, but I'm no Indian maiden. Atkinson, that's a different story. She confides her secret desire; says she is
going to marry a park ranger and live in the woods all of her life.
Can you imagine? Stuck out in some cabin a million miles from
nowhere? She's not telling us everything, but we can wait. She's been
getting a lot of letters, sometimes two in one day, from somebody
named Forrest somewhere in Germany. He's probably someone she
knew before. Are we supposed to believe Forrest is a forest ranger?
Maybe we are. My aunts would say, "Josette, megirl, you never can tell
about people." Love is in the air, seems like, for everybody.

Blackie calls me from San Raphael—his beloved rustbucket Victory ship has docked. I barely have time to wash my hair and steam
my dress blues before someone is yelling down the corridor, "Der-
mod-dee! Man waiting!" My hands are shaking so I can't get the ends
of my butterfly tie even. I whip the knot out three times before Corman takes pity on me and ties it precisely.

"Don't be such a fidget, honeychile. You remind me of that old
Navy song 'I need a guy to tie my tie . . . '" She tweaks the ends of the
tie and pats it under my lapel. "My grandmother always says," here
she drops into an exaggerated syrupy voice, "a gentleman caller will
think a lady is entirely too eager for his company if she is ready when
he calls."

"JesusMaryandJoseph, Corman. You and your grandmother. That sweet old gal has more rules than the Twelfth Naval District." I grab my newly buffed purse and start to leave, but Corman, laughing, blocks my way till she hands me a pair of spanking white gloves. Doggone. If I ever get out of this consarned Navy I'm going to start a whole new fashion for ladies: bare hands, blood-red nail polish, lots of rings and bracelets. I grab the gloves and push past. "See you later, kiddo."

Blackie, whip-thin and lithe, darker than ever from being in the sun so much, his crooked grin whiter and more dazzling than I remember, chases away all the tiredness I feel about sailors in general when I see him. He is leaning against the bulkhead, nonchalantly flirting with the MAA just to pass the time. She's ignoring him pointedly as she puts mail into the mail slots on the wall behind the desk. He unwinds himself casually when I come through the swinging door. Can't look *too* eager, I remind myself. "Hi, Toots." He grins his little-boy grin and raises one eyebrow quizzically.

"Nope. No way. Didn't get engaged or anything while you were away, just in case you were about to ask. Tolliver did, though. You'll never guess who to."

"You and me gotta lot of catching up to do. Let's go get some chow." He grabs my hand, making tingles go all the way to my shoulder, and pulls me out of the barracks. He acts like he wants to kiss me on the steps outside, but I won't let him, not with the shore patrol watching. Imagine. In broad daylight. I'd die before I'd have one of those SP guys smirking at me, watching while I turn into goo. Wait till later, megirl.

Sea stories: about storms and fights, the girls in the South Seas with the big knockers, buddies. Sea stories, a screen for things guys don't want to talk about unless they are good and drunk; guns and smoke, fire in the paint locker, magazines blowing up, death raining down from the sky or sucking people into the sea, bloody bodies, noise, heat, the smell of death. I have trouble looking at the newsreels when I know it is all censored and measured for me. What must it be like to be there, with no escape? Not to talk about it now. He's stateside, safe for now, scrubbed, shaved, barbered, poured into illegal, skin-tight tailor-mades, wallet bulging with sea pay and gambling winnings, ready for a nice stateside meal served on tablecloths in the Shadows on Telegraph Hill, with a nice, clean stateside girl to listen

wide-eyed to sea stories. Blackie's stories were funny ones; tricks they
played on the Old Man, foul-ups in communication that made for
massive snafus. Stories about fights; it seems if Blackie can't get his
hands on the Japs he will take on anybody: Marines, Mexicans, Limeys,
Aussies. AWOL tales where they didn't get caught, one time he did
and they busted him back to coxswain again. He gets busted so often,
usually for fighting, he just keeps two jumpers in his seabag, one with
a coxswain rating and the other with two chevrons under the embroidered crossed anchors for when he is a bosun.

As I listen, my mind drifts, I'm hearing his words but not really,
I'm breathing the fragrance of frangipani, watching the Southern
Cross wheel around the velvet Pacific sky, watching the dolphins
dance in the phosphorescent wake. By the time the waiter brings the
chocolate cake (where did the Shadows get the sugar?) and ice
cream, he's running down a little. He leans back in his chair and
says, "I sure like your new garrison hat, 'sbettern those old white
upside-down pots you had before. You're looking good, Toots."

I smile, hoping I can look mysterious, like Gene Tierney in all
those movies. Actually, I'm not feeling good-looking or even mysterious. All the Noxema in the world doesn't seem to have any effect on
the whiteheads on my forehead, all my uniform skirts are too tight,
by the time I get out of this Navy I will be oldandfat. What can I do
but smile? No fair complaining to someone who just got back from
Out There. Blackie is looking at me with his quizzical look.

"Howsabout it, do you want to go or dontcha?"

"Do I want to go where? Sorry, I was thinking about something
else." Daddy's right to call me a daydreamer. One of my besetting
sins, as they say.

"I just ast you if you wanted to go sailing with me over'n Oakland.
Buddy of mine says they rent dinghies there. I can teach you to be a
real sailor."

I lean back in my chair and laugh so hard I start crying. The head-
waiter looks over at us with a worried look on his triangular face.
Blackie comes around and whacks me a good one on my shoulder.
He hands me a glass of water. I swallow a couple of sips and wipe
tears from the corner of my eyes. Blackie is looking at me with his
"I'll-never-understand-dames-but-you-gotta-put-up-with-'em" look. He
waits for me to regain my powers of speech. "Sorry, Blackie. Of course
I would love to go sailing with you. Not in these heels, though." An-

other paroxysm shakes me. He looks like he's really getting exasperated. "Tomorrow?"

"Can do. We ain't leaving till Tuesday." I put my finger to his lips
and indicate the hovering waiter. "Oh, hell," he says, his face darken-
ing dangerously, "Tokyo Rose always knows where our ships are before our friggin' brass makes up their friggin' mind. 'Scuse the French.
What's so funny?" He looks baffled.

I think of all the cartoons of sailors taking their girls rowing in
Central Park and almost start to laugh again. "It's so funny, you know,
you just get back from sea duty and you want to go *sailing*.
Tomorrow's Sunday—1100 okay? 1300 better?"

"1300, affirmative. You dames is nuts."

Life is so symmetrical sometimes. So are sailors, I would say.

CHAPTER 22

Toot, Toot, Tootsie

Blackie's buddy is right. They do rent dinghies by the hour at Lake Merritt; the size of large rowboats, they have a mast, a triangular sail, a tiller, and appropriate ropes, even if I'd never dare call them ropes. The sky-blue paint is flaking off both the two boats that are left by the time we get there, both cockpits awash with a thin scum of brackish water, but we pick the cleaner one and Blackie leaves his ID with the grizzled old guy in the baggy pants who runs the boat concession by the rickety dock.

It's a fine day, and Lake Merritt is a pretty place. Oak-land has such a pretty name, but most of the flatland we pass on the train after we come over the bridge from TI doesn't seem to have any trees at all, just ugly, dark-green shingled flats, foreign-looking churches with steeples that look like onions on top, factories and warehouses, lots of shipyards and docks, with miles and miles of gray hulls, superstructures sticking up into the air all pointy. It's prettier up in the hills where Oak Knoll Hospital is, maybe they even have some oaks up there, but you don't catch me by any hospital voluntarily. Thank the good Lord for small favors, I didn't end up a hospital corpsman. I would be so terrible at it. All those hurt guys. I shiver.

Lots of people are out enjoying the beautiful Sunday, bicycling around the path or picnicking on the grass. Whole families, not like 'Frisco, where all you see is service guys and their girls. On the way to the dock Blackie had stopped to throw a ball back to a fat little blond kid about four years old. The boy's eyes got wide and then merry as he chased the ball; when he caught it he turned and saluted Blackie smartly. Blackie returned the salute. "You'd think," he said, almost as though he was talking to himself, "you'd think that all you would miss at sea would be dames. Naturally, you miss dames but geezt, you know you never see any kids. No old people, neither." I squeezed his hand and he squeezed back.

We cast off, and as the steady, light breeze bellies out the little patched sail we fly across the lake. We can't be going very fast, but fast enough to stream my hair out behind my head like a figurehead on a clipper ship. The trouble is the lake is so small that we have to tack all the time. Fly along, come about, fly along, come about, don't jibe, don't get dizzy. Blackie, true to his promise to make a real sailor out of me, puts his arms around me, with his brown hand over my paler one on the tiller. Can't say I mind—and I don't feel it necessary to mention that Sheila's Uncle Harvey, the rich one, had taught us all a little sailing back home on Lake St. Clair. There really isn't room aft for both of us and the tiller, it's easier to take turns. He moves to the seat amidships and sits facing me. He's wearing just his bell-bottoms and his skivvy shirt, which looks too small but shows off all the muscles in his shoulders and chest. He really is a cute guy.

"Starboard! Starboard!" he shouts. I put the tiller over. "Thought for a minute you was gonna drive us right up onto the grass." I just look at him, every time you get a guy in a boat he immediately turns into Captain Bligh. Let's change the subject along with the tack.

"Blackie, can I ask you something?"

"Fire away." He turns to scan the upcoming shore, "you're luffing, trim her to port. Whaddya wanna know?"

"How come you're not like the other guys? You never try anything . . . you know? Nothing serious, I mean." A little necking now and then doesn't count.

"Want me to?" He grins, scratches his chest.

"Stay where you are. I was just wondering. Tolliver had a terrible time with Whatzisname, C.C., him wanting her to go to the Russian River with him for a weekend, every time somebody in the barracks is late we all worry . . ." my voice trails off. Why did I start this dumb conversation, anyway?

"No sweat, Toots. I just go to Market Street and find a girl after I get you back in time." He's earnest with explanation.

I don't think I am hearing right, but of course I am. I'm not so dumb that I don't know about the prophylactic station by the bridge, even though the shore patrol always tries to position themselves so as to block the sign when we Waves come by. I must be looking bewildered. He continues, "'Way it is, there's three kinds of people. Men, women, and the other kind of women." Now here is a concept they never explained much at St. Aloysius'. There, if you wanted to know what a harlot was, even if it is in the Bible, you never asked anybody. No-siree-bob, you quietly looked it up in the big dictionary in the library, but that never told you much. I sit up, rigid with interest to learn about the Real World.

"You mean, you mean—you have a date with a prostitute after you bring me home?" I feel my mouth opening and closing like a gaffed fish.

He grins at the word "date," his maddeningly innocent choirboy grin. "Sure, Toots. All the guys do, that saves the nice girls for when we want to marry them." He shrugs, holding his hands out palms forward in a what-can-you-expect gesture. I'm not sure what to say, what to do, and the sheet rattles through my nerveless hand, the sail flaps free. Blackie makes a lunge for the sheet and misses. How do you stop this consarned thing? I throw the tiller over hard and Blackie ker-splashes into the drink, almost swamping us with a huge wave of not-so-clean water.

My whole life flashes in front of my eyes, even though I am not the person who is drowning. My life has been so dull lately that I haven't been able to find anything to make an Act of Contrition for—now this will probably make the papers back home. The *Detroit News* will headline LOCAL GIRL HELD IN INVESTIGATION BY NAVY, the *Free Press* will say NORTHWEST WAVE DROWNS LOVER IN CALIF. LAKE—CLAIMS ACCIDENT. You know how they always exaggerate, he's not really my lover, even if I do love him. Do I? I wobble wildly, trying to think what to do, but nobody has ever taught me the "Man Overboard Drill." I stand up to look for him and almost capsize. I plunk down on the wildly rocking seat. He's gonna kill me, I think irrationally. No, I've killed him. Oh God, what have I done?

Blackie grabs the gunnel behind me. He's looking sheepish, actually more like a big old Labrador surfacing, his curly black hair all slicked back and dripping, his dogtags hanging down his back. "It ain't deep," he spits out water with his words. He starts rocking the dinghy wildly like he is trying to hurl me in, too, but I hang onto the gunnel for dear life and give him my best "Don't you dare" look. He pushes the boat back the 300 yards to the sailboat house and glares at the gap-toothed old guy, who grins and makes cracks about calling the Coast Guard. I think Blackie is going to deck the old guy; good thing he doesn't, he'd kill him. I've never seen anybody so mad. I mean, small boats are what bosuns *do*. Blackie ducks into the park head to wring out and dry off. I sit on the nearby bench with all the lovers' initials scratched inside hearts into the thick layers of paint— parks and romance do seem to go together.

One part of me is still enjoying the lovely Sunday summer after- noon, the sunlight making dustmotes dance as the shouting kids scuff up the ocher paths with their little sandals; another part is feel- ing guilty. Sort of. If any of Blackie's buddies ever find out he went into the drink from a rinkydink dinghy on a little bitty lake in a park, he'll never hear the end of it. Most of those buddies have the sensi- bilities of a brass monkey, once they get ahold of something they never let go, oh dear. Maybe they won't ever find out. A whole 'nother part of me is wondering who decides which are the set-aside bunch of maidens that our heroes can marry and which are the others who are there for their convenience? Once upon a time I might have an- swered that the pope did, but people don't seem to consult him about every little thing here like they do back home in St. Aloysius' parish. Did anybody ever ask me whether I enjoy being in the corral of eligible virgins for marrying purposes, while maybe the gals on Market Street were having all the fun all this time? Or is it just the sailors who are having all the fun? This is fair? How can I find out? Can I change my fate?

Blackie comes out of the head, wrinkled and damp, but basically in uniform. He doesn't say anything, I don't dare ask him if he thinks I dunked him on purpose. Did I? Didn't I? He's angry: silent-mad, glaring-mad, don't-say-anything-to-me-mad, I-don't-want-to-talk-about- it-mad; he hails a Navy jeep with a timid four-eyed pharmacist's mate at the wheel and makes the guy drive us to the station. The medic zooms through the quiet summer Sunday streets, determined to get rid of us as soon as possible before he has to admit Blackie's scaring him. He's scaring me, too, but I start breathing again when his face lightens and he relaxes a little. "Nobody'd ever believe it," he grins. "C'mon, Toots, let's get you back on time. Howsabout some Chinese food first?"

As soon as my head hits the pillow that night my aunts are all there. Some nights it just doesn't pay to go to sleep. To sleep, to dream. Blackie had dropped me off, looking more bedraggled than roman- tic, but in charge of himself basically. He just punched me a buddy blow on the chin and said, "See ya, Toots." Is that the same as Sayonara? He didn't even tell me not to get engaged or nothin'. You really did it this time, megirl.

They are grouped around a microphone, like so many overage Andrews Sisters. Aunt Geraldine has a pitchpipe, she sounds the note, and her sisters harmonize—"Don't make my girl a sailor, the weeping mother said . . ." Right on cue Mother lifts the teensy veil attached to her hat and delicately pokes at her eyes with a lace-edged hanky. Aunt Cecelia, looking tiddlier than usual, puts her arm around Mother on the one side while Aunt Teddy, looking pink and pregnant (oh no, not again, Theodosia), leans on the other side. Their voices blend. "A man in every lake is not—not—not the life she learned from me . . ."

I am standing pigeon-toed, looking up at the microphone. I'm wearing my Shirley Temple dress with the polka dots that sticks out all around. "You aren't really the Andrews Sisters," I pout, my finger poked into my cheek alongside my dimple.

"Don't be, Don't be *impertinent*. Don't be *impertinent. Impertinent. Impertinent,*" they wail. I tap dance out of the room, nobody pays any attention. Aunt Geraldine sounds another note on her pipe. Why did I ever let them go to boot camp with me? I am in despair. I cover my hands with my ears and run away, but I can still hear them.

"Don't do that ship sailing down the bay one, I hate that one." They don't. Worse.

"Bell bottom trousers, coat of Navy blue, she can climb the rigging like her Daddy used to do . . .

"To do—

"To do, to do-oo—oo—oo."

The dream is so silly it wakes me up. Silly old aunts. Silly songs. I lie in my bunk cocoon half awake, listening to the rustles and breathing of the people in the bunks around me, so familiar and comforting after a demented dream. I haven't told anybody about Blackie falling overboard, just said that sailing was fine and dandy. It was pretty funny, but guys never like people laughing at them. Even if I never see him again, there's no point in having everybody laughing at him. Something has changed somehow, I don't miss him, actually I'm kinda mad at him. I can see through the window a cold and distant star shining all by itself in the blackness, I wish on it. I wish I knew what to do.

***

Our starchy MAA, who's really not so bad when you get to know her, hands me a fistful of mail and a package when I get in from the gunshed at 1630. Nothing from his Nibs, Mr. Bosun Blackie Gilbert Taranto, but I'm not expecting anything. The package contains cookies from Aunt Cecelia and on top are two pairs of white gloves I must have left behind. I have to laugh when I recognize Aunt Geraldine's decisive handwriting on the blue envelope, I am still chuckling at her with the pitchpipe in my dream. Aunt Geraldine is not laughing, I read that she is upset, she is not happy; Cousin Consuelo, her lone chick, her hope and joy, is determined to leave the convent instead of taking her final vows. Would you, dear godchild, Aunt Geraldine writes, would you write and dissuade her? Not me, negative, no way, sorry, Aunt Geraldine. I will write Consuelo, but I'll tell her she should do what she wants, whose life is it anyway?

Mother's letter is cheerful for a change. Daddy is feeling stronger every day and able to sit outside on the porch for an hour or so. Michael had written them—says Germany is a pretty country, what's left of it. He should be coming home soon; like everybody else he has to wait for transport. Michael had sent me a letter, too, not a V-mail because it has pictures in it. Must be Nuremberg—before our guys blew all the swastikas up. How'd that get through the censors? Leave it to Michael. All the letters I had written to him over the months had finally caught up with him in one big bunch—good thing I had numbered them on the envelope so he could read them in order.

Thank the good Lord, I'm almost home free. If Michael makes it home in one piece, I'll know for sure that I haven't Grandmother Scanlon's Second Sight. I thought Daddy was going to die and he didn't. I used to have awful presentiments about Michael, I was always lighting candles when I thought they might do some good. I'd hate to know when people are going to die.

I'm just starting to read Aunt Teddy's letter on her usual violet-scented paper—something about rationing hadn't been lifted yet—when Corman, who had been sitting at the table going through her usual enormous pile of mail, gasps and chokes. She runs out of our cubicle, her chair crashing behind her. She slams into the head, hooks the hook, and stays there for an hour, even though we take turns urging her to come out or at least tell us what's wrong. When she finally comes back she's composed, but her face is red and blotchy. Obviously she has been crying.

"Hilliard's buddy found my address in Hilliard's gear. He's missing and presumed dead—doesn't say what happened. I don't want to talk about it, okay?" The rest of us, even Tolliver, are too stunned to say anything. Hilliard, that baby, he can't be dead, he's too young, he's hardly lived at all. Corman waves away suggestions of going to get some chow with us, silently gets into her pajamas, climbs into her bunk, and turns her back on all of us. Poor Corman, her grandmother didn't hold with unladylike public displays of grief. Wonder what Corman's mother is like, she only talks about her grandmother.

After chow I take my letters I haven't read yet topside to the lounge. Seems like the best thing I can do for Corman is leave her alone. Tolliver joins me, looking subdued and twiddling nervously with her engagement ring. "I'd just die if anything happened to C.C."

"How 'bout that?" I don't know what to say.

"It's all in the hands of the Lord, I guess," she says, like she is looking for someone to agree with her.

"You just keep right on believing that, Tolliver. You just keep steady." No point in telling her that I'm not so sure that the Lord paid any attention a-tall. I'm not convinced that it was all those novenas that brought Michael through; besides, he isn't through yet, the war isn't over. I'm glad Consuelo did all that praying for me, though. If God is paying attention, He'll be unhappy with me. Maybe I shouldn't be so definite about it. Maybe I should just say that God marks the fall of every sparrow.

Poor Hilliard.

The "better" the war news gets, the worse it gets in a way, because that brings everybody closer to the invasion of Japan, but at least Okinawa has been "secured," as they say. The Japanese general and his aide committed hara-kiri. Suicide is a sin if you are Catholic, but apparently not if you are a Japanese general. Roman generals used to fall on their own swords—same thing. Isn't it peculiar that Catholics seem to have more sins than almost anybody? The list of things a person can go to hell for forever and ever is pretty long, Tolliver will find out soon enough. She's taking a quickie course in instruction from the chaplain's assistant, so she can marry C.C. and live happily ever after when the war ends, if it ends.

All of our guys on Okinawa who are still alive must think they have seen a foretaste of hell right here on this earth. The Japanese fight like devils and won't give up. If that's what it's like on that rocky tunneled island, imagine what it will be like when we hit the Home Islands. The bay is filling up with ships riding low in the water, loaded with stuff to transport over the thousands of watery miles between here and there. The Big One is coming, that's for sure. I wonder if Tokyo Rose knows when? She sure knows a lot, she drives the guys crazy by announcing all the fleet movements that are supposed to be so secret, then she teases the poor guys by telling them that their wives and sweethearts are taking up with 4-Fs and chairborne officers stateside. That drives the poor guys half-mad with jealousy, but there isn't much they can do about it, being so far away. She broadcasts better music than the Armed Forces Radio, so they listen in spite of themselves. So they say.

Surprise. Blackie calls me from San Raphael before they leave. I thought he was long gone, because he had planned on leaving the Tuesday after our misadventure at Lake Merritt, but something snafued like it always does and they are still tied to the dock across the bay two weeks later. Never a mention about not calling all this time, he sounds just like he always does, like he is getting ready to tell a joke; he says they won't be gone long this time, which must mean they are only going to Pearl, otherwise he'd be gone months like the last time.

"You okay?" I ask. He could have gotten pneumonia or typhoid from swallowing that murky water.

"Affirmative. Ol' Dr. Jack Daniels fixed me up just fine. Alls I was was a little hungover. Howsabout yourself?"

"Fine. I'm just fine." This conversation isn't going anywhere. Should I tell him I'm putting in for bosun? 'Tain't funny, McGee.

"Lissen. I'll see you when I get back. I got something to ast you. It's important. Don't get engaged or nothin'." There is a big silence on the line like something big is about to come across. I wait. "See ya around, Toots." The line goes dead, I'm holding the receiver in my hand stupidly. "Toot, toot, Tootsie, goodbye," I think to myself. I'm just your stateside girl in this particular port. Well, Blackie, meboyo, you aren't the only pebble on the beach; there's always another streetcar along in a few minutes. Etcetera, etcetera. So why do I feel so rotten? I slam the receiver into the cradle. Why is life so complicated?

CHAPTER 23

Anniversary

Jenson is in pretty bad shape. All of us are running down like an un-wound alarm clock, except maybe Tolliver, who's too starry-eyed to notice anything. Corman is really depressed, sometimes teary, even if Hilliard was only her number four fiancé, but she's melancholy and worried about all her other guys. We all kidded her about Hilliard, him playing grown-up in his sailor suit, but he did remind us of our own kid brothers and we miss him, too. I've got a different worry—what if I turn down Blackie, I can feel he's working up to propose, what if I turn him down and nobody ever asks me again? Corman keeps telling me I still have my interesting future in front of me, maybe she's right. Jenson won't talk to anybody. She's never been that gabby, but this is different, she's gotten thinner, her elbow and wristbones stick out like she could stab somebody with them. Now she's in sick bay again and couldn't even go to the city with us for my birthday dinner. Finally Corman calls a council of war in the top-deck lounge—she's getting worried that the Chief will get into the act. He's such a big, gray worrywart and we certainly don't want him worrying poor Jenson right home.

"Maybe you can get her to go see Lieutenant Kaufman, or even the chaplain," I say, thinking I'm being helpful. "Maybe they can do something. Find out what's bothering her. She's just worrying herself sick about something." I cough a little, Camels are too strong for me but I forgot my Pall Malls.

"Praise the Lord, Dermody. Not the chaplain. He'd turn her in for sure." Tolliver's biting her lip and picking at a thread in her hem that's come loose, sort of subdued and not mad. I don't get her drift, but I don't half the time anyway.

"Tolliver, I keep telling you, if you're going to be a Catholic you can't go around saying 'Praise the Lord' all the time. Try something Latin, *Deo Volente*, maybe. *Gloria in excelsis*."

"Stow it, you dummy. Why can't you ever be serious? We are supposed to be thinking about Judy."

"Knock it off, you two." Corman gets up and dusts her hands together. "I'll go see her in sick bay, see if she's in trouble or anything."
She's bustling like her old self, like she's glad to have somebody to
mother-hen again. Take her mind off Hilliard, probably.

"I'll go with you," Tolliver turns to glare at us, "howsomever, *ladeez*,
as far as the Chief is concerned, Jenson caught bronchitis from his
damned damp gunsheds. Okay?"

Atkinson arrives just then, heaving up the ladder, wearing her
satin warm-up jacket. "What is it with you gals?" she asks their departing backs.

"Beats me. They're going to sick bay to see if they can find out
what's bothering Jenson."

"She caught bronchitis from those damned damp gunsheds, din't
she?" She helps herself from the open package of cookies Corman
had left behind.

"Affirmative. Confirmed. Who won today?"

"Armed Guard. We skunked 'em. We always do. Western Sea Command people are terrible ballplayers."

How come Atkinson's war is different from my war?

Tolliver is so mad she's spitting bullets when they get back to our
cubicle right before lights out. Corman is calmer, a little, so we get
the story from her. It turns out, as any fool could have seen, Jenson is
suffering from a broken heart. Some of us are swifter than others,
maybe, but I never would have believed it in a million years—Jenson
is in love with that awful Lt. Beverly Woodley. I can't even imagine
how she got promoted. "How can she be . . . how could she?" I ask,
while it is sinking in. "Judy's such a nice girl and that . . . Woodley
person is awful. I mean, besides, besides . . ." I stutter to a stop, out of
breath. The world has turned silent, so strange, like we aren't in a
noisy, busy barracks at all.

"Honeychile, you never can tell about love." Corman doesn't look
all that convinced, really, when she finally answers.

"Didja hear what . . . that lieutenant did?" Tolliver's sputtering
like she's fulminate of mercury about to go off. "That Beverly Woodwhatzername who was so smashed at that party, she up and married
some bird colonel and transferred to Washington D.C. Din't even tell

Judy or nothin'. Just let her find out from some cat at the Twelfth
Naval District headquarters." She turns her head like a searchlight,
looking at each of us in turn. "Don't none of you say nothin' to nobody. Understand? Nothin'. No-bod-y. I'll skin you alive if you do.
Ain't nobody's business." She looks pointedly at me, her strawy hair
escaping into strings around her flushed face, her hillbilly accent appearing again to add urgency to what she's saying.

"I didn't say anything." I'm feeling aggrieved so I pout. "Why do
you think I'm such a blabbermouth, anyway? Why should I tell anyone some dumb, stupid, fat Wave lieutenant got married anyway?"
Actually, I think, Beverly Woodwhatzername is not all that dumb, stupid, fat (well she really is a pudge), she's just not a very nice person
and we all hate her and we would hate her even if Judy wasn't our
shipmate . . . my Examination of Conscience is running out of control but Corman interjects.

"'Cause it's important, that's why." Corman wearily waves her
graceful hands, the ones that describe the flight paths of enemy aircraft so elegantly. She's been separating Tolliver and me since boot
camp, it's practically automatic by now. "Judy could get a Blue Discharge if the Navy finds out she's been carrying on like that. She
could even get the brig . . ." The thought of our pale friend in the
brig is so mind-boggling, we exhale a collective gasp. "A discharge
other than honorable. All her life. No benefits . . . no GI Bill."

"That's dumb." I'm beginning to see the light, I'm beginning to
get the familiar angry, agitated feeling I get when the situation is too
dumb to be believed. "But there were lots of gals at that party . . . so
that's why we left in such a hurry, Coralee."

"You're smart, Dermody. Real smart. You know that?"

"Aw, stow it, Atkinson. What are we going to do now?"

"First thing is we gotta cheer Judy up. We're her friends. You
might even say, sentimentally, shipmates." Corman waits for the titter,
nobody obliges, we all just share the same stricken expression. "Second thing is we cover for her. Least we can do." Corman's voice trails
off.

"Oh, I get it. We can say her guy got in the way of a Jap torpedo
off Leyte." Tolliver looks gleeful.

"That's not true, Tolliver." Even I can hear the Miss Priss in my
voice. Where do I go to get out of this one?

"There's worse things than lying." It's Corman talking to us and to herself. "My grandmother always said the highest virtue for a woman was kindness. This is a kindness for Judy."

"Aw, come on, Dermody. We're all in this, none of us want to see a nice girl like Judy get an undesirable discharge for some dumb Navy rules. It ain't nobody's business but her own." Tolliver wipes her pudgy hand across her forehead.

I must look more bewildered than usual. "But . . . but . . ."

"Anybody doesn't wanta lie, just keep your goddamned mouth shut." She looks at me like she's getting steamed again, but Atkinson intervenes, passing the almost empty cookie box around.

"Our biggest problem is Judy. We have to cheer her up and get her on her feet again, so she doesn't give herself away. Nobody on TI will want to rat on her."

"You're real smart, Atkinson, you know that?" She throws a pillow at me. Tolliver whacks her a good one across the shoulders and pretty soon we have a terrific pillow fight going—until the killjoys in the next cubicle start yelling, "Knock it off in there. Knock it off."

Jenson gradually gets better, physically at least. They let her out of sick bay and she's back at work, not coughing so much you can worry. We try our best to mind our own business but still be on her side, but the person who helps bring her out of her deep blue mood is a big, ruddy sailor named Rudy. It's not a romance as far as we can tell. One day he's just there on the quarterdeck, asking for her. He likes ice cream as much as she does—we see them head to head over double chocolate fudge sundaes at the Ship's Store. *Deo Gratias.* Who would think it would be a big blond guy with chemical stains on his hands who would fatten her up? None of us can, and God knows we try. We all like him, he's hearty and harmless. All of our scrapbooks get fatter when Rudy comes around to pick up Jenson, because he has printed out our snapshots and even shown Judy how to use the enlarger in the darkroom at the Rec Center. Turns out he is Alan A. Rudolph, the photographer's mate who took a famous picture of the explosion on the deck of a flat-top when it took a kamikaze; he even had his picture in *Life* magazine. Long about Kwajalein his number came up and he was in the hospital for a long time. Now he's here on easy duty, recovering from something or other; if a person is not in a wheelchair or showing evident scars nobody asks, just assumes it's Section Eight, battle fatigue.

"You look like Mutt and Jeff," Tolliver says, as she runs into them in front of the Rec Center. She's so original, but she does get away with more teasing than anyone, which I can never understand.

"Knock it off," Jenson says, but she doesn't sound mad. They do make a funny-looking couple, he is as big and bluff and ruddy as she is delicate and pale. He takes pictures of all of us, but he has a whole file of pictures of Jenson which emphasize her pale ethereal look, her long neck, and her large dark eyes. 'Sfunny—we just see a skinny, anxious, pale wisp of a girl. Shows you what a camera can do; in some of Rudy's pictures she looks like a pensive fawn.

"Here're the prints of your last roll, Irish." He hands me the fat envelope. "It's mostly you and your Market Street Commando. You two look pretty good together."

We do. Blackie and I make a triangle leaning toward each other in front of the Pepsi-Cola Center in the snapshot Corman had taken on one of our double dates, his gob hat almost falling off the back of his head, my garrison hat as rakish as I can manage, our grins almost identical, having such a good time together. My heart leaps and flops, sighs and putters along. I say, "Thanks."

"C'mon by the darkroom, Tuesday at 1700, and I'll show you how to enlarge your pix, 'tain't hard, even for you." He grins, knowing I won't pop him.

"Thanks a heap, but I'm not stupid enough to get in a small, dark, locked room with you."

"Suit yourself. All the gals on this whole entire island are afraid of me, except Judy here, that right, kiddo?"

What an act. He's not dangerous, he's just, well, sort of patched together and fragile. Jenson plays along, "Damstraight, Rudy." They are good for each other while it lasts.

The big push is coming, we all know that. The Waves get to stand and watch the laden ships weigh anchor as the tide turns and head out in the sunrise, but the guys who have all their arms and legs and are reasonably patched up, like Rudy, have to say "So long" and move into the compound at the end of the island where they have to stay before they embark. Jenson says she isn't broken-hearted, she told us all along that he was like the big brother she always wanted, but we all miss him. The sailors, cosmopolitans all, shrug, "Say la gare." Corman laughs with me when we finally figure out that they are saying "C'est la guerre." "That's the frigging war for ya" is what they mean.

People come. People go. Maybe we'll see Rudy's name in *Life* magazine someday and say we knew him when. Maybe we won't. Maybe Michael will come home speaking terrible French. Maybe German. Just come home, *mein bruder. Mach schnell.*

So Judy seems to be okay for now. We don't know whether her heart is broken so bad it will never mend. I still don't understand it all, even though I know more than people think I do. I even figured out Mona's is a lesbian bar, but it isn't something I can talk about much. Sister Francesca Amelia used to reiterate, "Hate the sin, love the sinner." I didn't understand it then, but maybe I am beginning to now.

We've got other things to worry about. Tolliver's C.C. has gotten himself nominated for the Navy Cross for some particularly daring rescue in twenty-foot seas. She's frantic that he's going to let it go to his head and heroic himself right into a watery grave before she has a chance to marry him. She has us all keeping our fingers crossed, even saying prayers for them.

Atkinson has the most vitality of any of us. She's changed; from a homely, unwanted, awkward girl, the orphan kid nobody ever wanted, she's turned into this star athlete with her picture in the *Masthead* every week. Our ARGUARD softball team is the winningest in the whole Twelfth Naval District. It turns out she's not as impervious to Cupid's arrow as she lets on—there's this guy she used to know in high school, the one who wants to be a forest ranger and live in the woods forever, who's been writing, saying he should be demobilized soon, and will she marry him? She writes him at least two V-mails a day. She says she tells him she doesn't see how she can marry him when there is still a job to do against Tojo and the Son of Heaven. Hope he believes her. We think that she doesn't want to miss the finals, the playoffs. Her team would miss her pitching. You can hardly blame her.

What with all the romances, broken hearts, dead fiancés, and terminal tedium, we are there every day in the gunsheds, splicing the films together to last through one more day of teaching. They're getting pretty raggedy. Atkinson has turned out to be a wonderful teacher, patiently dealing with the skinny pinch-faced street kids from Oakland or Newark as well as the raw-boned farm kids, each as shy and awkward as she used to be. We can only hope that we might, just

might, teach them something that might save their lives someday. It's
been such a long time since "Praise the Lord and Pass the Ammunition" at Pearl Harbor. Even now our puny 20mms don't always do
much against a kamikaze or a torpedo. Don't think about it, megirl,
you'll drive yourself nuts.

Just in the nick of time, for our morale at least, comes the Waves'
third birthday party. All 700 of us on TI, all spiffed up in dress blues,
dazzling white gloves rising and falling while we pass in review before
the commodore and his party. Guidons, "Eyes Right, Hand Salute,"
the whole works. I do love a parade, I still do. Really. It's nice that the
whole Navy goes to so much trouble to say "Well done" to us, just
when we are beginning to wonder collectively and individually what
the hell we are doing here. Our own Ens. Marylou Bauzer, the high-
strung, long-jawed Waves officer sent out to replace our unlamented
Lieutenant Mac, steps out sturdily in front of Armed Guard company.
Lieutenant Kaufman's Western Sea Command marches behind us,
followed by Receiving Ship and the others. The bands are playing,
the flags are whipping in the wind, the commodore is dazzling in all
his gold braid. A person would wonder how Admiral King and all the
rest of the brass, with the whole other half of the war to win, had
time to write letters commending the fact that the Waves had
released enough men to man two whole task forces. They probably
had their yeomen run them out. Nice to hear, anyway. Even better
than the parade is the birthday dinner in the Waves galley, which by
this time has been feminized with chintz draperies at the windows.
The mountains of fried chicken on platters, piping hot and steaming
deliciously, make me wish I could wrap a few pieces in a napkin and
send them on to Buddy. Civilians haven't had much chicken lately,
nor birthday cake with frosting. Not to think of it, if this war goes on
much longer even Buddy will be in it. Spare us, O Lord. *Parce Deum.*
    I didn't have a date for the birthday ball until Tolliver enlisted
one of C.C.'s flying buddies, name of Purvis. He's not my type; he's
chunky for a flyer, his eyebrows grow together, he's got a cleft in his
chin, and he's full of himself. For one night, what's the difference?
Blackie's not the only pebble on the beach.
    At 2000 he walks with me into the foyer of the Ad Building, which
has flags of all the Allied countries hanging from poles jutting out
from the balcony. Since the United Nations has come to San Fran-

cisco you see the rows of flags wherever you turn. They make a brave show of color, most everything around is Navy blue and white, or that tiresome Navy gray. Perhaps to show what sports they are they give gardenias to the girls as we walk in. Most of us pin them in our hair, so we look like tailored Hawaiian maidens twirling to the syncopation of the Hunter's Point Band. Purvis is a total drip, with his sweaty palms and jokes. If you can call them jokes. "What's the definition of an Indian squaw? A pistol-packing mama with a rear gunner." Hardee, hardee, har har. Blackie, old pal, where are you when I need you? I ignore Purvis's jokes as politely as I can and concentrate on the music; it's hard not to have a good time when you have a gardenia in your hair, the music is good, and you can see your shipmates around you having a good time, too. Tolliver looks opalescent, little pearly beads of sweat on her short upper lip as she swoons and dips with the magnificent C.C. Corman is here with the fiancé who says he used to be a jazz musician; he's jitterbugging rings around everybody, flinging his long arms and legs around so folks have to back off. I do hope she doesn't choose him, he looks mean. Atkinson is here with Gus, who turned out to be a baseball player, too. He dances like an LST wallowing through heavy swells, but Atkinson is enjoying herself. Lieutenant Kaufman is dancing cheek to cheek with some Seabee captain. That's funny, I thought her husband is in the Army.

Just when we are about to drop from nonstop dancing they call an intermission and trot out the entertainment. An ethereal Wave I never saw before, but maybe I just don't recognize her in her frothy ballet costume, does a beautiful solo. Next a few more acts: three gals harmonizing "Accentuate the Positive" like the Andrews Sisters, a couple of sailor clowns, another dance act, and a sing-along. We do "Waves of the Navy," of course, "Anchors Aweigh," and then sing "Happy Birthday" to ourselves. Flushed and happy we can tackle the buffet. The Navy really can throw a party.

I reach under my jacket to undo the button on my skirt, then think better of it. If it is going to pop, let it. Purvis eats like there is no tomorrow, but at least when his mouth is occupied he isn't telling jokes. When we are all stuffed to the Plimsoll line, another band takes over, this one more swing than jazz. Way too soon it is 2400, the magical midnight hour when all the little sailor girls will turn into pumpkins if all the little sailor boys don't sashay them back to the barracks toot sweet. It's been an okay evening, but I'm not sorry to say goodnight to old Purvis by the barracks steps. I'm not quick enough, he manages to plant a gluey good-night kiss before I can disentangle myself.

"I'll call you," he promises as he turns to go. "Count on it."

"Fair enough?" I answer like a dope. I mean "why bother?" but I have a feeling he's taking it as encouragement.

Maybe I should become a professional card player. With my unluckiness at love I must be destined to be a winner at cards.

CHAPTER 24

War Ending

After the Waves birthday party it's business as usual: back to the gun-sheds, back to the same old jobs, back to the same old reluctant platoons clumping in and out. We are used to that but now I have the added job of avoiding Purvis's phone calls. He's making me Nervous in the Service, that's for sure. I told him I wasn't interested. Did he listen? It's like talking to a stone.

I tried telling him that I'm already married, but he has a friend in Personnel who checked my Service Jacket in the files. Tolliver, who's feeling responsible because she got me the blind date in the first place, offers to tell C.C. that her old pal Dermody has VD, so C.C. would be sure to tell his old buddy-buddy about it. "That'll take the wind out'n his sails," she chortles at the very thought.

"I'm gonna make you sor-ree, Tolliver. If you tell anybody that awful lie, even a hint, it will be sooner rather than later. The very idea . . ." I hear myself sputtering.

She sticks out her lower lip and looks aggrieved. "Just trying to help."

"JesusMaryandJoseph, Tolliver, have you lost your mind? When I want your kind of help I'll signal for it."

She just laughs.

The only thing I can think of to do, aside from praying Purvis will get sea duty, is to hide out until he gets tired. This guy wouldn't take no for an answer if a whole cargo net of ammunition boxes fell on him. I spend a lot of time in the library, I finally finish *Forever Amber,* which isn't so great after all the fuss about it, especially since several hundred others have read it before me and all the good parts are heavily underlined on pages darkened with greasy hands. Jeezus, if this keeps up I'll be forced to start studying the Bluejackets Manual and bucking for First Class.

Help. Tolliver is totally involved with True Love Realized, she is still pirouetting around radiating bliss. Jenson is still not well, wispier than ever, but soldiering on. I guess you can soldier on in the Navy. Corman is withdrawn and on the verge of tears all the time, Atkinson is hearty and triumphant. Blackie is God-knows-where; in my low moments I just know he's populating the environs of Oahu. I'm lonesome and restless when I wander into the craft shop behind the library. That's the same one where Calvin Jackson turned all those shell casings into umbrella stands and coffee mugs before he took up dancing.

The guy who runs the craft shop is bald, called Curly, natch. He's been working around the Rec Center as long as I've been on the Island, so I have no idea how come he's got such an easy job, he's probably been in the Navy forever. He can make anything out of wood and metal, he's a genius with his hands, but he has trouble with women—at least one woman. He putters around the shipshape workbenches, wailing under his breath, "Seven Years with the Wrong Woman." I've bunked with Tolliver and her dumb hillbilly music all this time—it still gets on my nerves, but the way I'm feeling now, there are worse things.

Curly is presently making a ship in a bottle, the genuine old-fashioned kind where you make a little teensy ship with the teeny tiny masts and yards hinged and attached to threads. When you poke the little hull and folded-up superstructure through the neck of the bottle, you hang onto the threads. Once the glue that holds the hull to the little painted plaster of Paris sea dries, you pull the threads. Zingo, you have a genuine square rigger with the spars and yards and rigging, all set like it's waiting for a crew of Little People to pipe themselves aboard. The one Curly is making is the most enchanting thing I have ever seen—tiny little gunports along the gunwales, tiny little portholes in the cabins, weeny anchor chain and anchor—a great thing to keep for the grandchildren. I would never have the patience or the skill to make one myself but I long for one; Curly makes me a deal, if I will bring him, smuggle onto the base actually, a bottle of Johnny Walker Red Label from the city, he will personally empty the bottle out and make me a ship. Fair enough. I shall christen her *Arabella*.

Market Street has a jillion liquor stores, but it takes us a while to find the Red Label that Curly specified. It gurgles alarmingly when we stroll through the gate, surely the Marines manning the post, their ears preternaturally sharpened from distinguishing the rustle of monkeys from the Jap snipers in the jungle, hear it. They are busy smashing their batons between the ankles of the guys in line, puddling good whiskey on the tarmac. The guys never seem to learn, always hoping that if they tape a pint under their bell-bottoms they can get it through the gate, even if it hardly ever works. I get more and more nervous as I hear the gurgle like the Hallelujah chorus in the brown bag I have in my arms, ostensibly loaded with bananas. The green eyes of the young gyrene look straight into mine, I'm sure he's going to turn me in, but he waves Atkinson and me on through. I don't think I'm cut out to be a smuggler. I can't stand the anxiety and the premature guilt about getting caught. Holy Mother, tell me, why am I such a dope as to risk trouble after all this time?

The worst part is that it turns out to be all for naught. Poor Curly gets taken with the DTs this very night and never gets to empty the bottle that was to be the home of my magical, miniature, square-rigged man-o-war *Arabella*. Too bad. Not so much "Say la gare" this time as "Say la vee." Poor Curly. I guess his bunkmates took care of the leftovers for him.

With all this going on I hardly pay any attention to the news and what's going on outside the Island. Amazing what skulking around to avoid someone can do to narrow your orbit. Purvis wasn't liable to *do* anything to me, but he's the kind of guy who thinks because he likes you you *owe* him something. Everything. Your time. Your phone number. Your life. The more you resist, the more he is convinced that you are really besotted with him and only playing hard to get. It's a weird feeling—like he's sucking the marrow out of your bones.

He caught up with me last Friday outside the Base Theater No. 2, where I was coming out of seeing *The Song of Bernadette* for the third time. I must have been feeling unaccountably uplifted and kind-hearted because I agreed to go with him to Trader Vic's the next day. Big mistake.

Trader Vic's is way out on San Pablo in Oakland. Purvis had borrowed a buddy's rattle-trap old car, a black Model A with a rumble seat and bald tires. Trader Vic has decorated his restaurant like a sailor's dream of the South Seas, before the jungles were found to be full of snipers, boobytraps, and jungle rot; lots of dark wood carvings of spooky masks and statues with pointed boobs like the business ends of torpedoes. Giant torches make spooky shadows that dance behind the artificial palm trees. Drinks with names like Fogcutter and Missionary's Downfall come in coconut shells or tall ice cream soda glasses with flowers on top. The place is crowded, as it always is, and for a little moment I am grateful to Purvis for bringing me here, one of the famous places. We order drinks with rum and pineapple and look over the menu, which is the size of a tabloid newspaper, finally ordering sweet and sour pork. From then on, until the frozen Mai Tai compote and the fried bananas appear, the evening goes downhill. First, he has saved up a whole seabag full of those dumb jokes he thinks are conversation; to make things worse, he emphasizes the point by pounding on my knee—the table is too small for me to scrootch away far enough. Then, after his fourth coconut full of rum and lime juice, he tells me solemnly that he is a direct descendent of Bonnie Prince Charlie. "Well, hi," I mutter under my breath, "I'm the Queen of Sheba." He's going to marry a rich society girl after the war and take his rightful place in Atlanta society. "Rotsaruck, Purvis, oh, gollygee, I have to be back by 2300," I lie, looking at my watch. We careen through the almost deserted (thank God) streets of Oakland back to the Island, he trying to handle the car and manhandle me at the same time, but he's pretty swozzled and not that much of a problem. I take a solemn vow never to spend another evening with someone, however royal, with sweaty wandering hands and a braying laugh. Sayonara.

Better I should devote my life to prayer and good works. Better I should put in for a transfer. Better I should go over the hill. Maybe I'll feel better in the morning.

Crabby from the effect of too many Missionary's Downfalls, I'm not ready to listen to Gus this morning. By this time I can thread my projector awake or asleep, hung over or not. "Great news, J-J-Josie." I ignore him. He won't quit. "Didja hear about Hee-ro-shee-ma? We flattened those Jappos. Dropped this here Atom-ick bomb on them."

"Go 'way, Gus. I got problems of my own." He picks me up and waltzes me, a navy blue Raggedy Ann doll draped over his huge arm, trying to shake some sense into my head.

"We did it, we did it! They're beat. They can't win. War's purtinear over—looky here." He waltzes me over to the divider shelf where we read the papers every morning. By this time the rest of the crew arrives and we crowd around to read what President Truman has announced. Seems we have dropped some kind of superbomb on the Japanese—one that harnessed the power of the universe. The paper says it has the power of 20,000 tons of TNT.

"Don't see where it says the Japanese have surrendered," I sulk. My eyes aren't focusing too well today.

"'U.S. OPENS SURRENDER ASSAULT ON JAPAN WITH NEW ATOMIC BOMB.' Says right here." Gus's big farmboy face is flushed with earnestness. "They ain't got a chance. Old Harry promised them a 'rain of ruin' if they don't yell Uncle right away."

"I'll believe it when it happens," D'Angelo, Jackson's replacement, mutters. He's so young he's hoping to see some action before it's over. Biff, bang, kapowee, you're dead. That's how Buddy plays war. D'Angelo isn't all that much older than my little brother. I think of Mischa and wonder if he survived "the Slot" on the way to Murmansk. I'll never know, will I? Maybe he will survive to become some kind of commissar in Odessa.

Chief heaves in. "Ain't no holiday I know of, ladeez and gentlemen. Man your guns. I'll let you know when the war is over. D'Angelo, where's the *java?*" He swells up and roars so loud the kid jumps two feet into the air, but he isn't really mad. He lets Tolliver bring her little blue radio in after chow so we can listen to "developments" between classes. Nobody's ever heard of Hiroshima, the Air Force must have looked it up so they would know where to drop the bomb; usually they go straight to Tokyo—everybody can find that on a map.

The voice of the announcer is edged with hysteria as he describes the new age that is dawning—the Atomic Age. He says that Hiroshima is an important place for transhipping materiel, with a quartermaster's depot and an ordnance plant. "Nobody knows what's left because," the announcer says, "there is an impenetrable cloud of dust hovering over the area." Dear God, what next?

As the day wears on, we get more and more reports—some of them from the little blue radio on the shelf and some from the guys who have buddies who are radiomen listening to the Armed Forces Radio. The Japanese don't know what hit them. Our transmitters in 'Frisco and Saipan are telling them that they don't have a chance. They had their chance last month when Truman offered them a chance to surrender. Too bad for them.

"Two billion dollars," Atkinson mutters. "What I couldn't do with two billion dollars. That's how much it cost." She shakes her head in disbelief as she unbuckles the harness from a guy and waves for the next one.

"Saved a bunch of lives, you betcha." Gus Mortenssen is more animated than I have ever seen him. "Those sonsabitches will surrender now and we won't have to invade."

"Now the frigging flyboys will think they won the frigging war," a grizzled gunner's mate with hash marks up to his shoulder complains. Wonder how he got stuck with the job herding recruits and flakeouts through gunshed drill? Just lucky, I guess.

"Halsey coulda beat them—with all the firepower on his battlewagons—just bring 'em up close to Tokyo Bay and pound the hell out of them. Navy does all the work and now they'll say the Air Force finished it." Shows how stunned we all are, nobody pipes up that the Air Force guys are Americans, too.

For some reason I keep seeing in my mind's eye the picture of Mount Fuji I saw somewhere, with the lines on a periscope lens in front; one of our subs had taken the picture from underwater. I wonder if it's still there, or does the marvelous new bomb only kill people? I feel sick to my stomach. Chief secures early so we can listen to our commander-in-chief on the radio. Everybody is talking about it . . . if the war is really going to be over . . . no invasion. Just bomb 'em to hell. Save our casualties. Can it be true?

Things get crazier. Purvis, thank God, seems to have disappeared. I can only hope that Winston Churchill has called him back to ascend the throne of Scotland. Our side drops another atomic bomb on someplace called Nagasaki. Same thing. Vaporized everybody. Everything. If you are the anxious, worrying kind you can worry about how close the Germans came to getting the atomic bomb first, Churchill says it was a near thing. Does that mean God was on our side all along? Some sailors swear that the other side had secret weapons, too, that lighted somethings swooshed by them at 500 knots over Kwajalein or Leyte. Who knows? You learn early never to believe sailors, but later on you learn it's hard to believe everything official either.

It has to be over soon, doesn't it? Russia has declared war on Japan and marched on Manchuria. The newspapers have maps with arrows like knockout punches encircling Japan from all sides.

Blackie is back, that old rustbucket must have gone full power all the way to Pearl and back to make it so soon to Sausalito. When he calls I don't tell him about Purvis. Blackie can't get liberty, the old man won't let any of his guys loose, but he's increased their beer ration 'cause he feels sorry for them. Blackie calls me every day with more rumors about what is going on, he has so many buddies in so many places that he collects a fine batch every day, all conflicting and all confusing. He doesn't seem real, just a voice on the phone every day.

We keep the radio on all the time in the gunshed now. The squawk boxes spit "Now hear this" constantly. "All hands—all leaves canceled. All hands confined to base." An hour later they announce that Starboard Liberty people can go. In between they announce really important stuff like Waves are not permitted to wear the Reserve Blue shirt in the Twelfth Naval District. (That's the pretty sky-blue one; no one ever said why they took such an attitude about it.) Then "All hands confined to base" again. With orders flying around contradicting each other and rumors flying around like tracer shells criss-crossing the sky, it's nice to get mail from home. At least there you know what to expect. Mother and Daddy had a telegram from Michael, he's definitely coming home, soon's he can get on a troop ship. Now that the war in the Pacific is just about over, that's really good news. What are you going to do with your life now, Michael? I wonder how much you have changed, you looked thinner and older in those snapshots from Germany—maybe it's because you were squinting into the sun that your eyes look so hollow.

What are any of us going to do? I think of my bedroom back home, all yellow and white ruffles with the Snow White lamp, and wince. For a minute I think of doing what that San Francisco Wave did—we read the story in the *Chronicle*. She left some of her clothes by the water near Cliff House so people would think she drowned, then she took off for Mexico. 'Twouldn't do, megirl, you can't speak the lingo. Besides her family found her and brought her back.

We talk about it all the time, what we want to do after the war is over and we get out. Gus is going right back to his farm, two of his brothers are going into partnership with him. His old father will be glad to give it up after trying to keep things going practically single-handed through the whole war. Atkinson knows that as soon as her infantryman gets home she's going to marry him and live in the woods somewhere and have half a dozen kids. Tolliver, to hear her tell it, is going to live in never-ending bliss with C.C. in a white-pillared mansion and raise a whole passel of kids, too. Corman is looking like the cat that swallowed the canary these days, she has plans, but she's not telling. She's probably going to marry the boy next door after all, good for her. She'll have to write Dear Emmett, Dear Chuck, Dear Raymond letters to her remaining fiancés, but she'll figure out a way to let them down easy. Jenson is going to get an apartment in 'Frisco and find a job in a photo shop. Some people are just dying to get home and others can't bear the thought. I never felt so betwixt and between in my life.

"You're not saying anything, Dermody? You going to marry Blackie?" Tolliver acts like she really wants to know.

"No way." I surprised myself, I didn't know I had made up my mind already. "He hasn't really asked me yet. Honest to God, I don't know what I want to do. I'm thinking of using the GI Bill to go to school. Maybe be a teacher."

"Hot diggety dog, you can get a MRS degree at the same time. It'll work out, pal." She comforts me with a pat.

"Yeah, thanks a heap. I'll write you when I decide."

It's so strange to be yarning and yearning about civilian dreams after so long in suspension, just trying to survive the war, do our job, and have a little fun along the way. Meanwhile, there isn't much gunnery instruction going on—if the war is already practically O-V-E-R, who needs it? We have a lot of time to chew the fat.

Ships' whistles start shrieking—the Japanese have capitulated. They stop. False alarm. Maybe it isn't a false alarm, maybe somebody who shouldn't announce it announced it first. Off again, on again, Finnegan, this has been going on for three days. Finally it comes over the radio. It's official. The Japanese have surrendered. The world goes mad.

CHAPTER 25

Blackie had been so insistent that I come with him, he figured I wouldn't want to miss anything as big as this. I am already wondering what I could have been thinking of when I agreed to come. Here I am, hanging onto my hat with one hand and holding onto the secure hardness of his left arm with the other. If I let go of one, I would lose my hat. If I let go of the other, I would be adrift, swamped by the sea of humanity surging wildly around us as we make our way to Market Street where the celebration is—everybody converging because the war is officially over. It's early yet, the sun is just going down. First the surrender was on, then it was off. After we dropped the atomic bombs the war was really over, but it wasn't official till now. The emperor had signed, saving face by saying he was only doing it to prevent further suffering. Shouldna started it, Hirohito. Somehow Blackie got liberty and at the last minute so did I—it must have seemed like a good idea to somebody to give *everybody* liberty. Let's celebrate, everybody. The war is over.

Blackie straight-arms a drunken Marine lurching toward me. The guy, his chest full of ribbons on his olive-green uniform, was already off balance and now falls against a light pole. He's scary, his face so distorted and red, his eyes so staring and all bloodshot. Blackie skedaddles me through a hole in the crowd. It isn't only the press of people that's crazy, it's the press of noise. Sometimes in church the organ will be playing and you can feel your armbone vibrating—this is a thousand times more so. All the ships' whistles are blowing, some steady, some rising and falling shrieks, never letting up; air-raid sirens are piercing the air; all the church bells are ringing, their bongs making the bricks in their towers reverberate; car horns are blowing, trolleys clanging, ambulances and paddywagons running their sirens; people all around are yelling and shrieking, hollering, crying, kissing and hugging. Betcha there's never been such a hullabaloo since the beginning of the world. Sound waves are pounding my body, I almost fancy I can see them. I open my mouth automatically to save my poor eardrums. This is worse than the gunnery range at Great Lakes, a thousand times worse. When I try to say something to Blackie the sound is snatched away by the gale of noise around us.

Blackie grins at me. "I wisht you was a boy. Then we could get drunk."

"You promised." I cling to his arm in a spasm of terror. Holy Toledo, he is maddening sometimes.

He just looks down at me. Did I doubt his word? He had promised me that if I would go with him to the Victory over Japan celebration he wouldn't get drunk. "What the hell, I been drunk three times already waiting on the false reports. Stick with me, Toots."

He's keeping his promise. He hadn't promised he wouldn't complain about it. "Geezt, we could have such a good time if you was a guy and we could get drunk together." I sigh. There's no way to have a discussion about why he hadn't chosen any of the shipful of neat buddies, each one equal to a tanker in his capacity for putting whiskey and beer away, instead of me. If he had, I wouldn't be here. In spite of his grousing he's having a good time protecting me. I fit neatly under the intersection where his arm sticks out in his straight-arm position—I can watch the goings-on from there.

We run into Tolliver, her hat askew and her face radiant, with her dazzling flyboy, but as the crowd pulled us apart Tolliver says, "We're heading for the Army-Navy Club." She beams as she indicates her lieutenant in his whites, "C.C. sez this here is too dangerous for ladies." Well, la-dee-dah. The crowd swirls them away. I see Corman in a conga line near Montgomery, but can't get near her. She waves and is gone—one, two, three, kicking across the street. All of the people around us are overexcited and looking stranger and stranger, except when a familiar face emerges from the crowd. Gruesome Gus appears briefly, then disappears down a side street with a civilian girl in very high heels, if it really is a civilian girl . . . she looks vaguely like someone I know, but I don't have time to worry over it. I think I see Lieutenant Kaufman riding on the back of a fire engine just as we reach Powell. You're seeing things, megirl, how could that be Lieutenant Kaufman, old and married as she is? She would be at the Army-Navy Club with all the other officers, wouldn't she? Nope. It's her, all right, shrieking like a girl and not looking old at all. I clutch at Blackie's arm, everything is so crazy. He sort of shakes himself, settling into his strength, but he looks flushed under his tan.

The streets are ankle-deep in confetti and torn-up phone books, with bonfires everywhere, casting a peculiar red light on every face, making them look like distorted masks. At the Admiral Dewey statue some overexcited girl has thrown off all her clothes and climbed to the top, throwing out her arms like the Wings of Victory. A beefy cop climbs up to get her down. She's feeling no pain, but he is, as he throws his coat over her. A circle of guys stand around, clapping and yelling.

Blackie keeps a lookout ahead. In all of the noise he couldn't confer if he wanted to; he just turns his head from side to side like a lighthouse beam, "Let's go this way. Let's not go down that way." He steers me like a tugboat as we zig and zag up Market Street. I'm getting annoyed.

"Hey," I yell, "what are you doing, jerking me around like this? We're just out to celebrate, dance a little in the street, do a little hollering of our own, aren't we?" He doesn't answer, maybe he doesn't hear. I put my hat in my purse so I don't have to hang onto it all the time.

It's fun, feeling crazy like everybody else, watching the sailors and gyrenes unwind the firehoses from the fire engines like a long, cold cooked spaghetti and play tug of war. It's still fairly early, like nine or ten o'clock but the paddywagons are making their way through the crowds, trying to clear the way for the immobilized firewagons. By an overturned taxicab, shore patrol are knocking guys out with their truncheons and stacking them into the paddywagons like cords of wood, sober or drunk, but it seems like almost everybody is drunk. It makes me feel sick to my stomach, feeling rather than hearing the thunk of the sticks on the skulls. I shudder and we move on.

We stand for a while to watch the sailors, Marines, and some Army guys push the cablecars around and around the merry-go-round turntable at Powell Street, like everybody is a six-foot-tall kid on some playground, a combination of madness and childhood. Blackie and I move along, arm in arm, not really going anywhere, just laughing and watching the action. The noise continues, the bonfires flicker red.

Somehow there is a change in the atmosphere. What had been celebrating crowds, grabbing ladies to kiss them in exuberance, has turned into marauding bands. They start smashing the windows of the liquor stores and passing out the bottles to the crowd. At first Blackie thinks it's funny. "Geezt, if'n you was a boy we could grab some, too." I hate to admit this. I just look at him with a killer look just like Aunt Geraldine's. I'm not being prissy this time, I'm really just plain scared.

The sound of breaking glass seems to overcome all the other sounds; guys in uniform, sailors mostly, run up and down the sidewalks, whooping and smashing windows. We can hardly walk from slithering and sliding on the shards covering the street. Fall down on that stuff and you'll be cut to ribbons.

"Let's get outta here," Blackie says. "Them guys is gettin' outta control." I shiver and move closer to his peacoat. He starts shouldering his way through the crowd, not ambling along, like we had been doing. "Make way! Make way!" he shouts, but who can hear him? We are almost to the Civic Center but Blackie straight-arms his way through uniforms and civilians till we get off Market Street, our brains paralyzed from the noise, and turn up California Street to Chinatown.

Yipes. Chinatown is worse. The Chinese have been fighting the Japanese longer, and they must have been saving fireworks for this day for a long time. With a war on, gunpowder needed, where had they hidden them—in the baby's bed, behind the clock at old St. Mary's? Anyway, from wherever, here they are, all going off like a million New Years at once. POP, POP—POP-POP-POP-POP. They come in long flanks like spare ribs that explode POP, POP, POPOPOP everywhere. The noise is bouncing back and forth between the balustraded neon-lit buildings that line the hilly streets. I can feel the shock waves and smell the gunpowder. Is this what battle sounds like? It's almost midnight and things have been going on for a while—the streets in Chinatown are six inches deep in scarlet firecracker paper. Every time somebody throws a fingerling firecracker into the air it starts a little fire, and usually somebody stomps it out. One army guy throws a firecracker right at me, it hits me on the leg as it explodes. As I lean down to assess the burn I catch a glimpse of the guy who threw it, his face all contorted and crazy. "Why me?" I mouth. He grimaces and shrugs.

Blackie puts his arm around my shoulder. "You okay? Show me the guy who did it, I'll kill him for you."

"Didn't see who did it," I lie. Lying is coming easier all the time these days. Better than having Blackie get into a fight and get hurt or hauled away in a paddywagon. He'd survive that, but how would I ever get out of here alive without him? We elbow our way through the crowd, trying to get somewhere more peaceful. Slow going.

"Banzai! Banzai! Banzai!" Six Marines are charging to the top of the hill, yelling. At first I think they are playing King of the Castle, then I see their berserk faces and wild eyes. People scatter in front of them, crowding out of their way, there's hardly room to move. Some other guys, equally drunk, join them and there is a furious stream of olive green and khaki attacking the top of the hill. Thank God for small favors, they hadn't brought their bayonets on liberty with them. The crowd is packed against the sides of the buildings. I'm more than ready to sound the retreat. I turn around and Blackie isn't anywhere. I'm swept away in the crowd, almost knocked down.

"Blackie, Blackie," I yell. Panic. Don't panic. Should I pray? Nobody, probably not even God, can hear anything in this hellish hullabaloo. Everywhere I look I see white hats and peacoats but none of them are his. Holy Mother of God, what do I do now? I move over by a dragon street lamp where a shore patrol is standing, looking for who to bonk next. Not much he can do all by himself in that berserk crowd. I just stand there, trying to think. I'm too terrified to think much, let me tell you. Fortunately, there's so much going on nobody notices I'm standing here all by myself. Just get me out of this one, God, and I'll never ask for anything else again.

Somebody grabs my arm. I turn to swing at him, but it's Blackie, looking worried. "Jeezus, I thought I lost ya." He tugs me fiercely through the crowd, cutting down an alley into a quieter street. He's trembling and has little drops of sweat on his upper lip. "Let's get outta here."

We walk down the uneven sidewalk on the back streets heading generally for the East Bay Station, holding onto each other. I'm not scared anymore, now that we are out of the crowds and the madness, but I cling to Blackie's arm just the same. I can feel the shudders still going through him. He has that white look, that pinched-around-the-mouth look, that guys get when they are going over the edge—heading for a Section Eight discharge from too much war. The guys in the bathrobes at the little hospital on TI look like that, sometimes we see them when they come out for a little sunshine. Blackie hardly ever talks about the war and what action he has seen, although he hinted he had a ship go down under him (who knows), but something has sure gotten to him this time. Who's taking care of whom? Not much I can do except squeeze his arm reassuringly. We walk along the quiet street for a while, not saying anything, just watching the little tendrils of fog curl around the tops of the buildings, reflecting red from the bonfires in some directions. The background roar of the crowd, the sirens, and the firecrackers still popping and reverberating are far enough away that our eardrums can recover a little. The foggy air is damp but at least it doesn't smell of gunpowder and smoke.

He wipes off his upper lip absentmindedly. "Too much noise, I guess. Sorry." I squeeze his strong square hand. He stops right there on the sidewalk and puts his arms around me, envelops me in his peacoat. He tips up my chin and kisses me. Pink champagne. My insides turn to pink champagne. Holy Toledo.

"I gotta idea," he says into my ear. "Let's me and you get married." The fog-haloed street light seems to blaze up, then subside.

"Are you kidding?" I can't believe I am saying this.

"Don't matter."

"It matters, believe me."

"If you was a guy, we could be buddies. You ain't, so let's get married. I'll buy you opera records. All the books you want. Think it over."

"You're sweet, but I think I'll pass." He is, too, sweet, in a funny-peculiar way. I feel like weeping. What's wrong with me? Three months ago I couldn't wait for him to ask me, now I'm perfectly sure I'm moving on without him. "Sorry."

"Suit yourself, but you're making a big mistake."

We reach the almost deserted station to find there are no more trains till morning. No way to get back to the base.

"Nothing to do about it," he says. "Can't put the whole frigging Navy on report. Whaddya wanna do, Toots?"

"I don't want to go out *there* again." In the distance the noise and the whistles are muffled, but it sounds like the riot will go on forever. "Guess we'll just have to stay here till morning."

"Fair enough, I'll get some java." He comes back with two steaming mugs of greasy liquid. Wonder where Jackson is tonight?

We settle down on the varnished benches and lean on each other.

"Can you believe it's over? We finally won. Everybody can go home. No more kamikazes. No more dying."

"No more chickenshit. 'Scuse me. No more general quarters. No more Jap subs."

"What are you going to do now, Blackie?"

"Ship over, I guess. Some of the guys say they are just gonna put an anchor over their shoulder and start walking till someone asks them what that thing is, then they'll settle down."

"You'll probably never settle down, will you?"

"Is that why you won't marry me?"

"I don't think I could live like your mother, always waiting for her man to come back from the sea."

"You'd get used to it. You should marry me and get used to it."

"No can do." Sometimes he makes me so mad, who does he think he is, anyhow?

"Whatcha gonna do then? Turn into an old maid sommers?"

"Silly boy. I'm not that old. Not likely. First I'm gonna buy me some civilian clothes. Then I'll apply for the GI Bill and go to school somewhere. Don't guess there'll be much call for antiaircraft gunnery instructors in peacetime." I yawn.

"You should marry me." He kisses me on the nose. He doesn't look angry or hurt. He's laughing. "Lemme know if you change your mind."

"I won't change my mind but thanks for the offer."

"Yes, you will. Just don't wait too long, though."

I'm too sleepy to answer. I don't think you ever said anything about love. You always call me Toots. Do you know my name is Josette? Do you call all the girls Toots? I guess guys who say things like "She walks in beauty like the night" or "Beloved, gaze in thine own heart" are few and far between these days. At least in the Navy. Come to think of it, back in Detroit, too. Too bad. I can wait.

This should be a big renunciation scene, like in the movies. The ghostly station, silent bodies stretched out asleep on the long benches, no trains due for hours. I should have glycerin on my eyelashes and barely held back tears. "No, I cannot marry you alas, but I will never forget what we had together." Alas, 'tisn't so. But 'tis so. V-J Day is something to remember.

"Goodnight, Blackie. Thanks."

"Thanks for what?"

"For not getting drunk. For taking me to Market Street and getting me back. For everything."

"Think it over, Toots."

"Goodnight."

CHAPTER 26

Well Done

This is the morning after to end all morning afters. We are all pretty ragged. Even Jenson, who hadn't even gone to the city, is red-eyed from lack of sleep. She and all the other girls who stayed put were up late playing cards, eating potato chips, and listening to the radio in the lounge. When I tell her she missed all the fun, she just grimaces. Not even a smile.

As people trail in we assess the damage. They must not be counting AOLs, Absent Over Libertys, down at the gate. There isn't a brig big enough to hold everybody if they whomped all the people who straggle in late, later, latest. Chief is staying out of sight, that way he doesn't have to ask for accountings. D'Angelo, our kid coffee striker, hasn't come back at all. Don't think about hospitals or brigs yet, maybe he's just sleeping it off somewhere. Corman has a bruise over one eye. "I fell, that's all." Nobody asked her. Tolliver is hung over and totally tuckered. She says there were seven seas worth of champagne at the Army-Navy Club. C.C. had passed out and she had the devil's own time getting a taxi to drop him off at his quarters. A likely story. We set up the guns, but nobody shows up for the first classes, so we just lollygag around, listening to the radio and swilling coffee, trying to keep awake.

"How'd you do with your Blackie Good Looker Lady Killer I saw you with last night?" Tolliver asks, blowing on her third cup of java.

"Fine. I lost him in Chinatown when the Marines went Banzai, but he found me again. Those guys were out of control."

"You know what she means," Corman chimes in.

"Oh, yes. He proposed."

"So?"

"So. I turned him down. He wants to be my buddy."

"Praise the Lord, Dermody. You're getting some sense at last." I can't believe this is Tolliver talking.

"Tolliver, I keep telling you, Catholics simply can't go around saying 'Praise the Lord' all the time," I say to cover my surprise. "You
gals have been giving me such a hard time about I should catch him
. . . all this time."

"Negative. You should wait for True Love, like me." Honestly, she
looks so smug I could kill her. On the other hand she may very well
be right. I start to cry. Blubber a bit.

"Tolliver's right, honeychile. Just another Wartime Romance." Corman puts her arms around me. I feel like a Tragic Heroine, but the
only hanky I have is one of the embroidered Hawaii numbers Blackie
sent me, which sets me off again. "There, there, your time will come.
Trust your old Auntie Corman."

"I don't believe you, any of you." I flounce out for the head, slam
the door. Someday, someday, just you wait. I feel silly talking to the
mirrors after a while so I go back. Nobody pays any mind. You can see
doomed Wartime Romances in the movies twice a week at any base
theater.

The first night of the celebration was a little wild, but mostly all in
fun, but the next night got nasty. I wasn't there, I flaked out long before lights out, most everybody I know did, too. Good thing. Better
just to read about it in the papers. Thousands of sailors poured ashore.
Pretty soon they had broken every window on Market Street, the ones
that hadn't been busted the night before. They didn't touch the
Pepsi-Cola Center; drunk or sober, I guess, nobody could bring himself to smash his Home Away From Home.

All hands are confined to base. How's that for too little, too late?
The brass are charging around or hollering over the blower trying to
sort out their personnel—who's in the hospital, who's in some brig
or jail somewhere, who simply went over the hill now that the war is
over. We don't have anything to do but sit around and count up
points for getting out. We get points for our age, points for how many
months we put in, points for combat, points for being wounded,
points here, points there. I add mine up. Twenty-one for age. Thirteen months in, only 34 points. No combat. No Purple Heart. Wouldn't
you just know? I'm going to be the last one out. Mrs. Lundgren sent
me a postcard last week reporting that Arvid is already out—all those
sorties wrecked European cities and added up to good solid points.
Arvid's English wife will join him as soon as she can get transport.

Some oceanliners have a whole complement of war brides and their babies coming across the water. Michael has plenty of points. His latest letter to me says that he has a French girlfriend—he is going to marry her but the folks don't know it yet. Rotsaruck, Michael. At least if she is French she is probably Catholic. More Wartime Romances all around us.

The city bigwigs in San Francisco are sputtering that they are going to bill the Navy for all the damage the rampaging sailors caused. The Navy, playing tough—who won the war, anyhow?—retorts that for a long time they have been thinking of moving the fleet to San Pedro. Somehow it all works out, somebody pays the enormous cleanup bill, the fleet is staying in the Bay Area. The papers are full of stories about large numbers of Japanese committing hara-kiri in front of the Imperial Palace. It must be terrible to lose, but it does serve them right. They ought to have known better than to mess with us. Halsey has taken his whole Third Fleet into Tokyo Bay—23 carriers, 12 battleships, 26 cruisers, 116 destroyers, and all the little ships, too. I hope it's a big bay, there would be hell to pay if they scraped the paint off of each other all mashed together like that. The Japs don't have any battleships left.

My parents called me last night to ask when I am coming home. "Well, folks, I signed on for the duration and six months, I guess you can start counting about now. Let's think March or April." I hear my voice, which for some reason sounds just exactly like Lieutenant Kaufman's cool tones. Mother sighs. C'mon, Mother, I think, we all have to face reality sooner or later. Daddy just harrumphs. Buddy gets on the phone, his voice squeaking and cracking, like it does when he is excited.

"Hi, Sis. Congratulations. You did it, shot 'em right out of the water."

"Thanks, Buddy, but remember I had a little help. How are you?"

"Fine. When Uncle Bud heard the war was over he got so snockered he tore up all his ration coupons. Now he doesn't have any. Doesn't need them for gas anymore, but does for meat. Aunt Wilma says she is going to kil—"

"Brian, Josette doesn't want to worry herself about all that." My mother has taken the phone away from him. Never change. If you don't talk about it, it never happened. "This is costing your father good money, Josette. I'm so thankful it is all over and God has kept you safe. Come home as soon as you can, Angel." Do I imagine it or do I hear the beginnings of a sniffle before we hang up?

Did you ever see a Navy of three and a half million people dissolve itself? It's like a parachutist who lands underneath his collapsed canopy and has to extricate himself. The Seabees or somebody have made great big signs out of rocks painted white on the hillsides, so the first thing that the thousands of guys coming home see is WEL-COME HOME on Angel Island or WELL DONE on Yerba Buena or GREAT JOB. When the survivors of the Japanese concentration camps see the signs, those who aren't on stretchers dance and whoop. Even with all the good news and happy homecomings there is sadness. We hear that Ensign Bauzer's father, who used to work for General Electric in China and had been interned, died of starvation two weeks before the Navy came up the river to liberate the camps in Shanghai. So close. Two weeks. Fourteen days. No wonder the guys believe in the number-coming-up business. If your number comes up there isn't anything you can do, or could have done, to avoid it. Kismet. Don't worry about it. Nothing you can do anyway.

The gunsheds are secured, left to the sand fleas and the damp cold. Glad to see the last of them; well, actually, we had some pretty okay times there. Wonder if Calvin Jackson is going back to Arkansas with his wad of savings to open the biggest chicken farm in the world? Will I ever know?

Tolliver doesn't have any more points than I do, but she has her flyboy lieutenant. Her plan is to marry him quick and get out on a pregnancy discharge. Lots of girls who are married are getting pregnant, presumably by their husbands, so they can get out quickly and ready the little nest for the returning he-roh. Actually, the brass has put out directives that wives of returning servicemen can apply for an early discharge, but Tolliver wants to start her family right away. She's not wasting any time, that girl. She's whizzed through Catholic instruction classes the chaplain insists on before he will marry them, she has gotten permission to wear a white dress uniform to match her resplendent groom.

They are married in the chapel next to the Rec Center, under the resplendent mosaic of the triumphant risen Lord. Tolliver looks as radiant as any bride you ever saw and C.C. as any bridegroom. It is so easy to feel happy for them, like a new life, a new era, is beginning and they are the symbol of it. I, of course, as the Catholic buddy and only Catholic Tolliver ever knew before Connery Caddo McLeod, got to be maid of honor. How funny life is. I figure the least I can do is give her my specially blessed Miraculous Medal as a wedding memento—look how miraculously it has performed for me. It is a beautiful wedding, flowers and rice and champagne afterwards at the Officers' Club. One little negative note, God help us, Purvis. He's C.C's best man, but he's not mine and I keep my distance.

After the gunsheds are secured, the Navy has to find jobs for all of us gunners. Typing, it turns out to be; we have to type forms to replace the point-rich yeoman who are gone with the tide. After all the trouble I went to in boot camp to avoid becoming a yeoman, here I sit, day after day, typing education records for the guys who are getting discharged. Painful. Painful. I have trouble making the consarned Underwood list all the classes the guys have had in the Navy between the little teeny lines. I decide I might as well do a little typing for myself so I ask Lieutenant Browning, who is filling in his time waiting for his separation to come through as the education officer, how I would go about going to the University of Chicago with the GI Bill. "I would suggest," he said, in a measured life-is-so-simple-once-you-get-the-hang-of-it voice, "that you send for an application." Will do. Can do. He helps me fill it out when it comes. No sweat. Around me, the few yeomen left who had gone to Stillwater and learned how to make the machines fly with never a mistake are clacking away furiously. They had even had lessons on how to put the paper into the machines properly. Oh well, none of them can break down a 20mm gun and put it back together again blindfolded. Big deal. At least I still have my rating, Specialist (G) Second Class. On the streetcars in the city the guys still stick their two index fingers into the air and wave them in an arc, going "ack-ack, ack-ack, ack-ack-ack" when they see our rating. Little do they know that the only thing I am shooting these days is a typewriter. I suppose if the Navy can stand it, I can. Duration and six months they said.

Corman and I are in Roos Brothers checking out civilian clothes when we run into Lieutenant Kaufman. We aren't buying anything

yet, just adding up costs and trying things on. A wool suit costs $29 or
$30, but we will have $200 to spend once we get our discharge allow-
ance. I am feeling the softness of a napped brown wool with a cardigan collar when I hear a familiar voice, "I don't really think brown is
your color, Josette." I turn abruptly and there she is, laughing a little.
"Are you ready for a change from Navy blue? Lots of changes in our
lives these days, are there not?"

"Yes ma'am. There sure are." I'm a little embarrassed, she doesn't
know that I saw her on the fire engine on V-J Day night. Corman saw
her that night, too; she comes up just then with a tan blouse in her
hand, one she found for the suit I'm not ready to buy. "Afternoon,
Lieutenant. I haven't seen you since you almost took a header off
that fire engine there by Turk Street."

Lieutenant Kaufman laughs and laughs. I swear that lady doesn't
have an ounce of mortification in her body. "That was one of our
more spirited evenings, wasn't it? I don't guess I'll see you girls anymore. My separation papers just came through. My husband and I
are leaving for Milwaukee next week."

"What are you going to do, Lieutenant?"

"Get my old job at the junior college back. Start a family, we've always wanted to have children. Well, goodbye. 'Fair seas and a following wind' or is it 'Fair winds and a following sea'? I never could remember. It doesn't matter anymore. I must run."

Never a hair out of place, I think, as I watch her perfect French
braid under her square white officers' hat recede through the aisles.
Aloud I say, "Start a family. I didn't know people as old as her could
start a family." Corman sighs.

"There's lotsa things you don't know, honeychile. I'm sure glad
you're going to that college in Chicago. Maybe that will help." She
smiles her dimpled smile to show me she isn't feeling mean. Maybe
she's right.

"I don't think brown is my color," I say, as I put the cardigan suit
back on the rack. "Let's go look at the City of Paris."

Blackie calls me . . . its Saturday night and he's lonesome. His ship
is fitted to leave for Peedro toot sweet. "Changed your mind, now
that you've had all this time to think it over, Toots?"

Be still my heart. "Negative."

"I think you're outta your head, kiddo, but suit yourself. Let me know if you change your mind."

Change my mind? I wouldn't marry Montgomery Clift if he was going to be at sea all of my life. I think of my aunts, living a life of martyrdom because they thought they could turn the feckless charming boyos they fell in love with into husbands.

"Don't wait too long," he says and hangs up.

I stand there, dead in the water in the corridor by the payphone in the Waves barracks. Does "don't wait too long" mean he has another girl waiting in Peedro? Honolulu? I'm still holding the receiver in my hand, but I don't have the number of his dock. I could at least have said goodbye and good luck. I hear a voice (Corman's? Tolliver's? Aunt Geraldine's?) in my head saying, "Let it go, megirl, you've got a life to live."

General Wainwright is back, rescued from a Japanese prison camp in China by paratroopers who were worried that the Japs might kill him after all, before the prison exchange people could get to him. It has been a long four years since he commanded the Bastards of Bataan—"No father, no mother, no Uncle Sam." We are marshalling for the victory parade for him, for all of us. For most of us this will be our last parade in the Navy, before they shake our hands, pin on our "Ruptured Duck" discharge pin, and say, "Well done." It's a beautiful blue-sky day, just little wisps of high cirrus like whitewash paint strokes high above. The sun is out early for San Francisco, too early it turns out. Market Street has trolley tracks, which are hard enough to march on, but the angle of the sun catches them just so and the reflections hit me right in the eyes. Hard to keep my eyes open and my head up. We move along, the old feeling of being one with many takes over. I love it. Our white gloves swing in unison, our polished Cuban-heeled shoes gleam in the light. "*Left, left,* what shall I do when I've *left?*" It should be perfect, we Waves pride ourselves on our drop-dead precision marching, our we'll-show-you-guys drill, but this morning some snafu has put our company smack between two marching bands. Our little ensign strains her vocal cords calling the cadence, but the girls aft hear one beat and the girls forward another. Drat. While I try to catch the cadence I wonder, what now megirl? The war is over, you've seen part of the world, you've come close to finding True Love, will you ever? Right. Right. Right. I can do anything anyone else can do. A lot of shuffle-skipping and peripheral peeking trying to get the synchronization together. Rats. There are moments when it all falls together and I can look at the happy crowds with their flags and listen to their cheering. But it doesn't last.

By the time we are approaching the reviewing stand by the Civic Center the drum and bugle corps in front of us is playing a rousing patriotic "Stars and Stripes Forever." Aft of us there is a band playing "Kiss me once, and kiss me twice, it's been a long, long time." That song is everywhere now—sort of the theme song of all the guys coming home. Confused, our company wobbles slightly, not much, not too bad. I can't see General Wainwright, but we know he is there, whip thin, proud and frail, behind all the flags. We hear "Eyes Right" and "Hand Salute." He takes our salute. We are part of it, too, we are part of the Victory against Germany and Japan, even if we never left Treasure Island. I can see Tolliver, now McLeod, looking as touched and proud as I feel, but she's muttering about getting the cadence, too. "This just about dogs it," I think I hear her grouse. We hear the announcer boom over the PA system, " . . . And now we have the Armed Guard Waves from Treasure Island. *Let's give these little ladies a great big hand.*"

Everybody does.

EPILOGUE

The war was over, the war was won, the world we knew was ready to return to "normalcy," a bright and shining prospect after four years of war and postponement. Many of my friends were more than ready to settle down and nest with their returned GIs, ready to produce a whole new crop of Americans. Little did we know that the pink and promising babies we were producing would be called the Baby Boomers. I wasn't ready to settle down yet, so I carefully cut the buttons off my elegant Mainbocher uniform to convert it to civilian wear and went to the University of Chicago on the GI Bill. After a few tentative romantic misadventures I met and married Lowdon Wingo, but that is a whole other story. We had two sons, moved around a lot, from Texas to Boston to Washington, D.C., to Chile, to Philadelphia, to California. I taught elementary school for several years. Now I am retired, a grandmother who writes stories.

Corman married Jack, the boy next door, after all, and went back home to Kentucky to raise a family. We lost touch after a while.

Tolliver went back to Maryland with her husband, who was slightly less resplendent in civvies. Her mother-in-law told her she cried for a week when she heard C.C. had married a nobody, but the marriage lasted and they had three blond children. Randall Junior grew up to be a congressman from West Virginia.

Atkinson married her forest ranger and moved to Oregon. They had five kids and now live in Montana where she taught high school for many years. We still write at Christmastime.

Jenson stayed in the Bay Area and got a degree in social work. She died in 1962.

Lieutenant Kaufman did have her late family, first a daughter, then a son. She got her Ph.D. in counseling and taught in colleges around Detroit. She has been a widow for many years, still has many gentleman friends—and, in fact, she still keeps in touch with every-body she knew on Treasure Island.

Jackson did survive and returned to Arkansas with his ill-gotten poker winnings stake. He and his mama bought a chicken farm and then opened a chain of Chicken Dee-lite restaurants. He's still short, but he's rich.

Blackie reenlisted and shipped out. After I turned him down for the last time, I never heard from him again. In my mind he is always rollicking and 20 years old. I think it is better that way.

ABOUT THE AUTHOR

Josette Dermody Wingo was born in Detroit in 1924. After World War II she attended the University of Chicago on the GI Bill, graduating with a bachelor of philosophy degree in 1948. While at Chicago she worked for Dr. Bruno Bettelheim at the Sonia Shankman Orthogenic School for emotionally disturbed children. She raised two sons and taught at the elementary level for several years before returning to school at Temple University, where she earned a master's degree in education.

She and her husband, Lowdon Wingo, currently reside in Santa Monica, California. She has volunteered at the *Los Angeles Times* Learning Lab, which emphasizes the use of computers to combat illiteracy. More recently, she has become involved in a community project for homeless families sponsored by the American Association of University Women. She has been a member of Waves National for many years. This is her first book.